The Spatialities of Europeanization

Europeanization is increasingly fashionable in the social sciences as a research focus as well as a backdrop for studies of the European Union and its relations with its member states. However, to date there is little consensus among the scholarly community over what Europeanization is or how it should be analysed.

Spatialities of Europeanization is the first work to comprehensively analyse contemporary research across the social sciences and humanities in order to bring together critically informed and previously unconnected contributions on this vital topic. The authors identify unexplored commonalities between these different research traditions as well as shedding light on its neglected geographical and spatial dimensions, which, they argue, are critical to understanding Europeanization in the twenty-first century. This book reflects a strong conceptual approach which is supported by detailed empirical materials drawn from interviews with policy elites at supranational, national and regional levels in the European Union who are engaged in short-, medium- and long-term EU policy planning and management.

Offering fascinating empirically grounded insights into why Europe's governance must now become more transparent and accountable to its 500 million citizens, this book will appeal to scholars and researchers in the fields of political geography, political science, international studies and European studies.

Alun Jones is Professor of Geography at University College Dublin, Ireland.

Julian Clark is Lecturer in Human Geography at the University of Birmingham, UK.

Routledge advances in European politics

The Spatialities of Europeanization

Power, governance and territory in Europe

Alun Jones and Julian Clark

Routledge
Taylor & Francis Group

LONDON AND NEW YORK

First published 2010
by Routledge
2 Park Square, Milton Park, Abingdon, Oxon OX14 4RN

Simultaneously published in the USA and Canada
by Routledge
270 Madison Avenue, New York, NY 10016

Routledge is an imprint of the Taylor & Francis Group, an informa business.

© 2010 Alun Jones and Julian Clark

Typeset in Times New Roman
by Keystroke, Tettenhall, Wolverhampton, UK
Printed and bound in Great Britain by
CPI Antony Rowe, Chippenham, Wiltshire

British Library Cataloguing in Publication Data
A catalogue record for this book is available from the British Library

Library of Congress Cataloging in Publication Data
Jones, Alun.
The spatialities of Europeanization : power, governance and territory in Europe / Alun Jones and Julian Clark.
p. cm. – (Routledge advances in European politics)
Includes bibliographical references and index.
1. Regionalism–European Union countries. 2. Central-local government relations–European Union countries. 3. Spatial behavior. I. Clark, Julian. II. Title.
JN34.5.J66 2010
320.44′049–dc22
2010001341

ISBN 10: 1–844–72167–1(hbk)
ISBN 10: 0–203–84774–1(ebk)

ISBN 13: 978–1–844–72167–2(hbk)
ISBN 13: 978–0–203–84774–9(ebk)

In memory of Richard Alec Clark,
Richard Owen Jones and Agnes Jones

Contents

Illustrations

Figures

Tables

Preface

At a time when the need for a united response to global challenges has never been greater – in terms of combating financial instability and climate change, and easing transnational flows of labour and migration – the European Union's capacity to act is in disarray. Simmering tensions exist between its member states over the need for financial subventions from 'West' to 'East' in the wake of global economic recession. Allegations of sleaze and corruption mire the workings of the Union's core institutions. The European Union itself appears tarnished by accusations of colluding in the United States-led 'War on Terror' through allegedly assisting in extraordinary rendition and the establishment of secret prisons, while, just months before assuming the EU presidency in autumn 2008, the Czech President, Václav Klaus, publicly questioned the Union's global role and poured cold water on its long-term political future.

Many of these issues spring from the increasingly vexed relation between the EU and its member states, a central focus of the rapidly developing research area of Europeanization. We are political geographers, and our interest in this topic grew out of a dissatisfaction with mainstream academic 'first generation' portrayals of Europeanization (in the political sciences especially) as 'transformation' of member states' polities, policies and politics towards an EU-determined norm. Even the case of the Common Agricultural Policy – the Union's single most substantive area of joint activity – casts doubt on this formulation, deriving as it does from EU policymakers building upon pre-existing heavily protectionist *national* agricultural programmes. But we also wanted to draw attention to the largely neglected wealth of literature on the multidirectional, millennia-old nature of Europeanization in the humanities, that is a testament to geographical propinquity, cultural richness and social diversity across Europe over many centuries. So the Europeanization puzzle, as we saw it, was not in establishing the precise degree of the European Union's 'impact' upon its member states. Rather, it was how and why these millennia-old processes had been harnessed successfully by state-based formations – most recently the European Union through its European integration narrative – and what the consequences might be for its half-billion citizens, now and in the future.

In the book, we have begun to explore the underpinnings of a more emancipatory politics of Europeanization not by disregarding the existing corpus of largely elite-based work in political science, but instead by scrutinizing this literature in detail, for our strong belief is that the 'tipping point' of a more liberating Europeanization is to be found through careful empirical analyses of the workings and operation of contemporary elite Europeanization spaces, discourses and practices. Consequently, in this book we have sought to make a focused, empirically driven contribution to leading-edge debates across the social sciences on different aspects of the Europeanization literature, including notions of 'impact', and 'goodness of fit', and projections of Europeanization beyond Europe's established borders.

The book forms part of our continuing project to build bridges between political science and political geography – a sub-discipline recently hailed by leading political scientists as one of the 'most exciting to emerge from the "spatial turn" in the social sciences' (Ethington and McDaniel 2007: 127).

This work has been some years in the making and we owe a debt of gratitude to many people, not least to the over 250 interviewees whose testimonies provide the backbone of our argument; to bodies who have funded the research, including the Leverhulme Trust, the British Academy, the University of London's Institute for Advanced Studies and the European Union's Fifth and Sixth Framework Programmes; to our thoughtful and considerate editors, Harriet Frammingham and Heidi Bagtazo, at Routledge; to colleagues at University College Dublin and the University of Birmingham for stimulating discussions on all things European; and to our wives, Jackie and Lucy, and our families for their unstinting encouragement and support.

Abbreviations

CAP	Common Agricultural Policy
CDOA	*Commission départementale d'orientation agricole*
CTE	*contrat territorial d'exploitation*
DEFRA	Department of Environment, Food and Rural Affairs
DG	Directorate-General (of the European Union)
EDO	*l'Étang de l'Or*
EMDA	East Midlands Development Agency
EMRAF	East Midlands Rural Affairs Forum
ENP	European Neighbourhood Policy
ENPI	European Neighbourhood and Partnership Instrument
ERDP	England Rural Development Programme
FBAS	Farm Business Advisory Service
FFC	Farming and Food Commission
GATT	General Agreement on Tariffs and Trade
GOEM	Government Office for the East Midlands
GOs	Government Offices for the Regions
GR	Government Region
LOA	*loi d'orientation agricole*
MAFF	Ministry of Agriculture, Fisheries and Food (now the Department of Environment, Food and Rural Affairs)
MEDA	development aid budget for Mediterranean countries
NCC	Nottinghamshire County Council
OECD	Organisation for Economic Co-operation and Development
PDRN	*Plan de développement rural national*
PMG	Processing and Marketing Grants Scheme
RDA	Regional Development Agency
RDP	Rural Development Programme
RDR	Rural Development Regulation
RDS	Rural Development Service
RES	Rural Enterprise Scheme

RPG	Regional Planning Group
TEC	Training and Enterprise Council
VTS	Vocational Training Scheme
WTO	World Trade Organization

1   Europeanization

A critical stocktaking

Introduction

Europeanization has become a fashionable term recently (Beyers 2004; Exadaktylos and Radaelli 2009; Graziano and Vink 2007; Rosenow 2009). For some, its significance lies in its role in the transition from government to governance in western European countries, its part in the internationalization of political actor networks and policy communities, and its promotion of the de-nationalization of the state. From this perspective, the state's position as bastion of economic and political sovereignty is being challenged by processes chiefly associated with the emergent European Union polity (Jones and Jones 2004). For others, Europeanization has opposite effects, strengthening the territorial state and state-based orders and creating more, not less, national government (Milward 1992; Moravcsik 1998, 1999). Between these two positions – as with debates on contemporary globalization (Dicken 2004; Held *et al.* 1999; Herod 2009; Martin 2004; Mittelman 2004) – there has emerged a growing literature on the permeability of the nation-state to Europeanization and the state's strategic capacity to mediate its effects (Goetz 2001; Goetz and Hix 2001; Green Cowles *et al.* 2001; Gualini 2003). More recently, Europeanization has been characterized by political sociologists as the product of global social movements as much as the transformation of institutions and governance (Delanty and Rumford 2005).

However, despite an abundance of work directed at calibrating its effects or merely treating Europeanization as a 'loose background concept' (Bulmer and Lequesne 2005: 11), far fewer studies have attempted to conceptualize Europeanization as 'something to be explained' (Radaelli 2004: 1) – that is, as a process, or perhaps more correctly a suite of processes. For, as Olsen (2002: 941) notes, Europeanization should be regarded not as 'an explanatory concept' but rather as 'an attention-directing device and a starting point for further exploration'. In our view, this represents an important research agenda, ripe for theoretically informed empirical analysis. While some authors are now advocating that studies of Europeanization need to be directed towards more social-theoretical conceptualizations linked to globalization (see, for example, Delanty and Rumford 2005), importantly this still shirks rigorous investigation of Europeanization's core meanings, scope and potential as a 'systematized concept' (Radaelli 2004: 2).

In this book, we seek to contribute to this development of more systematic understandings. We do so by critically examining some of the principal shortcomings of Europeanization research set out by Graziano and Vink (2007). In particular, we probe the Europeanization of political elites, the relationship between 'EUrope'[1] and its diverse territories, and the projection of Europe beyond its physical boundaries. We contend that the concept needs to be mapped out in terms of specific empirical contexts such as these, for, crucially, Europeanization is not an omnipresent transformation, as some of the literature attests. Rather, it comprises a suite of millennia-old socialization and learning processes recast and reiterated through daily exchanges among European elites, that shapes and is shaped by their personal goals and ambitions and is moderated by the historical and institutional circumstances they work within. One of our main contentions here is that elites have had disproportionate influence on or in Europeanization. While, therefore, Europeanization is multifaceted and multidirectional, we argue that elites have played a major role in defining and shaping this process for their own ends. (This idea is developed further in Chapter 2.)

Our concern is primarily with the context of the European Union. We adopt this focus because Europeanization's most recent instantiation lies in attempts by political elites to reorganize and orchestrate a distinctive European political space in the immediate post-Second World War period, in part as a response to international security and unfolding globalizing pressures. Among post-war European political elites, the response was to fashion a new narrative of European integration. Yet we also contend that Europeanization and European integration are all too easily conflated, a problem evident in much research undertaken so far. To some extent this is understandable, as the interrelationship between the two is complex: certainly the 'European project' has given renewed impetus and direction to Europeanization, which to a large extent is now influenced by the ebb and flow of European integration and the exigencies of EU policymaking. But we contend thtat Europeanization has always been moderated by much wider global fluxes. Indeed, one of the reasons why it has proved so intractable analytically is that its underlying socialization and learning processes respond not just to European integration, or to broader European narratives, but also to a multitude of varied and highly mutable discourses – academic, lay, business, economic and political – making any one single definition profoundly difficult (Graziano and Vink 2007).

Consequently, Europeanization has tended to be characterized in crude reductionist or opaque terms, for example as an 'impact' or as a phenomenon with multiple outcomes which might be positive or negative, intentional or unintentional, synergistic or conflictive, depending upon the research undertaken. Certainly in its most recent incarnation as the 'impact' of the European Union upon its member states, it has become more controversial and more publicized, creating the spectre of an insidious presence that is penetrating and transforming spheres of social life and areas of traditional concern in all European societies. This diffusion and politicization has created real difficulties for scholars of Europeanization trying to measure its dimensions objectively and to analyse its properties. In essence, what began centuries ago as a European 'way of doing things' has become a highly complex political, social and economic reality embedded in all work and leisure activities, one of a number of seemingly inescapable contextualizing frames for our daily lives.

Not surprisingly, researchers are beginning to acknowledge that greater clarity is needed in contemporary debate (Buller and Gamble 2002; Bulmer and Lequesne 2005; Featherstone 2003; Howell 2004; Radaelli 2004; Schmidt 2001; Vink 2002). All recognize the urgent need for a systematized concept of Europeanization which, as Bulmer and Lequesne (2005: 12) argue, 'ensure[s] precision of use, whilst not pre-empting empirical findings'. These and other authors have adopted distinctive 'takes' on Europeanization, assessing its effects variously as historical process, cultural diffusion, institutional adjustment and policy adaptation.

Our approach in this book is different. Rather than seeking to assess the 'impact' of this allegedly 'transformative' concept, we scrutinize the five-decade-old dynamic between European integration and Europeanization through the lens of European elite political praxis. In doing so, we are able to examine forensically the ways in which Europeanization unfolds in different elite contexts at particular times, thus bringing greater clarity and a more systematized understanding of its processual dimensions. We do so in the book in three ways.

- *Conceptualizing Europeanization.* Our first aim is to bring greater clarity to the issue of what Europeanization *is*. As we show in this chapter, few, if any, studies have set out, other than in general terms, what qualities Europeanization has or exhibits, obscuring new research possibilities. Likewise, faced with the multiplicity of discursive constructions of Europeanization, researchers have conceptualized it as (variously) a policy outcome, a trend affecting some policy areas but not others, a societal manifestation that is unrelated to or predates the European Union, or have denied its existence or importance. To an extent, these disparate terms of reference reflect Europeanization as a 'living concept' (Lehmkuhl 2007: 340) as much as the ways in which its manifestations have altered over the past fifty years. Yet few researchers have sought to theorize Europeanization as process (that is, its settings, contexts and associated actor behaviours and attitudes; see Radaelli 2000, 2003, 2004), which is what we undertake here (see Chapter 2).

- *Clarifying Europeanization and European integration.* Second, we aim to shed light on the interrelationship between Europeanization and European integration. For some, Europeanization is directly related to integration efforts. Others see it as a process, or set of processes, that relate to the 'European project' only in certain circumstances; or relate it to Europe rather than the emergent EU polity, and hence assert that it is not predicated on European integration. Similarly, some have depicted European integration as a state-led response to globalization, while Europeanization represents a more socially embedded multidirectional phenomenon, both responding to and shaping globalization. In the book, we seek to unravel the tangled relations between these concepts.

- *Mapping Europeanization contexts.* Third, by drawing upon empirically grounded case examples specifically undertaken for this volume, we offer a more nuanced and sophisticated account of Europeanization's core meanings, scope and potential strengths in terms of elite political practice – for example, its potential as a communicative strategy, as a learning mechanism, and as a means of bargaining and advocacy linking the European Union with the global, international, national and subnational scales. And by pooling the findings from our different empirical studies of the uses made of Europeanization by political and policy elites, we are able to establish whether commonalities exist in elite behaviours, and to characterize what these commonalities are, all aspects largely neglected in research to date on Europeanization (Bulmer and Lequesne 2005; Graziano and Vink 2007). As Laffan (2007: 138) comments,

> [M]ore attention needs to be paid to research on the EU cadre ... a significant interministerial cohort of officials who manage the interface of the EU and the domestic. We need to know more about their attitudes, practices, career trajectories and identities if we are to develop a deeper understanding of [Europeanization].

By way of contextualizing our arguments, in this chapter we provide a brief review of the burgeoning academic literature on Europeanization to show the ways in which it is currently highly imprecise as a concept, before demonstrating that there are pitfalls in using Europeanization unconditionally. On the basis of this review, we seek to develop a more systematized understanding in Chapter 2, one that informs our analysis of Europeanization as elite political discourse and practice in subsequent chapters. Chapter 1 concludes with an outline of the book's structure.

Disciplinary definitions and contradictions: the 'Hydra' of Europeanization

In Greek mythology, the Hydra was a serpentine monster with nine heads that posed a formidable challenge: as soon as one head was severed, two more would grow back in its place. Only by cauterizing each stump could the monster be subdued. In a sense, analysing Europeanization exhibits challenges similar to those faced in combating the mythical Hydra. As we demonstrate, in trying to define this concept, all too often researchers seem either to miss their target or to land a blow, only to see the emergence of new epistemological and methodological difficulties just as demanding as the last. Europeanization research has been undertaken from a variety of disciplinary perspectives – including political science, geography, sociology and anthropology – which we examine here.

Political science boasts by far the largest corpus of work on this topic. Nonetheless, researchers have not formed any consensus on what it constitutes, much less what its constituent processes might be at particular moments. Instead, work has focused broadly on the notion of Europeanization as transformation or adaptation emanating from the European Union, with these forces 'impacting' upon political institutions and policy procedures of member states (though latterly some authors have identified the 'uploading' by EU institutions of national policy paradigms and projects as part of Europeanization). Thus, Nugent (2003: 442) characterizes Europeanization as 'how national political structures, political actors, policy processes and policies are increasingly orientating, or are being oriented, in a European direction'.

Other authors have rallied behind this characterization. For example, Jachtenfuchs (2001: 250–51) maintains that the 'literature on the Europeanization of policies and politics started from the empirical observation that by no stretch of analytical imagination could political processes and policy making in an EU member state now be adequately understood without taking into account the influence of the EU', though the theoretical arguments and empirical observations 'lead to a complex picture with no clear tendency yet visible'. Ladrech (1994: 69) asserts that Europeanization is 'an incremental process reorientating the direction and shape of politics to the degree that EC political and economic dynamics become part of the organizational logic of national politics and policymaking'. This definition (which was instrumental in defining Europeanization as a distinct research area and precipitated a flood of writings in the 1990s and early 2000s) asserts that Europeanization takes effect upon the nation-state gradually, through exercising a normative influence on national political life such that an explicitly 'European' dimension is created in decision making and decision taking. From this perspective, Europeanization is situated nationally. By contrast, Green Cowles *et al.* (2001: 3; emphasis added) define Europeanization as 'the emergence and development *at the European level* of distinct structures of governance, that is, of political, legal and social institutions associated with problem solving among the actors, and of policy networks specializing in the creation of authoritative European rules'. The focus here is completely different, prioritizing research at a higher scale of political-administrative activity.

For Bulmer and Burch (1998: 602), Europeanization represents 'the extent to which EC/EU requirements and policies have affected the determination of member states' policy agendas and goals', and 'the extent to which EU practices, operating procedures and administrative values have impinged on, and become embedded in, the administrative practices of member states'. Thus, distinct from Ladrech (1994), prominence is given to change in national rule or norm formation rather than politics, implying that Europeanization should be viewed as the diffusion or transfer and absorption of 'European' norms by and among national administrations and executives. Another reading of the literature leads Bache (2003: 7) to conclude that Europeanization comprises 'a redirection of policies and/or practices and/or preferences in the domestic arena towards those advanced by dominant EU level actors/institutions', reinforcing the importance of the national scale as a research focus. This definition also unequivocally portrays the process as uni-directional – that is, as coming from the supranational and 'descending' to the national (cf. Green Cowles *et al.* 2001, above), reinforcing the notion of Europeanization as 'impacting' on member states. Bache depicts Europeanization as hierarchical, being 'advanced by dominant EU level actors/institutions', and therefore presumably 'received' by 'subordinate' national actors and organizations.

Goldsmith (2003: 116) also makes public policy the purview of Europeanization in stating that 'Europeanization refers to the process by which increasing numbers of policy arenas have taken a European dimension', emphasizing again its transformative impact. Likewise, Kohler-Koch (1999: 14–15) sees Europeanization as mechanism or transferral, specifically the ways in which

> EC governance is penetrating into the political life of member states and
> [how] its particular mode of governing may disseminate across national

borders . . . being a member of the EU is concomitant with the inter-penetrating of systems of governance; any polity which is part of such a 'penetrated system' is bound to change in terms of established patterns of governance.

This penetration is described as 'tentacular' by Laffan *et al.* (1999: 84), with Europeanization bringing about 'the interlocking of the national and EU levels in a system of collective governance'. Moreover, it is a process allegedly characterized by stealth-like qualities, aided and abetted by the European Union's labyrinthine nature, where the 'fragmented structure of the Union, a multiplicity of policy communities and the Union's myriad decision rules partially hide the breadth and depth of creeping European-isation'.

For Laffan and co-authors, Europeanization's breadth and depth are not only apparent in this penetration of national politics, and the growing salience of the Union as an arena of policymaking. They are also evident in the mobilization of national actors at the EU level, their alleged promotion of transnationalism, and the consequent adaptation of national systems. Once again, the emerging consensus among researchers seems to be that European-ization is transformative and directly attributable to EU membership. Smith (2000: 613), for example, focuses upon 'the ways EU membership itself changes, or perhaps "Europeanizes", the domestic politics of its member states', while for Ginsberg (1999: 443) it 'refers to a process by which European political cooperation moved closer to EC norms, policies and habits, without itself becoming supranationalized'.

Given this medley of theoretical pronouncements and definitions, politi-cal scientists have begun recently to take stock of the first decade of Europeanization studies (Bulmer and Lequesne 2005; Falkner 2003; Graziano and Vink 2007; Olsen 2002; Radaelli 2004; Trondal 2005). Importantly, Carlsnaes *et al.* (2004: 21) argue for greater theoretical rigour from researchers in their comments that

> [t]he concept of Europeanization . . . is . . . applied indiscriminately to a wide range of phenomena and under-researched in determining which outcomes are a function of Europeanization. Significantly . . . it can be argued that Europeanization is a descriptive rather than an explanatory concept. It describes a process of interaction rather than explaining how or why it occurs.

Radaelli (2004) detects a shift since the mid-1990s in the methodological perspectives used by Europeanization theorists. These 'first generation' studies conceptualized Europeanization as 'pressure' from the European

Union upon member states to subscribe to particular norms and practices, examining the resulting reactions and change domestically (typically via the transposition and implementation of EU regulations and directives). Subsequent work, Radaelli claims, has essayed an approach where Europeanization is one among a number of drivers of domestic change, requiring time-dependent or longitudinal study by researchers, and 'controlling' for these other drivers.

Buller and Gamble (2002: 4) have also argued for greater intellectual clarity from researchers, claiming 'we must . . . devote more time to the question of what Europeanisation actually is, before assigning to it any causal properties . . . the understanding of Europeanisation as a process whereby domestic politics is increasingly being affected by EU membership is rejected'. Following their own literature review, they conclude that early studies provide no fewer than five different interpretations of Europeanization. These are: (1) as the development of governance and institutions at supranational scale; (2) as distinctive forms of European governance, exported outside European territorial boundaries; (3) as the achievement of the political unification of Europe; (4) as 'a process whereby domestic politics becomes increasingly subjected to European policymaking' (pp. 18–19); and (5) as 'a smokescreen for domestic policy manoeuvres' – that is, 'the process whereby certain . . . domestic . . . actors will encourage or at least acquiesce in European Integration as a way of implementing domestic change, or legitimising the *status quo*' (p. 23).[2] Yet while recognizing that (5) represents 'a more complex phenomenon' than the 'top-down' conceptions of (1)–(4), these authors acknowledge that none helps 'answer . . . the question of what Europeanization is in the first place'.

Dyson and Goetz (2003) have also drawn attention to the varied characteristics ascribed to Europeanization, namely the implementation of EU legislation in a state, policy and learning transfer between different member states, the migration of powers from national to supranational scales, and changes within states consequent on EU membership. Another approach, proposed by Vink (2002: 1), maintains that there are 'thick' and 'thin' variants of Europeanization: 'thick' Europeanization occurs where national identities have been fundamentally changed. Conversely, 'thin' Europeanization occurs where the basis of national decision making has altered only in particular policy areas. Again, the result is Europeanization's portrayal as novel all-encompassing transformation of national identities, norms and beliefs. The contrary case – that Europeanization might be everyday, even mundane, sets of processes, working gradually and continuously to both recast *and* support these national characteristics, dependent on time, place and circumstance – is lost in assessments of 'impact' and calibrations of 'adjustment' within member states towards some EU-instigated norm.

Rather than describing different characterizations from the literature, Knill (2001: 33) argues that Europeanization is inherently too complex for any single definition. Instead, it comprises a range of interrelated process 'types', which Knill recommends be used to structure analysis:

> The first type refers to the growing authority and competences of EU level actors and institutions; the second type considers the impact of this growing authority and competences on domestic policies; and the third type focuses on interconnections and transfer mechanisms between European states, either with or without an EU focus.

This 'typology' approach to Europeanization has proved increasingly popular within political science. Howell (2004), for example, distinguishes between 'downloading' of Europeanization (i.e. from EU actors and institutions to member states), 'uploading' (i.e. from member states to the Union) and 'crossloading' (i.e. Europeanization that involves the exchange of best practice between member states in the absence of the active involvement of EU institutions). Similarly, Olsen (2002: 923–24) refers to five 'faces' of Europeanization: (1) changes in external boundaries; (2) developing institutions at the European level; (3) central penetration of national systems of governance by the 'European political centre and Europe-wide norms'; (4) exporting forms of political organization beyond EU borders; and (5) a political unification project – that is, a project aimed at intensifying the unification of the European Union. Some have favoured certain of these 'faces' rather than others: Bulmer and Lequesne (2005: 13), for example, prefer 'the first, third and fourth' of these faces, continuing, 'the key issue is that the term is clearly defined when it is applied'.

Following Buller and Gamble, Radaelli (2004) has argued that researchers should distinguish between Europeanization and related terms such as convergence, political [European] integration and harmonization. For Radaelli, the empirical focus should be exclusively on EU member states, based around understanding a raft of different processes.

> Europeanization consists of processes of a) construction b) diffusion and c) institutionalisation of formal and informal rules, procedures, policy paradigms, styles, 'ways of doing things' and shared beliefs and norms that are first defined and consolidated in the EU policy process and then incorporated in the logic of domestic (national and subnational) discourse, political structures and public policies.
>
> (Radaelli 2004: 3)

This striking omnibus definition identifies the undeniable importance of institutions to any grounded understanding. But while providing more tractability than many other interpretations, it is not without its shortcomings, since again there is an implicit impact of the supranational scale over the nation-state. Radaelli tempers this somewhat by acknowledging that decisions brokered by 'Europe' are nationally configured, while admitting that 'the idea of [supranational] impact' of Europeanization on the national 'is somewhat static and mechanistic . . . real-world processes of Europeanization provide [domestic actors with] considerable opportunities for creative uses of Europe. Domestic actors can use Europe in many discretionary ways' (2004: 3; cf. Bache 2003; Buller and Gamble 2002).

Crucially, however, Radaelli does not take this use of Europeanization on a routine everyday basis any further. And despite injunctions from all these authors for a more systematized and rigorous analysis of Europeanization, recent works continue to focus on its 'impact' on domestic administrative structures, for example using definitions such as 'domestic adaptation to European integration' (Bursens and Deforche 2008: 1), thereby directly connecting Europeanization with European integration. Similarly, Trondal (2002: 468) comments that 'European integration constantly penetrates and transforms the core elements of the governing dynamics of European nation-states [. . .] processes of European integration and national adaptation (Europeanization) have become two sides of the same coin'.

From this synthesis, what are we to conclude about political science representations of Europeanization? What is clear is that the great majority of authors portray it as incremental or revolutionary change in domestic preferences, polities, politics and policies. In all but a handful of studies, this directly results from the operation and functioning of the European Union, and hence is a comparatively novel (post-1957) phenomenon. In effect, Europeanization is the consequence of the operation of the European integration project. And either implicitly or explicitly, in virtually all accounts, Europeanization 'impacts' upon domestic arenas on a whole range of different issues; by definition, therefore, it is broad-scale in its effects. Hence, political science tends to portray Europeanization as dynamic change in domestic structures consequent upon EU membership – that is, as a *response* to European integration.

By contrast (admittedly based on a far smaller corpus of work), some geographers have begun to analyse Europeanization and European integration as change in statehood resulting from globalizing forces of socio-economic transformation. Swyngedouw (1997, 2000), for example, considers European integration as a state-led response to global economic change. Specifically, he conceives of European integration as a strategy for ensuring the pre-eminence of the nation-state as a site of political administrative authority by 'rescaling' powers to a new European scale, though this has only been achieved at the cost of divisive social change:

Perhaps the most important change associated with this rescaling process is the absence of structural redistribution programmes at the European scale. . . . The European geographical project has only the bare bones of such spatial redistribution mechanisms while ongoing economic homogenization and international competitiveness pressures feed the call for a reduction in national regulatory systems.

(Swyngedouw 1997: 174)

Over time, this 'reshuffling' of political and socio-economic powers, authority, 'know-how' and expertise between scales results in concentration of wealth and advantage in certain geographic areas, creating inclusionary and exclusionary political spaces:

The two or three speed Europe is not one linked to a geographical core or periphery in terms of their determination to accelerate integration, but is rather an internal differentiation between those who revel in and benefit from greater command over space on the one hand and those who remain trapped in the doldrums of persistent marginalization and exclusion on the other.

(Swyngedouw 1997: 174)

By implication, these rescaling effects depend upon Europeanization to create new spatialities of power across the European Union.

Sadler (1997: 311) also writes from an economic geographical perspective, and, unlike Swyngedouw, focuses specifically upon Europeanization rather than European integration, alleging that it is

a multifaceted process . . . a reorganization . . . such that the spatial frame of reference within which decisions take place, and the way in which these decisionmaking processes are spatially configured, have become qualitatively different from those spatial frames and organizational structures which characterised an earlier era.

This definition sees Europeanization recasting state-defined 'spatial frames' of socio-economic and political engagement. The result is that long-established national patterning of decision making gives way to a European patterning, which over extended periods has consequences for domestic governance and institutions. Change is thus implicit in this economic geographical 'take' on Europeanization. As yet, Europeanization has been little studied by the discipline; the geographer's contribution, therefore, has been to situate European integration and Europeanization firmly in the broader contours of globalization, a feature notably absent from many political science analyses (important exceptions being Rosamond 2000; Vink and Graziano 2007). However, while their contribution does offer this insight, the operation of Europeanization processes remains tantalizingly elusive.

Latterly, political sociologists have begun to wrestle with the hydra of Europeanization. Building upon the lacuna in political science – the absence of a contextualizing frame specifying the interrelation between Europeanization, European integration and globalization – this discipline argues that global social trends are at least as important as European integration in promoting Europeanization. A valuable contribution from this perspective is that of Delanty and Rumford (2005). Stating that '[c]urrent theorizing on Europeanization is primarily concerned with conceptualizing the emerging shape of the European polity', these authors assert that the problem with existing studies is that they focus on institutional processes and policymaking, which 'overshadow anything like a theory of society' (2005: 1), continuing: 'so long as Europeanization is seen as another version of nation-building, that is, as an exercise in supra-nation building, the current state of theorizing . . . will not move beyond a discussion on whether the EU can compete with the nation state' (2005: 4). Instead, they propose that Europeanization is 'a multidirectional process' with 'a strong discursive dimension' (2005: 18), requiring the use of a social constructivist approach to identify its processual dynamics. Hence, while acknowledging the importance of the global context in contextualizing Europeanization, these authors argue that consideration of its effects should not be restricted to considerations of statehood, as advocated by political scientists and geographers. Far more important from this perspective is analysis of Europeanization as a multifaceted process of social transformation. Similarly, from the perspective of anthropology, Borneman and Fowler (1997: 487) comment:

> As a strategy of self-representation and a device of power, Europeanization is fundamentally reorganizing territoriality and peoplehood. . . . Driven above all by the organizational and administrative power of the European Union, Europeanization is still distinct from the EU . . . the EU [is] a continental political unit of a novel order [while] Europeanization is both a vision and a process.

This review of the state of Europeanization research has revealed a bewildering variety of disciplinary definitions, seemingly shaped more by disciplinary perspectives than by empirical validation or concrete findings. Moreover, as will now be apparent, no single definition of Europeanization is entirely compatible with any other (although, significantly, there are complementarities, which we explore and develop in the next chapter). Consequently, there seems to be little consensus over whether Europeanization is a process, an output, an impact or, indeed, is even necessary; for, as Radaelli (2000) observes, if all political systems, processes and social practices have been touched by 'Europe', then all things are Europeanized, rendering the term meaningless.

The result is definitional problems and methodological contradictions for researchers that are not easy to resolve. So, there is little common ground within disciplines (much less between them) on how Europeanization data should be collected, how case studies should be constructed or what suite of methodological techniques is most appropriate. In turn, this has meant disparate points of entry and departure for analysis; a lack of clarity and imprecision in formulating basic understandings of Europeanization; and uncertainty in how to resolve these disciplinary dilemmas. Radaelli (2004: 22; original emphasis) reflects that this may be symptomatic of the 'bedding down' of a novel sphere of academic inquiry:

> It takes a decade or so for a new field of research to 'settle down' and clarify concepts and research agenda. Thus, although bandwagon effects exist, it would be unfair to argue that there is nothing new in Europeanisation. At least *some* work in this area has produced challenging propositions and fresh ideas.

Likewise, Töller (2004: 1) describes Europeanization research as 'still in its "infancy"', while Bulmer and Lequesne (2005: 11) suggest that it is 'at a relatively early stage of conceptual development'.

Equally, however, it could be the sign that the analysis of Europeanization has failed to find direction and impetus. As Roederer-Rynning (2007: 219–20) acidly observes,

> Although . . . studies . . . share a concern with investigating 'the domestic impact of Europe', they fail to provide a coherent or systematic defini-tion of Europeanization. Some ostentatiously place Europeanization at the centre of the analysis while abstaining from defining it. Others adopt changing understandings of Europeanization in the course of their analysis. Yet others just about stumble on Europeanization and discuss it almost by inadvertence or in digressions. Disorder may be inevitable at this early stage of research, though it raises real challenges for cumulative research.

To return to our analogy with the mythical Hydra, what is required is for researchers to find ways to cauterize the epistemological and methodological problems that are associated with all Europeanization studies. Certainly there are many pitfalls in using Europeanization unconditionally, the most important of which we examine next.

Examining Europeanization: avoiding the pitfalls

As Radaelli (2000) comments, the most fundamental pitfall is the possibility that Europeanization is redundant, a concept that brings little added value to research. Buller and Gamble (2002) argue against this position. First, they assert that the past two decades of European political science research have been dominated by work on European integration, specifically on the institutions of the European Union and examination of their formal operation, policy procedures and practices. Much of this work has been dogged by lengthy and increasingly fruitless debates on the nature of integration, and whether the emergent polity of the Union can be classified as an intergovernmental, neofunctional or *sui generis* organizational entity. They contend that these preoccupations have tended to overshadow exploration of the process interrelationships *between* EU-level institutions/'the supranational' and member states, for which Europeanization studies could potentially provide the main focus.

Recently, attention has been turned to the range of research design issues for Europeanization studies that arise from these debates over the nature of integration (Exadaktylos and Radaelli 2009; Graziano and Vink 2007). Two types of research design for empirical research of Europeanization have been identified: top-down and bottom-up models. In the former, empirical research assumes the presence of European integration, controls the level of fit or misfit of the EU-level policy vis-à-vis the member states and then seeks to explain the presence or absence of domestic-level change. The top-down model allows for a wide range of intervening variables or mediating factors (Exadaktylos and Radaelli 2009). The bottom-up research design, on the other hand, exogenizes the EU level and commences 'from the set of actors, ideas, problems, rules, styles and outcomes at the domestic level at time zero – in short, the policy system at a given time'. Such bottom-up studies, then, 'process-trace the system over the years' and attempt to highlight the 'critical junctures or turning points' that affect the domestic system (ibid.: 510).

Assuming, therefore, that Europeanization *is* worthy of our consideration, how can we be certain that researchers are investigating the same activity-related concept? One way in our view is to create typologies of Europeanization, as Buller and Gamble (2002), Howell (2004), Knill (2001) and Olsen (2002) have done, but to take these further by asking more searching questions: what underlying similarities do these typologies evince? In turn, what does this tell us about how Europeanization processes and contexts can be captured, and thus how the process can be theorized? Typologies offer a means of standardizing the comparability and exchange of data, hence giving a focus to academic debate and placing Europeanization analyses on a more systematic footing. We examine this approach further in Chapter 2.

A closely related problem is how to isolate Europeanization from other change processes, and, crucially, how to assign causality to any change identified (Exadaktylos and Radaelli 2009). For some (e.g. Buller and Gamble 2002), delimiting Europeanization from other global or national influences is best achieved by focusing upon policy areas where the European Union enjoys exclusive or predominant influence. For others, methodological safeguards help establish causality. Radaelli (2004), for example, considers that Europeanization must be shown to have preceded change in order to be correlated with it. Second, researchers should use counterfactual reasoning ('What if . . . ?') – that is, they should consider what might have happened if the alleged Europeanization had not taken place. Third, analyses should be sensitive to the 'complex sequences and time patterns' (Radaelli 2004: 10) underpinning Europeanization processes:

> One may well find that the [European] Commission failed to create consensus on 'genuine EU measures', and cooperation among certain countries proceeded along non-EU tracks. But these tracks would not have been discovered if the Commission had not contributed to agenda setting and socialisation.
>
> (ibid.: 10)

Haverland (2003, 2007) concurs with Radaelli's advocacy of counterfactual reasoning, and also suggests researchers include non-EU cases in their methodological design to act as a control. In Chapter 2 we consider in detail methodological safeguards used in this book.

As this chapter has shown, another pitfall is the inability to disentangle Europeanization from the operation of the 'European project'. A range of different interpretations of the Europeanization–European integration relationship is evident in the literature. For example, Buller and Gamble (2002: 19) infer a close interrelationship, noting that while European integration represents a process of convergence at EU level, 'Europeanisation denotes the consequences of this process which may have a variable impact at the national level'. By contrast, some see the interrelationship as indirect rather than direct. Goldsmith (2003: 112), for example,

> maintain[s] a distinction between formal [EU] integration, as evidenced through the treaty processes and acceptance of European Court decisions, and a more informal process of integration through the Europeanisation of public policy within the EU, as well as other more informal social processes – travel, cultural, educational – which EU citizens increasingly enjoy.

In a novel and rare analysis of Europeanization as process, Howell (2004) depicts Europeanization as multidirectional, with 'uploading' of member states' preferences and procedures to the EU level (termed 'En1'), and 'downloading' of policy programmes, inputs and outputs ('En2') to the national level, while 'European Integration comprises the environment on which Europeanization impacts or from which it emanates' (p. 9). However:

> it is more complicated than this with interaction between the two areas merging into one another for different lengths of time and at differing levels of intensity. This means that at different times the emphasis on Europeanization will either be based around mechanisms of change in terms of up-loading from the domestic to the EU level, downloading from the EU to the domestic level or crossloading though policy transfer.

This provides a more rounded depiction of the Europeanization/European integration dynamic than other studies, in line with Radaelli's recommendation that work be sensitive to 'complex sequences and time patterns'. One of our main aims in subsequent chapters is to bring further clarity to this interrelationship.

Europeanization studies have, we believe, a healthy future, but only if these pitfalls can be successfully avoided by researchers. For them to do so, we argue that Europeanization research needs to be steered by a number of guiding principles. First, we regard contemporary Europeanization processes as connected in some way with European integration, although the nature of this relationship needs further elucidation. Irrespective of whether this is a causal or a contingent relationship, our belief is that European integration has provided Europeanization in the late twentieth and early twenty-first centuries with a critically important focal point and a new operational logic. Thus, the first strand of a more rigorous account of Europeanization requires us to provide a *systematic focus for empirical work*: specifically, to delve into the substantive empirical contexts where Europeanization and European integration processes are interfaced, which is most clearly evident within the policy formulation and implementation processes of the European Union. In the political science literature, Europeanization is often invoked in relation to change processes affecting the trinity of polity, politics and policies, and of these it is arguably the transaction of politics among elite political cadres that will define, shape and project Europeanization within and beyond the EU polity in the twenty-first century. This provides the substantive empirical context for this volume.

Second, we argue that research needs to proceed from the basis that existing studies have a lot to tell us about Europeanization. While these have so far offered widely differing definitions and observations, each has applicability and validity in its own context and our feeling is that, cumulatively, they contribute towards a more holistic depiction of the broad contours of Europeanization. In Lehmkuhl's words, 'cumulating empirical and analytical knowledge' (2007: 338) provides substantial critical advantages. The second strand of systematizing the analysis of Europeanization therefore requires us to create *a systematic basis for theorization*, provided by examining these studies and identifying complementarities between them, enabling conceptualizations to be derived for empirical validation or refutation. Potentially these conceptualizations have a valuable role to play in deepening analyses and strengthening theorization.

This leads to a third guiding principle. Crucially, while existing studies add to the overall picture of Europeanization, very often they have not been anything like clear enough on how they contribute to a specific understanding of its multifaceted processes, or which aspects they seek to clarify. Scholars therefore need to be *systematic in specifying precisely the aims and the limitations of empirical research*, in particular citing what theories and methodologies they are using, how these relate to particular aspects of Europeanization, and the constraints that adoption of particular theoretical approaches might have (because of the multifarious nature of Europeanization, it is clear that some approaches will be more suited to exploring particular aspects than others). Consequently, the systematic analyses of Europeanization in this book are based upon applying appropriate theory to different sectoral and territorial elite manifestations of this elusive suite of processes. As we have argued above, only by focusing upon particular aspects of this multifaceted process – in our case, elite political discourses and practices – will our knowledge of Europeanization improve.

Synopsis

In the chapters that follow, we explore Europeanization in a number of substantive elite empirical contexts including different EU policy areas, various sites of EU institutions, in the offices and meeting rooms of key state actors from some of the EU's longest-standing and more recent member states, with diplomats actively representing non-European states' interests in Europe, and with local and regional governmental elites drawn from the four corners of the expanded European Union. On the basis of the primary research undertaken for this study, we argue that, in contrast to political science's focus on interests, institutions and ideas, elite political discourses and practice are more appropriately conceptualized around notions of power, governance and territory. Naturally, there are complex intersections and interrelations between these different concepts and we do not contend that the power–governance–territory triptych used herein is necessarily a 'better' categorical metric. Nonetheless, from our research, elite mobilizations of Europeanization seem to be preferentially channelled through these categories, as we demonstrate later. Consequently, the following chapters explicitly deploy this conceptual triptych. We explore, first, the individual power relations of elite political practice (Chapters 3 and 4), prior to examining the governance of Europeanization and its projection beyond EU borders (Chapter 5), and then consider the alleged 'impact' of Europeanization on the differentiated territorial mosaic of 'EUrope' (Chapter 6). Undoubtedly, power–governance–territory as an organizing template provides a 'fresh perspective' on Europeanization, as canvassed by Lehmkuhl (2007: 348). Moreover, by providing one of the first in-depth empirically sourced accounts of the Europeanization of elite political discourses and practices, we are able to respond to Laffan's (2007: 138) call for researchers to scope the 'attitudes, practices, career trajectories and identities . . . of officials who manage the interface between the EU and the domestic . . . if we are to develop a deeper understanding of [Europeanization]'.

Chapter 2 ('Theorizing Europeanization as process') builds on the diversity of perspectives on Europeanization presented here. In it, we draw together the definitions and meanings in the different academic literatures identified here that are complementary, and by elaborating their characteristics we develop nine conceptualizations. We show that each of these conceptualizations is underpinned by broadly similar socially conditioned change processes which can be categorized under power–governance–territory headings. These conceptualizations also help us to interrogate the relationship between Europeanization and European integration; what emerges is that European integration is best understood as a political narrative formulated by European elites as part of the post-Second World War settlement to redirect the millennia-old socialization and learning processes that constitute Europeanization. This contrasts somewhat with the approach taken in mainstream political science, which holds that European integration and Europeanization are 'two sides of the same coin' (Trondal 2002: 468). We then show how contemporary political science work relies heavily on new institutionalism; indeed, 'one might even go so far as to say that the Europeanization research agenda . . . exemplifies the institutionalist turn in the political sciences' (Vink and Graziano 2007: 13). New institutionalism professes to show how Europeanization can be comprehended as iterated rounds of decision making and decision taking by policy and political elites that follow particular criteria or 'logics'. In Chapter 2, we set out the new institutionalist agenda and its related research propositions, which we test empirically in Chapter 3.

In Chapter 3 ('Political elites and Europeanization: changing preferences in the corridors of power?'), we critically examine Europeanization from the new institutionalist perspective by drawing upon the testimonies of high-level diplomats and policy negotiators from the United Kingdom. Drawing on materials from interviews conducted with principal negotiators from the United Kingdom covering diverse portfolios including trade, agriculture, environment and external relations, we argue that there are difficulties in accounting for their behaviours, dynamics and identities in terms of new institutionalism's dependence on logics of 'consequentiality' and 'appropriateness'. In particular, Europeanization from a new institutionalist perspective fails to grasp the totality of relations between political spaces, actors and scales of EU governance. Consequently, we propose an alternative research focus based upon 'spaces of Europeanization' – that is, the multiscaled interaction of everyday practices, struggles and discourses among elites, and specifically their use of Europe as a discursive and instrumental resource with which to fashion Europeanization outcomes that favour their own interests.

As a conceptual motif, spaces of Europeanization enable the problem of the 'porosity' of existing new institutional studies to be overcome – that is, researchers' division for analytical purposes of Europeanization processes and outcomes into discrete institutional arenas, which often overlook crucial processual drivers or disregard contemporary social, political and cultural realities. In theory, new institutional approaches, through their rational, historical and sociological variants, can address this aspect. Yet the predominance of rational and, to a lesser extent, sociological accounts at the expense of historical institutional analyses has been noted (Bulmer 2007). This has tended to limit the effective analysis of ingrained norms and beliefs, administrative traditions, and associated socialization and learning processes, and to curtail insights into the temporality of Europeanization.

Such issues have a particular resonance among the EU-10 – that is, states that acceded to the European Union in May 2004 – which is the focus of Chapter 4, 'Spaces of Europeanization: central and eastern European elites and the 2004 accession'. Specifically, we examine these issues from the perspective of five central and eastern European states. Building on privileged access to Foreign Ministers and Ambassadors of Permanent Representations from each, we chart the Europeanization of elite political practice among these actors from accession negotiations through to full membership, the key issue areas and the main instruments and channels of Europeanization in each case. A complex and messy (re)articulation of national practices and discourses with 'EUropean' norms and standards of political behaviour appears to underpin Europeanization here, creating an unstable, and uncertain, communicative space for learning and socialization among EU member states in the twenty-first century.

Developing the spatializing motif, in Chapter 5 ('Discourses of Europeanization: the European Commission, European narratives and European

Neighbourhood Policy') we demonstrate the socially constructed nature of Europeanization spaces, with particular reference to the European Union's global activities. The chapter considers the EU's European neighbourhood by examining the difficulties facing the European Commission in 'European-izing' non-EU space. This chapter specifically addresses the lacuna observed by Lavenex (2004) on the extra-territorial impact of Europeanization. The European Commission is at the centre of these efforts through disseminating its market, democratic and governance norms beyond Europe's immediate territorial limits. These discursively based elite activities have resulted in a problematized space of agreements, concessions, diagnoses and actions. The chapter reveals that European elites are pivotal to the (re)production of this space by animating the negotiating order between 'EUrope' and its socially constructed neighbourhood, critically affecting the ability of the European Union to promote Europeanization outside of EU borders.

As we have demonstrated in this introduction, much has been made by authors of 'impact' and, latterly, 'goodness of fit' in the first and second phases of the Europeanization literature, which for us is a problematic formulation. We turn to this issue in Chapter 6 by considering Europeanization's alleged impact across multiple scales of political administrative engagement – an aspect which, again, is well suited to the spaces motif used in this book. Specifically, the chapter considers how EU policy rhetorics in agriculture and rural development have developed over time to define and manage rural territories in southern France and central England, a focus where the 'impact' of the European Union has frequently been invoked. We show evidence of a much richer and varied intermediation of EU policy templates by local territorial elites than can be conveyed through 'impact'/'goodness of fit', with a dominant monolithic mode based upon the Union's Common Agricultural Policy now being replaced by the evolving Europeanization discourse of 'multifunctionality', with regions and subregions grappling with this latest manifestation through learning and socialization processes based around reconfigured politics (including platform groups and partnership building), policies (stressing creativity and innovation) and 'sense-making' of multi-functionality to suit their own territorial agendas.

Finally, in Chapter 7 we reflect upon the opportunities and challenges revealed by spatialized understandings of Europeanization's processual dimensions. If Europeanization is about the everyday and the evolutionary, rather than the transformative, what new insights does this provide into the Europeanization/European integration dynamic? In terms of understanding Europeanization as process, and from a methodological viewpoint, what benefits and what disadvantages do spaces of Europeanization deployed here confer over new institutional approaches? And what are the prospects for Europeanization in an increasingly globalized world?

2 Theorizing Europeanization as process

Introduction

In this chapter, we address one of the key issues raised in Chapter 1: what is Europeanization? To do so, we draw together complementary definitions and meanings in the academic literatures and elaborate these characteristics into conceptualizations based on power, governance and territory. We use these three broad-based geographic concepts to address the hitherto neglected geographies of Europeanization noted by leading researchers of this topic (Goetz 2006, 2007). In each conceptualization, we pay particular attention to elite political practice and discourse. These conceptualizations also help us to interrogate the relationship between Europeanization and European integration, and, in particular, the ways in which European integration has been used by political elites as part of the post-Second World War settlement to channel and redirect the millennia-old socialization and learning processes constitutive of Europeanization. We then consider mainstream theoretical approaches within political science used to analyse Europeanization. To a large extent, these approaches have been rooted in new institutionalism; indeed, as Simon Bulmer (2007: 136) has recently made clear, 'Awareness of the new institutionalism is indispensable for understanding how Europeanization is theorized.' We conclude by setting out the overall methodological approach used here.

Geographical bases of Europeanization and contemporary approaches in the social sciences

Recent social science studies of Europeanization comprise a plethora of different theoretical approaches, empirical contexts and substantive analytical themes, and provide a rich resource for assessing the geographical bases of Europeanization. Within this growing corpus of work, a number of different conceptualizations have emerged, which we have categorized here using key geographical and sociospatial variables of: constellations of *power* (through the alleged diffusion of state-based orders across multiple scales or levels of administration; Marks 1993); changing patterns of *government and governance* (from hierarchical government to 'flatter', networked relationships; cf. Rhodes 1997); and organizing concepts of *territory/territoriality* which allow us to address the comparative lack of geographical consideration of Europeanization to date. We use this triptych of political-geographical factors to organize our analysis of contemporary approaches to Europeanization (see Table 2.1).

Broadly, the nine conceptualizations derive from different disciplinary traditions and therefore should not been seen as separate but rather constitutive of each other; clearly, for example, the lineaments of power are central to territorial and governance conceptions. Moreover, a growing corpus of work suggests that elite and popular understandings of Europeanization range across all nine categories, emphasizing that primacy should not be placed on one over others (Checkel 2007; Hooghe 2001). Crucially, we argue that by focusing upon the geographical bases of power–governance–territory underpinning these nine conceptualizations, a more holistic understanding of Europeanization as process can be derived, focused on the ensemble of relations animating each. We take the first step towards characterizing these relations here by outlining Europeanization's key underlying dynamics and mechanisms of change (see Table 2.1).

Power

Recent explanations of Europeanization utilize social rather than political theory, and have prioritized constructivist approaches to examine Europeanization's 'emergent social reality' (Delanty and Rumford 2005: 7; cf. Shore 2000). Key to this approach is how European social realities are constructed and projected through power relations, for '[European] identities . . . – typically social narratives – are usually fused with perpetually changing social practices and rituals, and thus subject to changes. Further, definitions and narratives of identities are always acts of power' (Paasi 2001: 19).

We identify three conceptualizations of Europeanization as constellations of power. Foregrounding its interrelations with globalization, the first foresees Europeanization as '*a multidirectional process of social transformation*' (Delanty and Rumford 2005: 7). Key dynamics of transformation include 'societal interpenetration' flowing from adoption of the Euro, the impact of multicultural societies on consumption patterns and lifestyles, and the importance of immigration, tourism and educational exchange among and between European states (see Borneman and Fowler 1997). Delanty and Rumford also emphasize Europeanization's role in the 'transformation of modernity'. Europeanization is thus fashioned from routinized social exchanges

Table 2.1 Europeanization as power–governance–territory

Key explanatory concept	Europeanization as	Linkage between Europeanization and European integration	Mechanism of processual change	Key underlying processual type
Power	1. Multidirectional process of social transformation (Borneman and Fowler 1997; Delanty and Rumford 2005; Taggart 2006).	No causal connection or relation. Europeanization is socially determined.	Modernization/modernity via discursive and socio-cognitive processes among multiple actors, organizations, institutions.	Societal interpenetration; discursive and socio-cognitive transformation.
	2. Global projection of European identities (Bicchi 2006; Buller and Gamble 2002; Jones 2006; Nicolaïdis and Howse 2002; Olsen 2002; Scheipers and Sicurelli 2007).	Explicitly connected. Europeanization as a process whereby the EU gains meaning, 'actorness' and presence.	Discursive construction and maintenance. Primarily communicative among multiple actors, organizations, institutions.	Discursive representation and projection.
Governance/ government	3. 'Smokescreen' for hegemonic national interests (Bache 2003; Buller and Gamble 2002; Kohler-Koch 1999; Radaelli 2004).	Linked but not causally. Europeanization as a hegemonic strategy used to maintain systemic national political advantage.	Reinterpretation by domestic elites of EU regulatory scripts.	Discursive appropriation; problem (re-) definition.

continued

Table 2.1 Europeanization as power–governance–territory

Key explanatory concept	Europeanization as	Linkage between Europeanization and European integration	Mechanism of processual change	Key underlying processual type
4. Emergent scale of supranational governance (Bache 2003, 2006; Buller and Gamble 2002; Green Cowles et al. 2001; Hughes et al. 2004; Knill 2001; Laegrid et al. 2004; Olsen 2002; Sifft et al. 2007; Stone-Sweet et al. 2001).	Explicitly linked. Europeanization as the pre-eminent scale of political integration, embodied in EU institutions and structures of governance.	Functional/political 'spill-over'; primarily coordinative effect among multiple actors, organizations and institutions.	Elite socialization.	
5. Reshuffling of territorial bases of authority (Adshead 2005; Baun et al. 2006; Buller and Gamble 2002; Bulmer and Burch 1998; Goldsmith 2003; Gualini 2003; Ladrech 1994, 2002; Nugent 2003; Olsen 2002; Rieker 2007; Schmidt and Radaelli 2004; Schneider and Häge 2008; Smith 2000; Trondal 2002; Vink 2002).	Explicitly linked. Europeanization as the 'impact' of a political integration process, with the reshuffling of policy programmes, procedures and mechanisms from EU to national scale.	Political and economic integration: primarily coordinative among multiple actors, organizations and institutions.	Elite bargaining; legitimization of 'technocratic' discourse.	

	6. Complex reconfigurations of governance (Featherstone 2003; Featherstone and Radaelli 2003; Grossman 2006; Howell 2004; Laffan et al. 1999; Major and Pomorska 2005; Radaelli 2004; Vetik et al. 2006).	Explicitly connected. Europeanization as a multiscalar process, involving interactive, iterated sequences of change and transformation within/between EU and national scales.	Nascent interlocking dependencies.	Social learning; network-building.
Territory/ territoriality	7. Reorganization of spatial frames of economic decision-making (Hudson 2003, 2004; Sadler 1997, 2000).	Connected, though European integration is shaped by globalization.	Emergence/consolidation of multilevel governance.	Social learning; problem (re)definition.
	8. Territorial propinquity (Falkner 2003; Goetz 2006; Knill 2001; Kohler-Koch 1999).	No causal connection and not necessarily linked. Europeanization is not restricted to the EU.	Political best practice, imitation, knowledge transfer. Primarily coordinative among multiple actors, organizations, institutions.	Network establishment, maintenance, elaboration. Consensus-building.
	9. Rescaling of territorial identities (Howell 2004; Jessop 2005; Leitner 2003; Méndez et al. 2006; Radaelli 2004).	Explicitly connected. Europeanization as articulation of national interests and identities.	Rescaling from national to EU levels to reduce 'adaptation costs' of European integration, shaped by European integration.	Elite advocacy/persuasion.

where power relations are diffuse, unpredictable and liable to change, creating a new model of modernity: 'It may be suggested that it is now modernity itself that is being constructed out of the current developments in Europeanization' (2005: 20; cf. Massey 2004). Importantly, Europeanization is here situated within global socio-political and economic contexts, though the failure of this account to explain polity construction has been highlighted (Weale 2007).

A second conceptualization by contrast is that of Buller and Gamble (2002), who describe Europeanization as the *global projection (or 'export') of hegemonic 'EUropean' identities by supranational political and policy elites.* Broadly, 'exported' governance encompasses the rescaling of EU policy narratives, norms, procedures and modes of operation globally. Europeanization becomes a substantive means of projecting 'EUropean' soft power by engaging EU interests, ideas and identities with state-based orders and global processes on favourable terms (Bialasiewicz *et al.* 2005; Jones 2006, 2009). Thus, 'claims to [EU] law [can be] . . . extend[ed] to . . . non-European spaces, subjects and events' (Bialasiewicz 2008: 18). Articulating interests in multilateral trade fora therefore constitutes Europeanization, as do the practical consequences of EU governance in areas such as trade, foreign policy, agriculture and environment. Understanding the social construction of Europeanization becomes pivotal, with its realization effected through discourses that provide the Union with meaning, 'actorness' and presence, for example in establishing EU boundary and region-building narratives (Jones 2006). Again, this is suggestive of socialization and learning in stabilizing, orchestrating and legitimizing EU 'presence' globally.

Third, Europeanization is depicted as the product of *hegemonic national interests.* Europeanization's penetration of domestic political life means it has become part of the political rhetoric of national actors, being used variously to justify unpopular decisions, bolster power positions and to reinvent policy dilemmas as 'problems', 'challenges' or 'solutions'. Buller and Gamble (2002), Radaelli (2004) and Falkner (2003) all endorse this view, with Buller and Gamble (2002: 23) describing a process 'whereby . . . domestic . . . actors will encourage or at least acquiesce in European Integration as a way of implementing domestic change, or legitimising the *status quo*'. The animating process here is discursive appropriation – that is, the 're-reading' – of EU legislation to further elite political priorities rather than the promotion of 'European' norms and values.

Government and governance

Unsurprisingly, given the breadth of work in political science, explanations of Europeanization based on government and governance are widespread. At least four, in our view, can be recognized. First, Europeanization is depicted as an *emergent scale of supranational governance* (Bache 2003; Buller and Gamble 2002; Table 2.1). Through the activities of EU institutions, this emergent scale variously augments or challenges the nation-state as the pre-eminent site of political authority. This conceptualization therefore evokes the closest possible link with European integration by identifying Europeaniza-tion as the processes that enable the quotidian operation of the 'European project'. These processes take effect through functional or political 'spill-over' – that is, the European Union's introduction of varied political and policy initiatives has implications for other areas (hence 'spilling over'), providing impetus for further integration. In contrast to territorial explana-tions, political behaviours among national elites are seen as converging towards a 'EUropean' norm through reflective argument, constructive debate and persuasion (Checkel 2005; Haas 1958; Nye 1970; Smith 2000).

A second, and related, interpretation views Europeanization as the *reconfiguration of territorial bases of authority*, the mainstream interpretation in political science (e.g. Adshead 2005: Schmidt and Radaelli 2004; Tonra 2001; Vink 2002). Implicitly, this portrays the supranational as a dominant scale of authority over the national leading to a characterization of European-ization as potentially transformative, with sudden or more gradual change in the attributes of nation-states including politics (political transaction and 'ways of doing things'), polities (institutions mediating political life) and policies (mechanisms delivering government mandates). These 'trans-formations' allegedly result from construction and diffusion of European institutions (formal (regulatory) and informal (norms, beliefs)) from the supranational to the national. Again European integration and Europeaniza-tion are very closely enmeshed, with Europeanization construed as modifi-cation (or radical alteration) of national structures resulting from European integration. Arguably, the underlying processes are elite bargaining and the fashioning of hegemonic discourses (often technocratic in nature) by national and supranational political and policy elites.

Third, more recently Europeanization has been characterized as an *ongoing multidirectional change in governance*, comprising the projection of national interests and identities to shape supranational policies, the assimilation by state actors of EU policy and political preferences, and the diffusion of policy and procedural know-how and expertise between states, with or without recourse to the European Union. Hence, 'Europeanisation attempts to capture the dialectical relationship between the actors and the system, the nation states and the EU as institutional entity' (Major and Pomorska 2005: 2). This represents the ultimate expression of Europeanization as transformation of statehood, with processual change imbricating activities of political and policy actors such that over time it becomes increasingly difficult to define actors as 'local', 'national' or 'supranational'.

A final conceptualization of Europeanization as changing patterns of governance has geographic disciplinary origins and is viewed as a reorganization of spatial frames of economic decision making (Hudson 2003, 2004; Sadler 1997, 2000). Thus, Sadler (1997) defines Europeanization as qualitative change in the long-established domestic patterning of economic decision making towards a more European orientation. The basis for this reorganization includes change in the identity of decision makers, qualitative change in factors considered relevant in the decision-making process, and structural change in the organizations shaping decisions. This suggests that actors are involved in a continual process of learning new roles and building new networks of relations that recast state-defined 'spatial frames' of decision making (Sadler 1997: 311) to suit new global economic imperatives. In turn, this implies that reorientation of domestic decision making on Europe is a response to globalization rather than European integration. This conceptualization therefore privileges Europeanization with a much wider spatial 'reach' than change in statehood: patterns of political, economic and social engagement are all reshuffled. Europeanization is thus a distinctively European-oriented learning process initiated by global rather than European socio-economic change.

Territory and territoriality

Work by political scientists has invoked two territorial explanations of Europeanization. Thus, Knill (2001) describes Europeanization as *transmission of tacit and codified knowledges between European states*, knowledges that need not be related to the European Union (Table 2.1). This definition is thus sympathetic with earlier humanities writings (Albrecht-Carrié 1965; Barraclough 1963; Beloff 1957; Bychkov and Bychkova-Jordan 2002; Chabod 1947; Davies 1990; Gollwitzer 1951; Hay 1968; Heffernan 1998; Pollard 1974; Seton-Watson 1985; Voyenne 1964), implying that territorial propinquity, socio-economic and market exchange or transactions, and historical and social affiliations all contribute to Europeanization's origins and persistence. Possible mechanisms by which Europeanization takes effect include generalized knowledge diffusion between European states (Goetz 2006), intentional exchange of best practice in specific public policy areas, and imitation by states of processes and procedures that are deemed 'successful'. Implicitly, this conceptualization describes a long-established embedded notion of Europeanization, predating the European Union.

A second territorial explanation of Europeanization – this time within the EU context – characterizes it as *rescaling of national identities and interests 'upwards' from states to the supranational [EU] scale* (Howell 2004; Jessop 2005; Radaelli 2004; Table 2.1). Here Europeanization is linked to intergovernmentalist understandings of the European Union – that is, as a mechanism for buttressing state-based orders. Elite socialization in the Union does not lead to a convergence in behavioural attitudes and values, as suggested by neofunctionalists, but rather to use of the EU institutional mosaic as an opportunity structure for national interest projection. The resulting rescaling has major economic benefits for national political elites, not least as a means of reducing adaptation costs of European integration. Again this offers novel insights into EU territoriality: while the European Union is dependent on knowledge flows from member states, its capacity for control is inherently limited by national interests (Moravcsik 1999). Hence, Europeanization can potentially undermine European integration efforts. In process terms, the emphasis would seem to be upon socialization, using elite advocacy and persuasion to promote national priorities through the routeways of supranational governance.

What, therefore, can we deduce about Europeanization from these conceptualizations in the social science literatures? First that Europeanization outcomes exhibit a tremendous variety and diversity, encompassing objective (i.e. material change in individual/territorial/state orders) and subjective (i.e. attitudinal, behavioural change) phenomena, which is strongly suggestive of the importance of hitherto under-specified or under-researched cultural, social and geographical contingencies in shaping these outcomes (cf. Bache 2006; Checkel 2007; Goertz 2006, 2007). Second, the imperatives of power–governance–territory deployed here emerge as substantive drivers of the construction and projection of Europeanization in the EU context – that is, territorial affiliations and community loyalties *as much as* the state interests so important in political science exert influence on how Europeanization is manifested and identified, and contribute to its role, purpose and functions in particular locales. Moreover, virtually all studies concur either explicitly or implicitly on the critical role played by elite factions in these processes of construction and projection, even if the accompanying politics (which involve diverse actors and stakeholders) are messy and contested.

Thus, while Europeanization outcomes are expressed territorially, the underlying processes are subject to shifting modalities of government and power that are not explicable through 'impact' or 'goodness of fit', as many political science studies aver. Rather, we argue that to understand the construction and projection of Europeanization in the EU context requires critical engagement with the ways in which different territorial sites of authority, supranational foci of power and networks of associated actors *intersect* in political struggles to shape Europeanization outcomes. As Byrnes and Katzenstein (2006: 284–85) reflect, 'the political contestation associated with . . . conflicting, or at least not readily congruent, understandings of "modern" and "Europe" is likely to significantly complicate the progression of what is usually called "Europeanization"'.

Europeanization and European integration

The nine conceptualizations outlined in Table 2.1 also enable some observations to be made on the interrelationships between Europeanization and European integration. Four out of the nine concepts depict or imply that Europeanization *predates* the creation of the European Union. While many studies in political science continue to represent Europeanization as a direct or mediated impact of the Union on polities, policies and politics (conceptualization 2), we argue that this obscures analysis of more profound processes at work that *cause* these alleged 'impacts'. Certainly, patterns of exchanges across continental Europe, founded upon migration, trade, (Catholic) religious observance, cultural exchange, political alliances and territorial closeness, have been transacted for millennia and plausibly could be said to have given rise to a qualitatively distinctive set of socialization and learning processes that preceded the emergence of nation-state loyalties and bases of political collectivity in the late sixteenth and early seventeenth centuries. It is these transnational socialization and learning processes, founded upon distinctive shared historiographies, geographies and repertoires of acculturation, that in our opinion come closest to what researchers term 'Europeanization'. Undoubtedly, globalizing forces of socio-economic change have influenced their purpose, intensity and character. Equally important, 'nationalizing tendencies operated in the opposite direction [and] arguably [have] been more powerful' across Europe for much of the nineteenth and twentieth centuries (Schalenburg 2006: 109). Yet, supported by continued exchange relations and territorial closeness, these processes have persisted, paradoxically being supportive of, yet transcending, national identities. There is also tremendous territorial variety in these patterns of learning and socialization, with Europeanization alleged to be occurring in fields as diverse as art, architecture, literature and diplomacy. Undoubtedly the capacity of these processes to 'tie in' to European cultural referents has contributed to their durability and ubiquity (see Featherstone 2003).

As the pace of globalization accelerated, direct attempts were made by European political elites to capitalize on these latent processes. The most important of these in the twentieth century was the narrative of European integration. Political elites were aware of the potency of continent-wide shared understandings and 'ways of doing things' that emerged from the territorial contiguity of states, and devised this overarching political integration narrative to harness these processes as a means of transcending the horrors of two world wars. The integration narrative has given contemporary Europeanization's learning and socialization a renewed emphasis, direction and purpose, focused since 1957 upon state (institutional and governance) change and meeting the needs of economic globalization.

Subsequently, and perhaps understandably, narrative and underlying process have tended to be conflated. Crucially, however, and in contrast to European integration, Europeanization is not politically constructed. Indeed, during EU crises when the pace of political integration has slackened, Europeanization has continued in its manifold forms, in a sense buffering the integration narrative against political 'disengagement', 'stalemate' or 'shock', and increasing its impetus and momentum in times of political agreement. Notably, when Pascal Lamy, ex-EU Commissioner for Trade and now Director-General of the World Trade Organization, described the French referendum result on the EU Constitution as 'a turning point in the history of Europe – a point when the French opted for no more political integration' (Lamy 2005), implicitly he acknowledged that the latent socialization and learning processes of Europeanization would continue irrespective of disarray in the 'European project'.

It follows that Europeanization can proceed independently of European integration; although over the past fifty years the integration narrative has been crucially important in shaping the focus of Europeanization's coordinative (socialization) and communicative (learning) processes, most often to meet the economic needs of EU member states – hence Pieterse's (1999: 5) comment that

> Europeanization since the 1980s unfolds in the epoch of accelerated globalization with transnational corporations as market leaders, which is now increasingly moving towards flexible accumulation and innovation-driven industrialization. Even so this is not simply a matter of economic determination. Throughout the process of Europeanization political considerations have interacted with economic parameters. European integration was founded on economic modernization but at every step along the way political considerations have been inseparably woven in.

It is this most recent incarnation of Europeanization – its coupling with the 'European project' – that we examine in subsequent chapters. In the context of elite political practice and discourse, our argument is that Europeanization is the product of very closely intertwined socialization and learning processes, whose specific effects are historically, economically, socially and *spatially* contingent.

There are, of course, sound precedents for focusing upon elite socialization and learning processes in this way. Both are implicit in mainstream European integration epistemologies; for example, neofunctionalism deals explicitly with 'elite socialization', which can be characterized as a 'deep' form of socialization among elites that over extended periods of time prompts a convergence of norms among them and to the creation and, allegedly, the assimilation of new values supportive of an integrationist vision (Checkel 2005; Haas 1958). Thus, in an early study Puchala (1972: 278–79) characterized the European Union as a 'concordance system' that tended towards consensual outcomes through deliberation and reflective debate among national delegations geared by what constitutes socially acceptable behaviour. In effect, distinctive 'supranational' behaviours evolve among national representatives in response to unspoken rules and the 'attributes of atmosphere' (Puchala 1972: 272) in EU decision-making fora, allowing, as March and Olsen (1989: 23) have it, a 'logic of appropriateness' to develop. By contrast, intergovernmental theory characterizes the European Union as an opportunity structure for the advancement of national interests, ideas and preferences, suggestive of a more 'shallow' form of elite socialization based around the development of strategies to secure specific objectives, with individuals learning from the mistakes and successes of implementation (cf. March and Olsen's (1989: 23) 'logic of consequentiality').

Having thus underscored the processual basis of Europeanization, we now consider how mainstream political science literatures have analysed Europeanization. As discussed in Chapter 1 and the introduction to this chapter, such work has emphasized new instutionalism and its numerous variants.

Mastering the Hydra of Europeanization: the scope of new institutional approaches

Political science's engagement with Europeanization has prioritized two particular institutional logics within the broad realm of new institutionalism. Most clearly, this engagement has relied heavily upon two different incarnations of new institutional theory, sociological and rational choice institutionalism. These are driven, to use March and Olsen's (1984, 1989, 1998, 2005) phrases, by 'logics' of 'appropriateness' and 'consequentiality'. Leading political scientists have argued that these new institutionalist variants provide sophisticated tools for analysing the outcomes of Europeanization and its impact upon domestic politico-administrative arrangements. Using these two new institutional approaches, so these commentors claim, yields important insights.

If one were to apply March and Olsen's 'logics' to elite political practice, two different accounts of this practice could be adduced. In Chapter 3, we adopt such an approach in order to examine whether elite behaviours can be understood through the lens of these two logics, and the extent to which these behaviours are culturally and nationally conditioned. This takes us to the kernel of what Europeanization is in terms of elite political practice – in particular, what it is to 'Europeanize' or to be 'Europeanized'. In order to contextualize this task, here we outline these two logics and how they might be applied to the Europeanization of elite political practice.

March and Olsen (1998: 951) define the logic of appropriateness as follows:

> Human actors are imagined to follow rules that associate particular identities to particular situations, approaching individual opportunities for action by assessing similarities between current identities and choice dilemmas and more general concepts of self and situations. Action involves evoking an identity or role and matching the obligations of that identity or role to a specific situation. The pursuit of purpose is associated with identities more than interests and with the selection of rules more than with individual expectations.

By adopting a logic of appropriateness, political elites therefore seek to engage with and to fulfil the role of being 'European', identifying and subscribing to particular formal and informal rules in decision-making and decision-taking contexts, acknowledging the importance of particular sets of values, and socializing and learning on, around and about these values.

We define a 'Europeanization context' here *as a formal or informal setting, event and/or arena that obliges or encourages decision making and decision taking such that prevailing domestic or EU norms are reappraised or re-evaluated in light of the other norm set.* These contexts may be epoch-making in scale and time, for example the continuing socio-economic/geopolitical reverberations in the European Union following the collapse of the EU Constitution or reactions to media depictions of the Union's handling of the international financial crisis, or – equally germane – the everyday, mundane, low-level negotiations between domestic and EU actors on sectoral or procedural matters. Inevitably, the logic of appropriateness means recognizing the value and importance of 'EUropean' values or European-level solutions within these contexts. However, different Europeanization contexts will prompt different responses from political elites: in effect, elites may not subscribe consistently to EU or to national values. In other words, this logic is not necessarily about redefining national ideas, norms or preferences towards a more 'European' orientation. Indeed, with (currently) twenty-seven players in the EU game, it may be advantageous for actors to mimic or adopt temporarily 'EUropean' values in one decision-making context so as to maintain or secure other 'held preferences' (be they individual, organizational or national) elsewhere.

March and Olsen (1989) stake a claim for this logic in the following terms, saying that it:

- enables coordination of many simultaneous activities in a way that makes them mutually consistent;
- facilitates avoidance of conflict with other actors;
- promotes shared codes of meaning, facilitating the interpretation of 'ambiguous worlds';
- delimits negotiating and bargaining within particular parameters;
- assists the enforcement of agreements;
- narrows down choices of particular solutions to policy problems.

To furnish insights into this form of elite behaviour, the relevant new institutional approach adopted by political scientists is sociological institutionalism.

By contrast, in their discussion of the logic of consequentiality March and Olsen (1989: 56) state, 'the core ideas are that individuals enter [into Europeanization contexts] with preferences and resources, and that each individual uses personal resources to pursue personal gain measured in terms of personal preferences'. Hence, collective decisions on Europeanization viewed through this logic reflect the power distributions of the individuals taking part, while relations between actors are determined by offering or withholding resources to create Europeanization outcomes that are acceptable to all. Dispute settlement is by negotiation based on argument and debate conducted according to certain pre-given rules. March and Olsen (ibid.) note that actors choose the options that have the best consequences as judged by the values the actor represents (these may be individual, organizational and/or domestic). In this case, the new institutional variant of rational choice institutionalism is used. As Featherstone (2003: 9) reflects, rational choice institutionalism is well suited to examining the 'complex interpenetration between the "domestic" and the European level [that] creates a variety of opportunities for actors to exploit'. The rational choice school asserts that institutional rules regulate the behaviour of actors in their rational pursuit of political gain, and, as a result, actors must quickly learn more accommodative norms and accept institutional values if they are to exercise influence.

Commentators have identified a number of advantages in using March and Olsen's two logics to illuminate Europeanization. Most clearly, the logics stress the importance of ideas (structure) and interests (agency), a critical feature of Europeanization however defined (cf. the nine conceptualizations identified here). Bulmer (2007: 50) argues that new institutionalism offers many benefits in exploring Europeanization, noting, for example, that the logic of consequentiality enables greater understanding of 'the ways in which actors' preferences [are] oriented towards institutional settings or rules. Institutions are regarded as opportunity structures or veto points; actors seize the available opportunities or are blocked by the veto points' (cf. Börzel 2005; Bulmer and Lequesne 2005). Another advantage is that sequenced use of both logics dependent on the stage of the policymaking process and the institutional attributes of decision-making fora enables us to 'model reality' more accurately, helping explain the messiness and incoherence of Europeanization processes and outcomes.

Overall, the new institutionalist approach also suggests that Europeanization's pace and direction will vary in different areas of elite political activity. For example, more developed areas of EU intervention will have more rules and procedures, less developed areas fewer rules, or none at all, all of which will alter Europeanization dynamics. Thus, Bulmer and Radaelli (2005) suggest that 'positive integration' – that is, full-blown EU policies such as the Common Agricultural Policy (CAP) – tend to favour sociological institutionalism – the 'logic of appropriateness' – as an explanatory framework for examining Europeanization. Conversely, in situations of 'negative' integration, such as the removal of national barriers to trade, where 'punitive' directives and regulations have been introduced, or where new policy initiatives are being attempted, rational choice institutionalism – the logic of consequentiality – will be more appropriate. This approach also provides a framework for generating research propositions, which we outline in the following section and problematize in Chapter 3.

Analysing Europeanization as decision making and decision taking by political elites

Europeanization as a logic of appropriateness depicts Europeanization contexts as settings in which political elites seek to coordinate their decision making and decision taking and make these mutually consistent through the adoption and application of 'EUropean' rule sets and behaviours. This coordination favours harmonious, concordant, decision-making and decision-taking outcomes among these elites over fractious or discordant outcomes. Specifically, elites adopt this 'way of behaving' since it can hold benefits: for example, the identification of new norms and codes of meaning, and by helping to clarify policy ambiguities. The result is that bargaining is kept within particular parameters, and agreements among elites are more easily enforced as they are self-regulated or 'policed' by all, creating identifiably 'European' solutions to particular policy 'problems'. In effect, this logic encourages distinctive modes of elite behaviour, or, in March and Olsen's (1989: 23) phrase, 'litanies of action'. Such a 'litany of action' for elites adopting the logic of appropriateness might address the following issues:

- What are the specific features of the Europeanization context within which elite activity is situated?

- What are the elite actor's duties or responsibilities within this Europeanization context?
- Based on the absence or presence of pre-given rules or 'EUropean' norms
  associated with the Europeanization context, what elite actions or behaviours are deemed 'appropriate', and what might be the consequences of
  their adoption?

Similarly, *Europeanization as a logic of consequentiality* has consequences
for elite behaviour. This logic sees policy and political elites enter into
Europeanization contexts with particular preferences and resources, with the
aim of pursuing domestic, state or national objectives measured in terms of
securing these pre-given preferences. From this perspective, Europeanization
contexts embody the relative power distributions of the elites involved, with
exchanges between them based upon offering and/or withholding resources
to create mutually acceptable outcomes. This gives rise to the following
'litany of action':

- What are the specific features of the Europeanization context with and
  through which elite activity is transacted?
- What are elite actors' preferences, goals and values?
- What are the consequences of the Europeanization context for achieving
  or delivering policy, or political elites' goals?
- In what ways do elites choose the alternatives presented by the
  Europeanization context that have the best consequences for delivering
  these goals?

Seemingly, therefore, the new institutional approach provides a highly
apposite means for examining Europeanized elite political practice. And yet,
applying new institutionalist approaches to understanding elite actor
behaviours in this way is not without problems. Thus, Kjell Goldmann (2005)
has argued that a more complete understanding of the political behaviour of
elites can be adduced by viewing the logics as not mutually exclusive but
overlapping very considerably. In particular, Goldmann argues that in
understanding high-level political behaviours using a two-logic approach,
there are substantial problems in 'classifying . . . decision processes, explaining political action, and taking a reflected stance on normative issues' (2005:
36). For Goldmann, March and Olsen's reasoning is problematic as it
conflates a variety of different subsets of political behaviours. Goldmann
notes, for example, that the logic of consequentiality comprises different,
competing, career, organizational and national agendas. Similarly, March
and Olsen's logic of appropriateness consists of individual rules and norms,
organizational obligations and national goals. In short, aggregating these

different political behaviours into two binary logics is not conducive to nuanced understandings of individual elite behaviours, and hence limits explanatory power and empirical scope.

Such a position would of course have substantial implications for existing understandings of Europeanization, which are based fundamentally on new institutional insights. For example, sociological institutional accounts of Europeanization depict its effects as transformative upon elite behaviour, as supranational norms and beliefs catalyse change in domestic values, opinions and attitudes, while rational choice accounts view Europeanization as the product of carefully judged and considered decision making by domestic elites in supranational policy contexts. Consequently, in the next chapter we use Goldmann's critique of the foundational logics of new institutionalism to develop a subtler and more refined understanding of Europeanization's dynamic relationship with individual elite behaviour; and, applied at the territorial scale, consider how the lack of spatiality inherent in many contemporary interpretations might be addressed.

Methodology

As outlined in Chapter 1, the conduct of Europeanization research has been the subject of much discussion recently, particularly in terms of developing effective approaches of implementing fieldwork (Exadaktylos and Radaelli 2009). A leading proponent in these debates is Markus Haverland (2005, 2007), who has called for research to observe a number of critical conventions in order to take account of the particular qualities of Europeanization's multifaceted processes. These conventions, Haverland argues, provide robust methodological safeguards to ensure that Europeanization research is grounded upon clear principles of cause and effect. 'Most studies [of Europeanization] focus upon the question of how the EU matters rather than to what extent it matters . . . there is still a need to better elucidate [Europeanization's] causal mechanisms' (Haverland 2007: 67–68). Here, we briefly outline how we have responded to Haverland's observations on methodological safeguards (each chapter contains further reflections on methodology in relation to the specific needs of the case study being examined).

Haverland identifies these 'causal mechanisms' as follows:

- 'The conduct of case studies remains important in Europeanization research' (2007: 68), in particular with theoretically informed comparative case studies now playing a critical role in developing more holistic understandings. We have responded to this requirement by conducting rigorous empirical examination of Europeanization in multiple policy sectors (Chapter 3); different territorial contexts (Chapter

    6); from the perspectives of 'novice' as well as highly experienced policy negotiators (Chapter 4); and through conducting research in different constitutional jurisdictions through analysis of the divergence of attitudes among member states over neighbourhood policy (Chapter 5).

- The deployment of 'multiple [methodological] strategies' in order to probe and substantiate Europeanization outcomes and impacts (Haverland 2007: 62). The chapters herein develop multiple methodological strategies, including building and projection of Europeanization discourses (Chapter 5), examination and analysis of elite political practices (Chapters 3 and 4), and intensive scrutiny of Europeanization's alleged 'impact' on national and territorial administrative and institutional arrangements (Chapter 6). Each chapter contains a dedicated section on methodological procedures, specifying these strategies in more detail.

- The 'need to better elucidate the framing, socialization and changing opportunity structures of Europeanization. Intensive case studies are indispensable for this' (Haverland 2007: 68). Dedicated research reported in this volume addresses this threefold requirement through analysis of policy framing of discourse (Chapter 5); analysis of the intensive processes of socialization and the steep learning curves expected of central and eastern European elites from the outset of accession negotiations to the European Union (Chapter 4); and through examination of the extent to which Europeanization has 'chang[ed] opportunity structures' within the French Languedoc and the English central Midlands (Chapter 6).

- '[I]t is a potential pitfall . . . that scholars following a particular strategy do not take into account the results of studies following another route' (Haverland 2007: 68). As discussed here and explored in Chapter 3, we have sought to do so by adopting a critical perspective on new institutionalism, widely regarded as the most influential and successful mainstream methodological approach in Europeanization studies.

As a further safeguard, in the following chapters we have added to Haverland's conditions by presenting dedicated case studies, which are all longitudinally based – that is, derived from Europeanization contexts where data collection and analysis were continued by us over an eleven-year period.

Thematically, the book examines a truly representative range of the European Union's Europeanization contexts and Europeanized spaces. Empirical materials are drawn from one of the largest primary data collection surveys ever undertaken of politicians, policy practitioners, diplomats and business representatives within domestic and EU contexts. Some 250 interviews were conducted by us between 1995 and 2005 in national capitals and territories of the United Kingdom, France, the Czech Republic, Poland, Lithuania, Latvia, Germany, Hungary, Spain, Sweden and the Netherlands, as well as in Brussels, Luxembourg and Strasbourg. Crucially, over this eleven-year period we returned to eighty respondents and re-interviewed them to validate their earlier responses, enabling interviewees to provide us with a more reflexive and nuanced interpretation of Europeanization.

The results reported are also based upon rigorous empirical investigations including changing rural and regional development agendas, environmental sustainability debates, and external relations and foreign policy strategies. We have been privileged in gaining access to leading representatives at the front line of Europeanization over the past decade at various defining moments in the European Union's development, including during difficult negotiations over the reform and future orientation of the EU CAP, changes to the arrangements for structural policies and the articulation of new governance agendas by EU institutions, the rethinking of EU external relations policies in the wake of 9/11, and preparations for entry into the Union of new member states in central and eastern Europe at a time of growing uncertainty over the nature, speed and direction of European integration following the derailing of the proposed European Constitution.

We have thus been able not only to explore the nature of the relationship between Europeanization and European integration, but also to validate our conceptualizations of Europeanization with elite constituencies from across the European Union. To our knowledge, this represents the first systematic attempt by researchers to refine definitions and understandings in this emerging research area. Our empirical materials comprise not only detailed semi-structured interviews but also corroborative use of secondary documentation drawn from national governments and EU sources, much of which was classified as confidential. The range and depth of the empirical materials contained herein thus provide an unparalleled treasury of information by which the processual nature of Europeanization can be investigated.

3 Political elites and Europeanization

Changing preferences in the corridors of power?

Introduction

As discussed in Chapter 2, a defining characteristic of Europeanization is the penetration of the European Union into the political lives of domestic policy elites such that change is effected in their established patterns of decision making and actor behaviour (Checkel 2005; Haas 1958; Hooghe 2005; Kohler-Koch 1999). Undoubtedly, clarifying Europeanization's effects upon individual political elites is an interesting challenge to researchers, and it is one that we address here. We do so using the analytical approaches of new institutionalism, which, as discussed earlier, has provided much of the theoretical impetus for many influential studies of the interrelations between formal EU institutional rules and procedures and informal norms and beliefs affecting individual actor behaviour (Beyers 2005; Caporaso *et al.* 2003; Checkel 1999, 2001, 2003, 2004, 2005; Stone-Sweet *et al.* 2001). In this chapter, we therefore critically examine Europeanization from this new institutionalist perspective. Drawing on interview materials conducted with principal negotiators from the United Kingdom covering diverse portfolios including trade, agriculture, environment and external relations, we argue that there are significant problems with accounting for elite behaviours, dynamics and identities in terms of new institutionalism's dependence on logics of 'consequentiality' and 'appropriateness'. In particular, Europeanization from a new institutionalist perspective fails to grasp the totality of relations between political spaces, actors and scales of EU governance.

Certainly, using new institutionalism to examine Europeanization and its interconnections with and effects upon the European Union's distinctive model of internationalization has provided the bedrock for very many studies. Yet it is not without problems, as recent analyses confirm (Bendor *et al.* 2001; Goldmann 2005; Muller 2004; Sending 2002). In particular, researchers find themselves caught in a maelstrom of debate surrounding the explanatory powers and empirical scope of different 'logics of action' – specifically, the 'logic of expected consequences' and the 'logic of appropriateness' – that underpin sociological, historical and rational-choice variants of the new institutionalism (Adler 2002; Caporaso and Jupille 1999; Goldmann 2005; Moravcsik 1999, 2001; Muller 2004; Sending 2002). These logics, originally expounded in the work of James G. March and Johan P. Olsen (1989, 1998, 2002), have been of seminal importance in developing new institutional theorizing by providing what some have described as a 'central dividing line between rationalist and constructivist [thinkers who] . . . bring to bear different conceptions of the rationality of action' (Sending 2002: 444).

In brief, the logic of appropriateness regards human actions as driven by rules of appropriate or exemplary behaviour set in institutional arenas. To cite March and Olsen:

> Rules are followed because they are seen as natural, rightful, expected, and legitimate. Actors seek to fulfil the obligations encapsulated in a role, an identity, a membership in a political community or group, and the ethos, practices and expectations of its institutions.
>
> (2002: 2)

On the other hand, the logic of expected consequences views actions as driven by expectations of consequences in which human actors choose among alternatives by evaluating their likely consequences for personal or collective objectives, conscious that other actors are doing likewise. Hence, a consequential frame sees political order as arising from negotiation among rational actors pursuing personal preferences or interests in circumstances in which there may be gains to coordinated action. European integration thus represents a collection of 'contracts' negotiated among actors with conflicting interests and varying resources. The political outcome achieved and its terms depend on the bargaining positions of the actors.

While March and Olsen (1998) viewed the two logics as separate explanatory devices, they indicated that any political action was likely to involve elements of each logic. This has not, however, stopped political scientists speculating whether and how the explanatory power and significance of the two logics varies in different decision-making settings where policy dossiers might be deemed to be 'low' or 'high politics' – issues that have profound importance in the myriad decision-making and decision-taking fora of the European Union. Foremost among those advocating the explanatory power of the logic of appropriateness set within broad social constructivist inquiry is Jeffrey Checkel (2003: 219), who argues that accounts of EU decision making relying on the logic of consequentiality lead to a situation where '[social] [i]nteraction [among political actors] drops out of the analysis'. On the other hand, Andrew Moravcsik (2001) has offered a highly critical view of constructivist approaches to EU decision making, contending that those who advocate logics of appropriateness cannot address a critical line of inquiry in Europeanization. As he maintains, 'Aren't most social actors constrained by structures and systems, rather than the direct manipulation and coercion of another social actor?'

Rather than emphasizing this binary distinction between the two logics, Kjell Goldmann (2005) has argued that a more complete understanding of the political behaviour of actors can be adduced by viewing the logics as not mutually exclusive but overlapping very considerably. In particular, Goldmann argues that when understanding high-level political behaviours using a 'two logic approach', there are substantial problems in 'classifying . . . decision processes, explaining political action and taking a reflected stance on normative issues' (2005: 36). For Goldmann, March and Olsen's reasoning is problematic as it conflates a variety of different subsets of political behaviours. Goldmann notes, for example, that the logic of consequentiality comprises different competing career, organizational and national agendas. Similarly, March and Olsen's logic of appropriateness consists of individual rules and norms, organizational obligations and national goals. In short, aggregating these different political behaviours into two binary logics is not conducive to nuanced understandings of individual actor behaviours, and hence limits explanatory power and empirical scope.

Such a position would have substantial implications for existing understandings of Europeanization, which are based fundamentally on new institutional insights. For example, sociological institutional accounts of Europeanization depict its effects as transformative upon actor behaviour, as supranational norms and beliefs catalyse change in domestic values, opinions and attitudes, while rational choice accounts view Europeanization as the product of carefully judged and considered decision making by domestic elites in supranational policy contexts.

Building on these debates, in this chapter we use Goldmann's critique of the foundational logics of new institutionalism as a starting point for developing a subtler and more refined understanding of Europeanization's dynamic relationship with individual actor behaviour – spaces of Europeanization – which forms the theoretical underpinning for subsequent chapters. To do so, first we develop 'ideal-type' propositions derived from Goldmann's work on the logics of appropriateness and consequentiality. That is, elaborating our approach in Chapter 2, we reflect upon what Europeanization at individual actor level would be like if Goldmann's observations were confirmed empirically. We then test these propositions through lengthy detailed interviews conducted with senior UK policy elites who were asked to reflect upon their career experience of, and participation in, negotiations in the European Union's Council Working Groups. We use their frank, revealing and highly perceptive commentaries to reappraise and re-evaluate the propositions derived from Goldmann's work to provide new insight into the processual basis of Europeanization at the level of individual political elites. From these interviews, we also seek to distil contemporary understandings of Europeanization in the Union's Council Working Groups.

The Council Working Groups provide an ideal laboratory for understanding Europeanization as political behaviour, for, as Checkel (2005: 810) notes, 'prolonged exposure and communication in European institutions promote a greater sense of "we-ness", as well as socialization dynamics', within which, he alleges, a 'shift has occurred away from a logic of consequences and towards a logic of appropriateness' (ibid.: 816). The behaviour of specific political actors 'operating in institutionalized environments in Europe' (ibid.: 814) represents an increasingly important focus for micro-level empirical work for, as Wallace and Wallace (1999: 59) contend, 'The intensity and intimacy of [policy actor] involvement is unparalled at the transnational level.' What is particularly evident is the need for empirical studies that, as Checkel (2005: 819) argues, 'capture both the constraining and constitutive aspects of the European project'. Thus, the processual basis of Europeanization as political behaviour resides in the constraining and constitutive aspects within which European political elites are situated and routinely operate. Consequently, we have an ideal situation in which to probe the logics of appropriateness and consequences and add to the growing body of work on the roles, actions and impacts of the Council in EU governance (Beyers and Dierickx 1997; Dahl and Giacomello 2000; Egeberg 2006; Hayes-Renshaw and Wallace 1997; Hooghe 2005; Jones and Clark 2002; Juncos and Pomorska 2006; Lewis 2005; Peterson and Bomberg 1999; Thomson and Hosli 2006).

Within this high-level diplomatic setting, Europeanization is at the sharp end of the juncture between supranational and national interests, ideas and political motivations, and seemingly Goldmann's argument that the two logics be seen as complementary rather than mutually exclusive in underwriting political action should be particularly apposite. Hence, in this chapter we seek to derive a more sophisticated understanding of the Europeanization of high-level political behaviour by examining:

1   the reflections of senior negotiators on their engagement with and participation in EU Council discussions, viewed through the prism of logics of appropriateness and consequentiality; and
2   the reflections of these negotiators on their own 'lived experience' of Europeanization, referring to specific policy dossiers for which they had personal responsibility.

Methodology

During 2004–6, semi-structured interviews were conducted with twelve UK lead negotiators of EU policy at Council of Ministers level. These negotiators were drawn from four policy areas – agriculture and rural development; environment; trade; and foreign policy – enabling us to compile a generic profile of the Europeanization of elite political practice. While this number might appear low, it represents a significant proportion of the most senior negotiators from the United Kingdom in Council decision making in these key policy areas. Moreover, the negotiators are drawn from one of the large voting blocs in the Council, which, as one author has argued, is significant in that the size of a country and its voting power in EU Council decision making may have an 'impact on the stability of European decision making' (Mattila 2004: 47). Additionally, from a Europeanization perspective, negotiators from large voting blocs may 'try to hang onto their national interests more often than . . . [negotiators] from small countries', thereby 'introduc[ing] instability [in Council decision making]' (ibid.: 46–47). The UK empirical focus therefore enables a thorough probing of the constitutive and constraining aspects of Europeanization in the political space of the Council. This space, as Hix (1999: 71) argues, presents 'significant cognitive constraint on all political interaction' even for those negotiators drawn from states that may be considered less supportive of increased integration (Mattila 2004; Naurin and Wallace 2008).

There has been growing empirical research on the workings of the Council. For example, Naurin (2007: 2) has analysed the presence of arguing and bargaining in the Council working groups and suggests that elite political actors are more likely to engage in arguing when 'they feel confident and in control of the decision-making situation'. By contrast, those negotiators who feel pressurized by the prospect of losing out in negotiations are more likely to adopt bargaining modes. Despite this important recent research on the nature and extent of deliberative supranationalism, the effects of Europeanization upon individual Council negotiators remain unclear. As Naurin (ibid.: 7) confirms, 'We need research designs which can say something about Council behaviour in general.' This is our empirical intention in this chapter.

Each interview had two substantive elements. First was a general discussion of the workings and operation of the EU Council Working Groups from the negotiator's viewpoint. Second was detailed analysis of the nature of decision making within the particular policy field the interviewee had responsibility for, and the interviewee's own experience of negotiating in that field. With each interviewee, we questioned whether consensus building was the prevailing feature in the routinized decision-making processes of the Council; explored the existence of overriding and long-standing values and norms associated with membership of particular Councils; and examined the extent to which these values and norms were shared among Council negotiators, thereby creating a constitutive belonging in which trust and mutual exchange are dominant. We then probed with the negotiators the extent to which this constitutive belonging set a context for strategic calculation, and asked them to clarify how this limited or enabled the scope of normative suasion. Finally, we attempted to capture the ways in which this constitutive belonging incorporated clearly identifiable 'appropriate' and 'inappropriate' behaviours for securing negotiator preferences.

In this way, detailed data collection on Europeanization as elite political practice was achieved. Interviews were undertaken immediately prior to negotiations or following their conclusion, thus providing a highly detailed data set and opening a window on how high-level negotiators prepared their own position prior to Council meetings, as well as their post-negotiation assessment of their own input to Council decision-making preparations. Negotiators referred to written reports of these meetings in order to reflect upon various forms of 'appropriate' and 'inappropriate' behaviour during negotiations, discussion of their negotiating tactics, the ways in which they made interventions during meetings, and assessments of the effectiveness of these interventions during these high-level discussions. Interviewees were also asked to comment on how they perceived their specific role at those meetings. Coupled with the safeguards identified by Haverland (2007) in Chapter 2, this methodology thus allowed us to explore fully with interviewees Goldmann's research propositions on the processual dynamics of Europeanization.

Applying Goldmann's propositions to political actor behaviour in the European Union's Council of Ministers

In a thought-provoking article published in the journal *Governance*, Goldmann (2005: 35) poses what he calls 'skeptical questions' about the logic of consequentiality and the logic of appropriateness that constitute the theoretical foundations of new institutionalism. Goldmann (ibid.: 35) formalizes these 'skeptical questions' as follows:

(1) [I]t is difficult to determine what kind of constructs the so-called logics are – whether they are to be seen as perspectives, theories, or ideal types; (2) the logics, far from being mutually excluding, overlap very considerably; (3) analytical utility is debatable not only in the case of the 'logic of expected consequences' but also when it is a matter of the 'logic of appropriateness'; (4) the normative virtue of substituting a 'logic of appropriateness' for a 'logic of expected consequences' is less obvious than March and Olsen's readers may be led to think.

Goldmann (ibid.: 35) continues, 'It is tempting to conclude that March and Olsen's approach has proven compelling because of its consequences for the scholarly community rather than by virtue of its analytical appropriateness'. Clearly, such questions have ramifications for all fields of inquiry using new institutional approaches, but, as Bulmer (2007: 51) notes, such implications are likely to be particularly relevant to EU studies, where 'an awareness of the new institutionalisms is indispensable for understanding how Europeanization is theorized'. As discussed earlier, March and Olsen (1998, 2005) do acknowledge that the complex realities of political decision making and decision taking will result, in effect, in the logics overlapping – the basis of Goldmann's argument. Crucially, where Goldmann differs, however, is to problematize the nature of this overlap and to hypothesize the way(s) overlap occurs, by arguing for a more nuanced appreciation of entanglements of individual actor rationales, affiliated organizational imperatives and national interests upon decision making and decision taking, which, he alleges, is intrinsically part of both logics of appropriateness and consequentiality.

We develop Goldmann's position here by presenting one means of exploring how this difference can be made sense of empirically. We do so by distilling Goldmann's argument into three analytical propositions (set out below) permitting detailed consideration of the complex overlapping realities of elite decision making and decision taking. We argue that these propositions are of particular relevance to conceptualizing a more sophisti-cated understanding of the Europeanization of elite EU political practice, by enabling us to explore the opportunities and constraints offered by March and Olsen's logics. These propositions highlight: (a) the overlapping nature of the logics, in particular conflation of actor self-interest with 'appropriate' behaviour in particular institutional settings (Proposition 1); (b) the fluctuating explanatory power of the logics at different times and in different negotiating situations (Proposition 2); and (c) the possibility that justifying decision making might be a more compelling *explanans* than internal motives – whether 'appropriate' or 'consequential' (Proposition 3).

Proposition 1: 'There remains a common situation in social life in which . . . self interest is defined as that which is appropriate in view of the fact that the actor is fulfilling the obligations of a role and is adhering to the imperative of holding a position' (Goldmann 2005: 41).

From our interviews with senior negotiators concerning the workings of the EU Council Working Groups, it became apparent that Goldmann's 'common situation in social life' – where actor self-interest effectively constitutes what is deemed 'appropriate' behaviour in particular institutional settings – also frequently occurs in EU diplomacy, making the distinction between March and Olsen's two logics fuzzy and problematic. This is hardly surprising: a negotiator's role, after all, is to embody and act upon extrinsic and intrinsic public obligations. These obligations routinely require following government instructions, acting to agreed negotiating scripts and positions, and reporting upon unfolding developments and countering those that threaten such positions. In these circumstances, therefore, it might be hypothesized that negotiators' 'self-interest' will often be determined by personal avoidance of actions that cede points to their peers or higher political actors, or that undermine a carefully prepared negotiating line.

Our briefing sessions provided some grounds for developing this proposition. In particular, senior negotiators within the United Kingdom's Foreign and Commonwealth Office (FCO), the former Department of Trade and Industry and the Department of Environment, Food and Rural Affairs (DEFRA) gave credence to Goldmann's statement, noting specifically how actor self-interest was often indivisible from the delivery of role obligations in high-level diplomatic settings. Importantly, this did not mean individual actors subordinating their interest and initiative in some way to 'higher authority', but rather their vesting their individual expertise and experience creatively to further national interest. We heard how this collective pooling of years of individual experience among senior negotiators, often from across a range of different government departments ('parent' department as well as other departments whose interests might be at stake in negotiations, or those that might have directly relevant expertise), provided the cornerstone for producing UK negotiating briefs for Council, which typically were highly specified (setting out negotiating objectives, milestones towards these objectives, red lines, etc.); on issues of 'high politics', the Cabinet Office and the Number 10 European Policy Office would be directly involved in coordinating the production and final content of these documents. Typically, the resulting briefing would be finalized only twelve to eighteen hours prior to a Council meeting to ensure that its guidance reflected the latest available intelligence. Understandably, this places senior negotiators under additional pressure since, as one interviewee pithily commented,

> I've had my briefing pack given to me as I'm leaving for the station, by which time everyone's gone home. So if you get a briefing that turns out to be complete rubbish – guff that you couldn't possibly say or use – nobody's going to be there for you to ring from the train or the plane. So, worryingly, there's sometimes a bit of winging it.
>
> (Authors' interview with FCO official)

Applying Goldmann's first proposition to Europeanization within EU decision-making fora therefore suggests that individual actor behaviours arise from a sublimation of the two logics to achieve the specific preferences of government.

Proposition 2: '[T]he relative significance of the logics varies with situation and issue as well as over time' (Goldmann 2005: 43).

Even if one accepts March and Olsen's logics as separate explanatory devices, Goldmann argues that neither provides a sufficiently robust or compelling explanation for decision making behaviour in all circumstances. Again, from our preliminary discussions with UK negotiators, events in the EU Council of Ministers provided examples of where, dependent on the stage reached in the negotiating process, it could be plausibly argued that 'variation in logics' occurred. There are a number of credible explanations for why this might arise. Perhaps the most common is that Council negotiators will strive to avoid actions weakening their position in relation to their peers or higher political actors, suggesting that a logic of expected consequences will predominate as negotiators battle to avoid 'ceding ground' or 'losing position'. Our preliminary discussions with interviewees certainly confirmed that, at lower levels of the Council's tiered decision-making process, negotiators tend to be preoccupied with not losing any ground in discussions. An apposite example of this was furnished by the United Kingdom's senior negotiator engaged in protracted discussions in the latest bout of Common Agricultural Policy (CAP) reforms. This negotiator commented how, in the Council Working Groups set up to examine different aspects of this reform, national representation was dominated by subject experts – leading to very prolonged discussion, with national representatives 'making heavy weather of everything' in their attempts to secure domestic advantage. By contrast, higher up the Council hierarchy, where EU diplomatic cadres took over, there was a greater sense among participants of the 'European' norms of consensus and compromise epitomized in the logic of appropriateness. Indeed, striking deals at the lowest level of EU Council decision making (i.e. a logic of consequentiality), in order, as one interviewee noted, 'not to lose the point higher up', fosters the development of habits of group loyalties, mutual confidence and trust typified by the logic of appropriateness. In essence, therefore, Goldmann's second proposition sheds new light on the importance of who is taking the decisions that comprise Europeanization, how these decisions are sequenced, their timing and their political salience. Again, this supports the notion of a blending of calculated strategy by individual actors with subscription to Europeanized learning and socialization strategies.

Proposition 3: 'It is not self evident that internal motives should be given priority in the search for the logic of an action. It may be just as relevant to be concerned with justifications because they may tell us something about the logic of the constituencies of decision makers' (Goldmann 2005: 42).

Here Goldmann takes issue with March and Olsen's notion that either logic should be prioritized to explain political action. Instead, it might be equally valid to focus upon how political actors justify their behaviours to the constituencies they represent and to whom they are responsible; obviously, the aftermath of any political decision comprises not only consequences for the negotiator, but, crucially, how this decision can be cleared with these constituencies. Thus, rather than socialization and learning promoting value change, as the logic of appropriateness suggests, or creating the conditions for hard bargaining around national political priorities embodied in the logic of expected consequences, certain sorts of political decisions may be taken on the basis of how well these can be 'sold' to the often disparate constituencies the negotiator represents.

Justification and legitimization can of course be derived through a variety of means (Habermas 1996; Heath 2001), and, crucially, are required for different constituencies – participants in the decision-making process, as much as the 'silent majorities' represented by decision makers in high-level negotiation (Kratochwil 1989). Thus, what has been termed the 'logic of justification' (Eriksen 1999) can be expressed as the utility of proposed decisions to affected constituencies; assertion of values that decisions embody and that constituencies might subscribe to; or to universally recognized rights that these decisions uphold (Fossum 2000). So, elite decision making and decision taking

> does not solely designate consistency or preference driven action based on calculus of success, nor merely norm conformity or accordance with entrenched standards of appropriateness, but rather public reason-giving: when criticized plans of action can be justified by explicating the relevant situation in a legitimate manner.
>
> (Eriksen and Fossum 2003: 28)

This latter aspect of 'public reason-giving' is crucial for elite actors, who require not only self-justification but also justification to peers. Equally important is the need to defend what might be perceived as 'failure' to key stakeholders and wider publics. Within EU decision-taking fora, it is widely recognized that there is considerable scope for policymakers within what is a relatively closed decision-making process (Grande 1996) to be ingenious in their defending of 'failure' in this way.

Our background discussions suggested that this logic of justification may be invoked where political elites deem the political salience of an issue to be low – that is, where national interests are not at stake or are negligible. We heard, for example, of cases where 'UK plc' was not directly involved in 'side agreements' to major policy negotiations, but where UK NGOs' and civil society groups' goals would be jeopardized. In these cases, 'picking a negotiating line, a way through that before you enter into negotiations with your EU partners' that provided 'adequate justification' for particular action being taken, became an important feature.

Applying this third proposition to Europeanization of individual actor behaviour explicitly recognizes the multiplicity of interests involved in this multifaceted process; individual actors, organizations, political parties and civil society groups as well as the 'national' interest, monopolized by government, have an interest in Europeanization outcomes. Intriguingly, applying this proposition to Europeanization also implies that the machinery of the Council seeks to manufacture justifications for national negotiators to participate in EU policy, rather than catalysing change in national values, or brokering consensus among competing national interests. If that is so, the routinized nature of political exchange and interaction within Europeanization might comprise logics of appropriateness and consequentiality interchangeably, creating a context in which it is, empirically, incredibly difficult to separate their influence upon the reasoning of political actors.

In the next section, we use these propositions to provide an overarching analytical framework for the empirical examination of Europeanization as elite political practice in the EU's Council of Ministers.

Building on Goldmann's propositions: actor understandings of Europeanization in Council negotiations

Having developed Goldmann's propositions by applying them to the specific case of Europeanization of individual elite behaviour, here we seek to critically examine each by drawing upon the 'lived experience' of senior UK policy actors. In interview after general discussion of the workings of the Council, respondents were asked to critically engage with each of the three propositions and to reflect upon whether and to what extent these described their career experience of, and participation in, high-level negotiations in Council. We present their verbatim responses to each proposition here, with the aim of establishing fresh insights into the Europeanization of political elites. In particular, we examine the extent to which political actor behaviour in Council decision-making arenas confirms Goldmann's propositions on the alleged chaotic and problematic nature of Europeanization.

Interviewees' experience of Council-level negotiations ranged from twelve months' to over thirty years' engagement, and this interviewing range enabled us to explore what Checkel (2005: 802) describes as 'senses of community and belonging' in EU decision-making institutions and probe the complex processual dynamics of Europeanization. All twelve interviewees were members of the Senior Civil Service at either Assistant Director (Grade 5; PB1) or Director (Grade 3; PB2) level, and hence used to agreeing strategic aims with Ministers and possessing great experience of communicating those aims to their peers from other states in high-level EU negotiating fora. A requirement for each interviewee was that they had been entrusted with leading on specific, often highly complex, negotiating briefs, requiring them to act on their own initiative during often lengthy negotiations, thus allowing us to explore fully March and Olsen's logics. From these interviews we also sought to distil contemporary understandings of Europeanization in the EU's Council of Ministers.

Proposition 1

Interviewees emphasized the critical importance of a detailed strategic framework within which their decision taking in Council could be situated. As discussed above, these frameworks – usually taking the form of highly detailed briefings, or a briefing pack – represented the culmination of considerable effort by responsible arms of the national bureaucracy to reach agreement on what constituted 'appropriate' goals and suitable strategies for lead negotiators in Council. From these documents – and building upon their own individual experience – interviewees described how they adopted specific 'roles' to play in Council, the importance of which could not be overestimated:

> You are stuck if you go to Brussels without understanding what role you are playing, and what is one of a number of negotiating frameworks. You have got to have the basic knowledge to do that.
>
> (Author's interview with UK environment official)

For some interviewees, these 'role' obligations were firmly associated with particular Council fora. For example, negotiators identified certain practices and well-defined understandings and interests that contributed to the 'atmospherics' of Council meetings, subtly influencing their behaviours and, through them, the outcome of Council politics. As a UK environment policy negotiator explained,

> [Role obligations] are a very important driver. Let's take it at the level of discussions in the Council of Ministers. There are some Councils that regard their job as being the collective defence of a particular interest, and the Agriculture Council is the obvious one, where the majority of members see their job as protecting the interest of the farmer. There are members of the Agriculture Council who will explicitly take this line and so, you know, we 'are here in Brussels operating against our colleagues back home'. The Environment Council is to some extent like that too. There are the 'green ministers' and there is a green baton which is handed from one Council presidency to the next. This is not

metaphorical – there is a real baton, and this was handed over across my place at the Council last Friday.

(Author's interview with UK environment official)

Such comments would favour a logic of appropriateness, depicting Council actors as carefully calculating and seeking to maximize given interests, adapting their behaviour to the norms and rules favoured by the EU Council community. Yet the detailed guidance and specification of 'appropriate' behaviours distilled in negotiators' briefings and the prevailing 'atmospherics' of Council seemingly only provide a framework for what is often hard-fought negotiation. The weight of responsibility on the shoulders of lead UK negotiators really arises from the imperatives of holding a position while respecting these 'atmospherics', as a UK environment policy negotiator, commenting on his recent involvement in an Environment Council meeting, explained:

You don't ever go into the Council chamber cold. What basically happened last week is that the Department looked at the proposals, saw how they might affect our work, and made a judgement about whether or not they would be acceptable to us in their present wording. [We] reassured ourselves that we know what the consequences will be if we were to implement them in their original state, whether that would be acceptable to us, and what we would want out of them as a member state, bearing in mind political considerations – what the policy flavour of the day is, as it were. So the Department did that sort of assessment and then there was an agreed formal position in the Cabinet office, and there were mechanisms to do that. And then as negotiator it was down to me.

(Author's interview with UK environment official)

Thus, the framework of appropriate behaviours provides the context of and the parameters for very carefully calibrated decision making and taking by high-level negotiators, the scope of whom, to judge from interviewees, varied with their skills, aptitude and experience. So, for one Grade 5 negotiator recently taking up an entirely new brief in international trade:

No, no, I rarely said anything off my own bat and didn't dare let our negotiating position unfold [without consulting colleagues]. I had two phones going at any one time when I was in the room, so I rarely said anything off my own bat. We got the agenda on Monday morning (though it's sometimes much later than that) and then got the Commission briefing and cleared the lines across Whitehall that were necessary for that particular meeting which was [in Brussels] on Friday.

> We had a coordination meeting on Wednesday morning here [in London] and we just went through the agenda and the subject expert said what the issue was about, what their recommended line was and then the various others, the more strategic overview bods, chipped in, saying, 'that's a load of rubbish because of X, Y, Z' and then we thrashed it out there. Then it was formalized and written up. I was given various specific lines to take at the Friday meeting. However, an AOB [any other business] issue came up on the day and I was on the phones straight away.
>
> (Author's interview with UK trade official)

Here the interviewee's comparative lack of experience is compensated by the formidable resources of the 'Whitehall machine' to make Europeanization a finely judged process of individual actions and calculation, hedged about by organizational goals and national priorities. More strategic calculation in meetings necessitates a finer-grained knowledge of the behaviour of particular actors around the Council table, accrued through repeated socialization in EU arenas. As a UK negotiator explained,

> One of the tricks of securing your objectives in the Council is to plan for what you expect the partners to be saying and allow for the 'line-up' you expect to see in the negotiation. And it's not only a factor of the subject matter that's being dealt with: it's a factor of the personalities you're dealing with too.
>
> (Author's interview with UK environment official)

Similarly, the capacity of negotiators to spot the opportunity to use particular bargaining strategies within Council, and the ways they might exploit these opportunities, varied. Not surprisingly, perhaps, a common strategy – widely considered 'appropriate' behaviour – is for negotiators to contact other partners before meetings to agree common positions, as a UK trade negotiator explained:

> In the meetings for specific issues, my tactics would be pretty straight-forward, such as phoning up like-minded colleagues in advance, discussing things in the margins of meetings, et cetera. I don't believe that could be considered as inappropriate.
>
> (Author's interview with UK trade official)

Interviewees agreed that 'inappropriate' behaviour included reneging on agreed points, being over-critical of the European Commission and its services when decisions 'go against' their national delegation, or refusing to cooperate with the Commission to find a solution to particular negotiating difficulties and stalemates. The evidence for these inappropriate behaviours was articulated by one interviewee as follows:

> Of course, it would be very politically expedient to say this is due to a load of Eurocrats in Brussels but at the same time this doesn't actually happen very often – even by our political masters – simply because they know that we have to have a good working relationship [with the Commission], and as soon as you start playing that card, all the goodwill and favours that you get will be cut dead. Or, the next time that you need something done, something critical, there's some reason why 'it can't be done' for us.
>
> (Author's interview with UK trade official)

> Well, we had our own agenda, obviously, and there are things which I didn't say in open forum, there are things I wouldn't say, things I knew and did not volunteer, and things that I took someone over to one side and discussed with them only before the meeting began. I mean within the constraints that I had to operate in, then that's not devious or inappropriate as such. It was vital to secure our own agenda.
>
> (Author's interview with UK agriculture official)

> If a particular member state has a problem with an issue, then the Commission will pursue it individually with that member state and they will try and set up meetings and keep a dialogue going until they can resolve it between themselves so that we can arrive at a consensus . . . it is always a negotiated consensus where not everyone is happy all of the time, and you kind of accept that you will win some and you'll lose some and that everyone is always open to working with the Commission on kind of sticking points . . . the shutters rarely go down.
>
> (Author's interview with UK agriculture official)

The tenor of these observations was about flux in motivations, rationales and use of a multiplicity of different techniques, particularly by lead negotiators in Council. Thus, when asked specifically about the different motivations or logics of decision taking in the Council, all interviewees found it profoundly difficult to disentangle 'appropriateness' from 'consequentiality', partly because of the classic iterated nature and lengthy character of Europeanization:

> If you've been in discussions and negotiations with your EU partners for several months on a major package, it's about an issue which you've

absorbed, rather like cold which comes up through your feet when you've been standing on a concrete floor for a long time. Most of the interaction we will have had with our EU partners will have been done at official level, by people like me, who will have deeply imbibed what the issue is about. So, you don't find yourself surprised by what you are being asked to do.

(Author's interview with UK environment official)

An excellent example of the way in which Europeanization has political behaviour blending appropriateness and self-interest was articulated by one senior trade negotiator, who explained bluntly:

If something is particularly controversial and it requires me to take a position, then I would always get political clearance. These dilemmas of [appropriateness and consequentiality] don't churn through my head: so long as I've got political clearance, frankly I don't care.

(Author's interview with UK trade official)

There is therefore much to suggest that strategic calculation in Council decision making takes place in an institutional context of policy cooperation and consensus building, tending to confirm Goldmann's first proposition about the 'blurring' of decision-making logics. As Wallace and Wallace (1999: 35) reflect, 'The relative solidity of the [European Union's] institutional casing imposes a distinctive structure on the negotiating process and helps to consolidate the results.'

Proposition 2

At certain times and in certain situations, respondents confirmed that they had adopted what might have been perceived by other negotiators as 'discordant' behaviour, or even positions 'antagonistic' to other negotiators, to secure their objectives. As one interviewee commented,

There are distinctive styles of negotiating among different member states. I always tend to keep my contributions very short, sharp and sweet. By contrast, the ones that have been there longer tend to ramble on and on . . . as I don't have ten years of that crowd, I can't . . . the southern member states tend to be more garrulous, if that's not being too stereotypical . . . but I don't know whether that's because they've been doing the job for years.

(Author's interview with UK trade official)

Moreover, even among negotiators, awareness of appropriate behaviours apparently varies between individuals, depending on their own experience and training. Thus, routinized behaviours among some negotiators may pose difficulties for others, as a UK foreign policy negotiator involved in EU neighbourhood policy revealed:

> The committee meeting that I attend comprises senior officials from the member states, and it's a deeply political process. There are people engaged in this committee that were there in 1995 and they have an immense background of knowledge, they help you inordinately but they are very much constrained in the way in which they do things. There's a real stylistic difference in the way in which they do things, so you inevitably end up talking to people from the newer generations of diplomats around the table. We are taught to negotiate differently, I think.
>
> (Author's interview with UK diplomat)

Similarly, Checkel's (2005: 811) observation that 'those agents with extensive previous professional experience in . . . international policymaking settings are more likely to internalise supranational role conceptions . . . than those who are . . . "parachuted" into international settings' appears substantiated by the contrasting views of two UK officials of the EU 133 trade committee: one new to the brief and one a long-serving career negotiator. Take the comments of the new appointment:

> You just hit the ground running and do what needs to be done. I see it very functionally: go in, get what we want, and come out again. If we know that we're not going to get what we want, then at least I'm on record as having said what we needed to say. It wouldn't bother me to contradict or confront the Commission; that's part of the role . . . people do. I don't particularly think that that sort of atmosphere dominates the meeting. It's all just quite frank discussion.
>
> (Author's interview with UK trade official)

The career diplomat with over three decades of EU negotiating experience maintained:

> The great thing about the 133 Committee is that it has no power. It's advising the Commission on policy in the role that it carries out in negotiating on behalf of the EU and that gives the individual delegate – and I know, as I've attended one of the 133 Committees – the freedom to say what he or she thinks because there's no voting; the 133 Committee doesn't decide anything, it advises. It's chaired by the Commission, so

it's not as if there can be a mood in the Committee or which could be summed up by a chairman against what the Commission chooses to conclude. I just don't recognize that description of the 133 Committee because that atmosphere enables delegates to wax lyrical. The notion of 'going in and getting what you want and then going out again' is the opposite of the constitution of the 133 Committee. The constitution of that Committee is that the individual delegate has to devote the effort that's necessary to influence the Commission.

(Author's interview with UK environment official)

Crucially, here 'appropriateness' and 'consequentiality' logics would be interpreted and deployed in entirely different ways by these negotiators, as neither has 'read' the informal institutional norms and conventions – or indeed the formal role of this Committee – in the same way.

Respondents also emphasized that as individuals they worked within wider decision-making environments. Routinely, negotiators with particular skills and experience – inherently favouring particular decision-making logics – are therefore deployed by national governments for particular effects:

People who come from capitals can't have the kind of camaraderie that goes between those who are Brussels based and who probably do know each other very well because they probably cover two or three committees together, swapping notes and so on. However, there's also the tendency for them to go slightly native, which is why people like me go out there every week to be a sort of counterweight to that.

(Author's interview with UK trade official)

Consequently, while Checkel (2005: 806) argues that '[n]ational officials heading to Brussels may already be highly pro-European', it is important to recognize that many may not be so.

Proposition 3

Goldmann's contention that 'internal motives' may not provide the real focus for decision making and that justification of decisions instead is the driver has substantial ramifications for Europeanization – particularly on issues of sub-optimal decision making or topics of 'low politics' where national interest may not be at stake. As a UK trade official confirmed, this justification of political behaviours does not require any reference to the internal motives of individual actors:

We have to be very acutely aware of not simply trying to satisfy UK plc but also NGO interests and broader society goals, and you are always pulled in contradictory directions between what, say, the CBI might say, and what politicians might say, and what developing countries might say. So you can't always get what you want.

(Author's interview with UK trade official)

In other words, national delegations constantly need justifications for taking action – and equally for *not* taking action, so-called non-decisions (Majone 1989) – to satisfy the myriad constituencies of interest they represent. Moreover, if justification rather than internal motive is important, it suggests that the dynamic of the Council, and particularly its consensual basis, tends to operate against persuasion of the sort proposed by Checkel. As one UK agricultural negotiator pithily put it, 'You can't convince other negotiators that it is in their interests to be hanged in the morning.' Thus, applying Goldmann's third proposition to the operation of the Council, rather than attempting to change fundamental national interests (key negotiating goals, 'red lines', etc.) and key negotiating preferences, the Commission and the Council presidency are constantly seeking to generate justifications for member states to 'buy in' to EU political projects. As interviewees reflected, this might merely take the form of reassurances to national delegations:

[I]f they're worried about something fundamental, you can't tell them that black is white. But if it's a matter of interpretation, the Commission might be able to offer reassurance without needing to change the text. They've resorted rather more to making bilateral undertakings, which are not recorded publicly, to different delegations: 'Don't make a fuss about this, why are you worried about that aspect, I can assure you that when it comes to it you won't have a problem on that particular point, it's not our intention at all to . . . So, you can soothe people's fears in the margins up to a point, but I wouldn't describe that as redefining their preferences.

(Author's interview with UK foreign policy official)

Certainly, the idea that negotiators can be persuaded to redefine their preferences and interests through the offer of side payments and complex issue linkage is not borne out by interviewee comments. As a UK environment policy negotiator explained,

There's remarkably little of that. Up to ministerial level it does not apply at all. Within any individual bit of activity you'll probably be thinking, 'on balance, this is probably all right because while that's not as good as I might like, that gives me one of the really important things'. You go into most negotiations with a clear idea of the things you have got to get, and if you don't get, then you can't sign up. I think that even when you get Ministers putting together packages – this is most obviously true in the Agriculture Council and probably also in the European Council – what you are thinking about is 'overall, is this something which meets more of my requirements than delivers things that fail to meet my requirements?' rather than this mechanical trade-off. There isn't in negotiation, I find, much of that trade-off going on. Participants don't say, 'If I give way to you on article 3.1 will you give way to me on article 4.5?' There isn't as much of that as you might think.

(Author's interview with UK environment official)

Political elites' insights into the processual dynamics of Europeanization

In the preceding sections, we have seen how UK negotiators involved in Europeanization explain their behaviours and actions in ways that cannot be understood simply in terms of March and Olsen's logics of appropriateness and consequentiality. Building on Goldmann (2005), we have identified several important points about the constraining and constitutive aspects of Europeanization, and sought to winnow its processual dynamics. From the preceding analysis, we contend that the key dynamic of Europeanization of individual actor behaviour in Council is the commingling of the two logics to satisfy career, organizational and national goals while as far as possible acting 'appropriately' by observing the Council's 'attributes of atmosphere' (Puchala 1972: 282). The result is a suite of processes that maintain and sustain the European Union, and are indicative of a profound relationship between the political project of European integration and a 'way of doing things' among EU political actors that are constitutive of Europeanization:

- Decision-making processes are routinized; the prevailing feature is consensus building.
- There is recognition among negotiators that there are prevailing and long-standing values and norms associated with membership of particular Councils.
- These values and norms are shared among Council negotiators and create a constitutive belonging in which trust and mutual exchange are dominant.
- This constitutive belonging is the context in which strategic calculation is made and limits placed on the extent of normative suasion.
- This constitutive belonging incorporates clearly identifiable appropriate and inappropriate behaviours for securing negotiator preferences.

Paradoxically, while there has in recent years been much academic discussion on Europeanization and its inherent characteristics, there has not been a

corresponding engagement and clear understanding among policy practitioners of Europeanization's precise attributes and processual features. It
was thus instructive to finish our discussions by asking respondents what they
perceived to be the salient features of the Europeanization process. Under
questioning, its multifaceted and complex nature came over strongly in the
various ways that UK negotiators tried to conceptualize it. Critically, from
their comments it is apparent that Europeanization bears upon the totality of
relations between political spaces, actors and scales of EU governance. UK
negotiators offer four broad interpretations of what we term here *spaces of
Europeanization*:

1   Europeanization as the use of EU arenas for the projection of national
    interests, though where clear differences among participants are recog-
    nized and respected:

> Never underestimate the extent to which you don't understand
> where the other guy is coming from. And that's true right across
> the piece. And of course, where they are coming from is a
> symptom of where this 'thing' called Europeanization stops
> short. There is a still a wide variety of difference in the ways in
> which they do things across the member states and in different
> policy areas in different member states as well.
> (Author's interview with UK agriculture official)

2   Europeanization as an emergent scale of supranational governance
    within which actors subscribe to an 'EU way' of doing business (that is,
    pressure to resolve differences between member states is, in effect, a
    consensus-building activity that motors integration).

> I think there's probably a book to be written there about the role
> of that pressure to resolve problems in driving policy integration
> in lots of ways that integration isn't being driven. This could be
> what you might call 'Europeanization'.
> (Author's interview with UK environment official)

3   Europeanization as a reshuffling of territorial bases of authority and
    alterations in the ways in which national interests might be represented.

> The cooperative atmosphere that exists between the member
> states is pretty strong. You see that in international negotiations,
> where the tasks are carved up between different negotiators
> and delegations, when you are sitting at one of these major

international negotiations. I would therefore say Europeanization is the need to adapt to a developing spread of European
competence in decision making.

(Author's interview with UK foreign policy official)

4   Europeanization as a complex reconfiguration of governance in which
over time it becomes increasingly difficult to define actors as 'national'
or 'supranational'.

It's very difficult to single out what Europeanization might be
because EU activity really is, I think, a form of domestic policy.
You don't step out of your domestic arena and go into another
one. There's really no boundary in the things that we deal with,
which are largely EU driven, between thinking about them as
EU activities and thinking about them as domestic activities.

(Author's interview with UK trade official)

Importantly, these four conceptualizations proposed by political actors map
onto the categories set out in Chapter 2 and provide key avenues linking
academic and policy practitioner interests around which further empirical
testing and verification of Europeanization's processual features should be
prioritized. Consequently, we focus academic scrutiny on these areas in the
following chapters. First, however, we consider what spaces of Europeanization might comprise.

Towards spatialities of Europeanization

As we have seen, explaining and understanding Europeanization and its
impacts upon political structures and processes in the European Union is
replete with difficulties. Specifically, as this chapter has demonstrated, probing
Europeanization's effects upon individual political actor behaviour in the
European Union presents particular challenges to researchers. We have
investigated the processual dynamics of Europeanization in the Union through
a focus on one facet – that is, the role of domestic political elites in mediating
Europeanization through their participation and active engagement in decision
making in the European Union's Council of Ministers, the Union's foremost
decision-taking body. Given the difficulties that scholars have encountered
with understanding and explaining Europeanization, this chapter has furnished
a clearly defined entry point into this research area, and, critically, one that is
amenable to empirical testing and scrutiny. The empirical work supports and
builds on our conceptualization and typologies of Europeanization elaborated
in Chapter 2 and elsewhere (Clark and Jones 2008; Jones and Clark 2008).

Our entry point has been recent critiques of the new institutionalism, an analytical approach critically important to current conceptualizations of Europeanization. The logics of appropriateness and consequentiality have become, in themselves, foci of much critical debate in political science over their utility for interpreting individual political action. In this chapter, we have sought to examine the utility of these logics in explaining the behaviours and activities of EU negotiators from the United Kingdom. Using their testimonies, we have endeavoured to gauge their personal 'lived' experience of contemporary Europeanization in the European Union's Council of Ministers.

What is evident from their testimonies is that these logics do not adequately capture the juxtaposition of different behavioural reasoning and stances adopted by UK negotiators during the period 2004–06. Moreover, while much of the literature contends that Europeanization involves domestic precepts moving inevitably towards a convergence around a 'European' norm, crucially the testimonies of UK negotiators appears to cast doubt on this assertion. Indeed, the findings presented here would suggest that European-ization *is not transformative* but, rather, is attenuated through consensual behaviours, attitudes and opinions in the EU negotiating context such that domestic norms are not compromised. In fact, the analysis presented here suggests that they may even be furthered or advanced. Europeanization thus emerges as the nuanced articulation of disparate (individual; organizational; national) interests set within highly circumscribed EU decision-making and decision-taking fora. Fundamentally, while these EU fora facilitate cooperative discussion and consensual behaviours, they do not necessarily lead to the refashioning of embedded norms and beliefs or the remodelling of deeply etched understandings among UK negotiators.

Now that we have identified some of the shortcomings of the new institutional approach, are there indications provided by UK interviewees around which we can develop a more holistic understanding of the European-ization of elite political practice? Importantly, all respondents acknowledged, either explicitly or implicitly, the importance of the reshuffling of established constellations of power, the transition from government to governance, and the political geographical drivers of territory and territoriality, aspects identified in Chapter 2 as outcomes of Europeanization. But more funda-mentally, underlying these power–governance–territory outcomes is the rescaling of authority, identities and knowledges between the individual, the local, the regional, the national and the global. Recent work in geography on the political economies of scale (Leitner *et al.* 2002; Leitner 2003; McMaster and Sheppard 2003; Paasi 2001; Scott 2002, 2005; Swyngedouw 1997, 2000, 2005) is therefore useful in progressing processual understandings of Europeanization, for, as Paasi (2001: 8) comments, 'The emergence of the EU provides the most recent and powerful expression of the European politics of scale in the age of globalization.'

In our view, three findings from this work by geographers are particularly instructive here. First, as scale is socially produced rather than pre-given or static, it follows that quotidian social exchanges between actors create distinctive scaled visions of what it is to be European, and what roles and responsibilities this entails. Second, scale is relational, implying that Europeanization is fashioned from the melding of these different scaled visions; in effect, Europeanization is interlinked, nested and constantly (re)produced through the cross-cutting activities of actors (cf. Bache 2006; Geyer 2007). Third, scale is mutually interpenetrated. Hence, although Europeanization is actively (re)produced from interrelations that originate locally, regionally, nationally and globally, these cannot be disentangled meaningfully.

Taken together, this is suggestive analytically of an approach that examines how power–governance–territory is interwoven in spaces of Europeanization that cut across scales, imbricating multiple actor and institutional activities. As we have seen in this chapter, some of these spaces are specialized and relatively autonomous, with their own dynamics, discourses and clienteles, focused for example on territory–community values, the state, its actors and agents, or particular instantiations of power embodied, for example, in specific policy regimes or thematic areas. Notably, the broadest social space of Europeanization, European society, is composed of all these constituent aspects.

Spaces of Europeanization are thus constituted from meetings and intersections between networks of relations stretching out across different scales (Massey 1994, 1999). Such spaces display a spatial and scalar tension derived from the multiple politics of Europeanization they are constituted from, in which powerful individuals, groups and institutions seek to promote their own material and ideological visions of 'EUrope' at the expense of less powerful groups advocating divergent visions. These spatialized politics are shaped by factors including local and national state attitudes and values towards the Europeanization context in question; class, gender and ethnic divisions, and the way they link to EU identities; and the micro-geographies of everyday worked life of specific actors, and how these structure social interaction and the action frames of actors towards Europeanization (i.e. their type and level of engagement).

It is the politics of these spaces – the practices, struggles, and discourses produced by people's everyday patterns of living and working – that determine the (re)production of Europeanization, by precipitating change in actors' identities, powers and resources. As spaces of Europeanization are so heterogeneous (not only cutting across scales, but morphing with place and policy area, for example), it is only through examining particular spatialized politics that sense can be made of underlying process. That is, these politics demonstrate the multifarious ways in which actors employ their common stock of knowledge about 'EUrope' and European identities to meet their strategic needs and purposes (cf. Checkel and Katzenstein 2009; Passerini 2002). This has echoes in Jerneck's (2000: 37) description of it as 'a certain "civicness"', based on trust, shared rules and norms. As such, it paves the way for 'civilised and constructive means of mutual problem solving . . . the political dialogue in Europe has moved . . . from simple to complex and more sophisticated learning'.

A range of different empirical approaches for capturing the interweaving processes of power–governance–territory is possible, with the primary goal of interrogating particular spaces of Europeanization and the representative and participative politics therein. We argue for a number of reasons that the triptych of power–governance–territory offers a promising analytical approach to understanding the role of elite political practice in Europeanization. First, it furnishes a more holistic, less porous and reductionist, account that specifically addresses the 'elusive fluidity' of the processes of Europeanization. Second, it highlights Europeanization as an organic, processual suite that is dependent on the activities of many elite actors operating at a variety of scales and levels, rather than simply a transformative outcome deriving from a monolithic European Union. Finally, it reveals how Europeanization is mediated through power relations between actors and social structures within boundary-spanning networks, such that quanta of identity and territorial specificities are exchanged through socialization and learning processes.

In order to exemplify the interweaving processes of power–governance–territory, in the following chapters we present three further contemporary case studies of Europeanization (see Table 3.1). In the first, we consider the activities of senior EU policy actors and political elites from five states acceding to the European Union, demonstrating how the political dynamics within high-level policy spaces is predicated on cross-cutting loyalties to state, nation and 'EUrope', leading to the fashioning of distinctive constructions of Europeanization. Here Europeanization depends fundamentally on the use of EU arenas for the projection of national interests, though clear differences among participants in those arenas are recognized and, more often than not, tolerated. The second case study examines how elite constructions of Europeanization are projected beyond the European Union; here, politics arise from these constructions encountering third-country preferences and expectations of 'EUrope'. Finally, we examine Europeanization through the lens of European territorial reshuffling in which alterations occur in the representation of national interests.

Table 3.1 Spaces of Europeanization by chapter theme

Chapter title	Europeanization context	Processes
4: Spaces of Europeanization: central and eastern European elites and the 2004 accession.	Accounts from high-level policy elites from five central and east European states directly involved in 2004 accession to the EU. Formalized policy areas, novice and expert policy elites; domestic/supranational.	Establishing/building networks of relations; learning formal rules and informality; learning technocratic language; learning through emulation.
5: Discourses of Europeanization: the European Commission, European narratives and European Neighbourhood Policy.	Dilemmas facing EU, member state and third-country political and policy elites in fashioning of the European Neighbourhood Policy for the Mediterranean. Domestic supranational/global.	Building consensus; articulation and projection of EU region-building narrative.
6: Territorial spaces of Europeanization: narratives and politics of multi-functionality in English and French rural areas.	EU, national and territorial elites' involvement in introduction of new forms of territorial governance within the EU CAP.	Regulatory scripts as 'heuristic templates'; mediation/reinterpretation of templates by domestic elites.

4 Spaces of Europeanization

Central and eastern European elites and the 2004 accession

Introduction

In Chapter 3, we argued that while new institutionalist approaches provide a valuable 'way in' to conceptualizing Europeanization generally, at the same time they exhibit certain weaknesses, not least in terms of explaining the role of individual actors in instigating, promoting and projecting Europeanization. To address this difficulty, we advocated a more holistic approach based around the notion of spaces of Europeanization: multi-scaled arenas defined and delimited by quotidian activities of diverse actors (including policy and political elites, the focus of this book), and made and remade by them through their everyday actions as these relate to 'EUrope'. One of the principal attractions of this form of conceptualization is the way in which detailed scrutiny of what we term here the spatializing political practice[1] of elite actors can be facilitated – practice that is often conducted at a variety of geographic scales, thereby furnishing new insights into Europeanization as process. Specifically, spaces of Europeanization comprise discursive and essentialist components that are (re)produced through mediations and intersections between spatializing political practices of different actors – whether 'EUropean', member state or 'third country' in origin – with these practices given purpose and meaning by the territorially defined norms and beliefs of elites relating to what it is, or what it means, to be 'EUropean'.

Here we exemplify this argument by examining elite representational practice associated with the 2004 accession to the European Union of central and east European states. We show how central and east European assertions of sociospatial concepts were embroiled in complex ways with enactments of these spatializing practices – that is, how elite assertion and performance of concepts such as space, territory and positionality created novel forms of politics pivotal to the reproduction of Europeanization. We contend in this chapter that spatialized political practice typically finds expression in one of two ways. The first is elites' explicit use of sociospatial concepts in contexts with which they are familiar to further their strategic goals and to assert their legitimacy as actors with political counterparts. The second expression is more subtle, whereby elites, encountering new political contexts, need to reappraise what might be termed their sociospatial lexicons in order to develop spatializing practices that are effective and 'licit' for these new contexts. Spatializing political practice can thus derive from elites' mastery of sociospatial concepts, or their adaptation to new sociospatialities. Unfamiliarity provides valuable prompts and cues to fashion new spatializing political practices, or to elaborate new permutations of existing practices.

We deepen our understanding of spaces of Europeanization by providing a longitudinal study of spatializing political practice among central and eastern European[2] (CE) political elites in the wake of accession to the European Union in 2004. Our analysis presents an actor-based perspective of how CE elite political practice sought to engage with the Union's dominant sociospatialities – a byzantine mix of space, place, scales and networks – in order to assert their bona fides as 'EUropean' actors. In contrast to new institutional approaches, by focusing upon spaces of Europeanization we can place the analytical focus firmly on the elusive fluidity and processual dynamism of Europeanized sociospatial practices.

This approach chimes with recent contributions to the sociospatialities literature. For example, Brenner (2009: 134) notes how 'periodization' of sociospatial relations requires researchers to demonstrate how continuities and discontinuities in these relations emerge, and (citing Jessop and Sum 2006: 327) how 'path-dependent "conservation–dissolution" moments can occur'. Undoubtedly, one such 'moment' for CE elites was the break-up of previous state socialist sociospatialities, obliging them to refashion their sociospatial vocabularies to suit novel EU institutional contexts.

Our analysis proceeds as follows. First, in order to explore the substance of spaces of Europeanization, we go beyond the new institutional literature, reviewing the diverse work on spatializing politics to provide key themes for theorizing elite spatializing political practice. We then consider the ways in which EU decision making is organized, and the norms and conventions that political and policy elites need to observe to assert their legitimacy within 'EUrope'. Drawing upon detailed semi-structured interview materials with high-level CE and EU elites compiled over a two-year period, we then piece together how CE elites attempted to play out these performative requirements through their own spatialized political practice, taking us to the heart of what it is to be European and to Europeanize. Crucially, such practice sought to mediate Eastness (defined by Kuus (2007a: 150) as 'an inscription of identity – a process by which places, events and societal developments are endowed with a likeness to the "East" as distinct from [western-dominated conceptions of] "Europe"'), while enhancing Europeanness ('proximity to or distance from an idealized [notion of] Europe'; ibid.: 150). We demonstrate how, since accession in May 2004, interpretation and performance of spatialized political practice has impinged upon and exaggerated a politics of difference and hierarchy within the European Union.

This chapter thus directly responds to Schimmelfennig and Sedelmeier's (2007) assessment of the perceived inadequacies of existing Europeanization research on central and eastern Europe, which has tended to rely heavily on rational choice and sociological institutionalism as explanatory motives, and which has tended to focus upon either pre-accession or post-accession politics rather than providing a more encompassing longitudinal analysis, which we do here. Moreover, through our focus upon elite political practices, we provide a novel means of conceptualizing the varied influence of EU interventions and historic and cultural legacies on these practices – a theoretical objective prioritized by Schimmelfennig and Sedelmeier.

Theorizing elite spatializing political practice

There is now a substantial literature on spatializing politics within the social sciences, originating in philosophy, sociology and anthropology (see, for example, Bourdieu 1977; Foucault 1972; Lefebvre 1974, 1991; Tilly 1977). Thus, Tilly (1977, 1992) shows how, over time, space has been continually enrolled by actors both as arena for popular protest globally and as a medium for articulating and enacting collective political struggle or so-called 'contentious politics' (McAdam *et al.* 2001: 5). In geography, the initial focus of spatializing politics was upon the reproduction of space and social relations of production associated with advanced capitalism (Harvey 1982, 1990; Smith 1987, 1992; Soja 1980), but recent theorizations have successively built upon these insights to highlight the myriad ways in which political activities and actions (in fields as diverse as class, labour, gender and race relations, environmental activism and local–global social movements) shape and reshape sociospatial concepts, including place, scale, territory, positionality and mobility (e.g. Brenner 2004; Brenner *et al.* 2003; Brown 2000; Massey 1994; Rose 1996, 1999; Soja 1996, 1999). For as Massey (1992, 1994, 1999, 2005) argues, the defining attributes of these concepts are their contingency and malleability, confirming space as inherently representational and politicized.

Drawing upon Tilly's ideas, Leitner *et al.* (2008: 158) have teased out how actors' political practice mobilizes sociospatial concepts. Thus, 'Discussions of the spatiality of contentious politics seek to analyse the ways in which geography matters to the imaginaries, practices and trajectories of contentious politics.' These spatializing politics might involve (re)structuring of networks to develop new spaces of empowerment or resistance; challenging geographical positionings of place; or upholding existing hierarchical and hegemonic conceptions. The critical feature is that political strategies mobilize sociospatial imaginaries, political strategies define how sociospatial concepts will be mobilized – even reimagined – and political strategies determine how these reimagined concepts will be deployed. As Bialasiewicz (2008: 71) comments, ultimately 'all representations of space, all geographical imaginations, have political effects'.

Among the most influential work on spatializing politics remains that of Henri Lefebvre (1991; see Elden 2004). Through developing a now celebrated triad of ways of rethinking space – as representations of space, spatial practice and representational spaces, respectively – Lefebvre offers a framework for anatomizing the intrinsically social and political qualities of spaces of Europeanization. For Lefebvre, this triad of spaces is co-constituted, with each existing simultaneously yet having particular characteristics. The notion of *representations of space*, for example, crystallizes how actors grapple with space in the abstract, typically by assigning codes, beliefs and imaginaries that imbue it with particular qualities. Simultaneously, Lefebvre alleges that representations of space play a critically important role in shaping actors' quotidian social and political practices by providing structures around and through which they live and work – their *spatial practice*. And in combination, spatial practice and representations of space assist in understanding the opportunities and constraints upon actors' everyday performativities – that is, their *representational space*.

Certainly the notion of parsing social constructions of space with power and action has become a commonplace in studies of spatializing politics in a variety of empirical contexts (e.g. Allen 2004; Bærenholdt and Simonsen 2004; Brenner *et al.* 2003; Faulconbridge 2007; Herbert 1996; Law and Hetherington 2000; Leitner *et al.* 2002; Martin and Miller 2003). Moreover, while Lefebvre and others focus upon spatial intersections with everyday political struggle, the insights they offer can plausibly be applied to elite political contexts – particularly, we argue, to contexts such as the European Union, where quotidian elite political practice underpins sociospatialities. For, while popular politics have their own spatializing expressions and practices, crucially elites are conditioned by prevailing societal mores and behavioural norms. Indeed, as society's representatives, elite spatializing political practice needs to reflect wider social contexts if it is to be rendered credible (Agnew 1995; Agnew and Corbridge 1995; Feldman 2005; Ó Tuathail and Agnew 1992; Shore and Wright 1997). Furthermore, for elites, performing 'appropriate' spatialized political practice is crucial to asserting their authority. That is, in elite circles, defining who is and who is not a 'legitimate' actor is based invariably on espousing recognized, 'licit' sociospatial imaginaries and demonstrating command of the full vocabulary of 'appropriate' sociospatial practices flowing from these imaginaries (Agnew 1995, 2001; Bialasiewicz and Minca 2005).

We argue that this broad-based notion of elite spatializing political practice can helpfully elucidate the essence of spaces of Europeanization in the elite context of decision making in EU arenas. It does so by opening a window on how such arenas provide opportunities for elites to come together, mobilize sociospatial concepts and the more complex societal-wide imaginaries that derive from these, and display 'licit' behaviours to secure their strategic goals. It is through these contemporary elite practices and performativities that the institutional memories and the sociospatial concepts constitutive of elite Europeanization spaces are reworked.

The European Union's sociospatialities

The European Union's closely interwoven sociospatialities (comprising multiscaled governance, scale and space-spanning networks, and multiple decision-making arenas) and the diversity of sociospatial conceptions among its member states make it simultaneously a melting pot of, and incubator for, sociospatial practices. Importantly, these are actualized by and through its elite actors (cf. Bialasiewicz *et al.* 2005). Such practices take a very particular form, transacted in decision-making or decision-taking fora that to date have served to reinforce elite power by effectively excluding popular scrutiny – much less participation – in EU governance.

Elite spatializing political practice has thus provided the backbone of post-war European integration efforts, enabling societal-wide sociospatial relations to be shaped and directed to serve elite purposes. In effect, the 'everyday politics' of the European Union is an elite activity (Abélès 1992; Shore 2000). While this elite form of European integration is waning (witnessed by popular expressions of Europeanness in tourism, sport, gender relations and green politics, for example (Checkel and Katzenstein 2009; Imig and Tarrow 2001), and in the emphatic results of the 2005 constitutional referenda and the 2008 Irish referendum on the Lisbon Treaty), undoubtedly it remains the foundation of the 'European project'. Hence, study of the spatializing political practice of EU elites is highly significant: indeed, with 'EUropean' policies and politics now affecting the livelihoods and political freedoms of almost half a billion people, arguably their examination has never been more important.

Unquestionably, the accession of eight CE states[3] to the European Union constituted an epochal event in the Union's spatializing politics. While a coherent political narrative existed for this event (the 'reuniting of Europe' after decades of partition and occupation, Nazi and communist), it still represented a grand spatializing political bargain involving EU and CE elites in intensive negotiations. Importantly, accession negotiations were conducted in the shadow of complex sociospatial imaginaries mobilized by CE and EU elites, focused on CE desire to reduce 'Eastness' (distanciation of sociospatial concepts and practices used by central and eastern Europe from those of the European Union) and to assert their 'Europeanness' (extolling shared sociospatial concepts and institutional memories through use of 'legitimate' sociospatial practices). Consequently, one can think of Europeanization as a process of shedding Eastness.

Spaces of Europeanization and the 2004 accession

To recap, spaces of Europeanization for the 2004 accession comprised rival representations of EU space (i.e. spatial norms and beliefs pertaining to the 'east' and to 'Europeanness'), mobilized by EU and CE elites; and associated spatializing practices, maintained and sustained by these practices across multiple scales of political engagement. *Representations of EU space* effectively provided a template for CE and EU elite behaviour and political action during and after accession. But this repertoire of norms offered elites radically different readings of CE entitlement to EU membership. On the one hand, they asserted CE belonging, geographical proximity and cultural closeness to 'EUrope'; on the other, they bristled with claims of CE difference, marginality and cultural exclusion.

The reason why these competing representations held such a grip was that both drew on deeply embedded European historical-geographical mores and traditions. Assertions of CE 'belonging' derived from geographical patterns of migration, trade, (Catholic) religious observance, intellectual endeavour and territorial closeness transacted for millennia across the continent, which, as discussed in Chapter 2, plausibly could be said to give rise to continent-wide 'European' 'ways of doing things' constitutive of Europeanness (Albrecht-Carrié 1965; Barraclough 1963; Barzini 1984; Beloff 1957; Bychkov and Bychkova-Jordan 2002; Chabod 1947; Davies 1990; Geyer 2007; Gollwitzer 1951; Hay 1968; Heffernan 1998; Pagden 2002; Pollard 1974; Voyenne 1964). As Seton-Watson (1985: 14) contends,

> Nowhere in the world is there so widespread a belief in the reality, and the importance, of a European cultural community, as in the countries lying between the EEC and the Soviet Union. . . . To these peoples, the idea of Europe is that of a community of cultures to which a specific culture or sub-culture of each belongs. None of them can survive without Europe, or Europe without them.

Yet other historiographies provided radically different representations of EU space, which, over centuries, west European elites have habitually used for more divisive purposes. Hence, with the schism of the Church in the eleventh century and the emergence of nation-states during the seventeenth century, 'western' political elites largely commandeered 'Europeanness' for their own purposes (Huntington 1993). As Wolff (1994: 358) powerfully demonstrates, the imaginary boundaries dividing Europe were recast in the seventeenth and eighteenth centuries by western interests 'entering, possessing, imagining, mapping, addressing and peopling Eastern Europe'. This resulted in framing territory to the 'East' as somehow inherently less 'European' than territory to the 'West' (Agnew 2005; Feakins and Bialasiewicz 2006; Spohn and Triandafyllidou 2003). According to Scott (2005: 434), even in the late twentieth century this 'manifested itself in a condescending attitude towards central and eastern European states and a general negative stereotyping of the "East"' by western European elites.

Not surprisingly, CE states founded their accession strategies on imaginaries extolling their 'Europeanness'. But negotiations were conducted within the reality of *EU spatial practice* (that is, the way social space is organized and how norms govern 'legitimate' actor behaviour) that had its own, very particular, features. Most clearly, acceding states needed to transpose and implement the entire body of EU law, the *acquis communautaire*, establishing the Union's many policy regimes; and to meet and observe the Copenhagen criteria, a codification of the democratic and liberal intergovernmental norms expected of 'EUropean' states. But arguably more important were *uncodified* aspects of EU spatial practice to which all policy and political elites were required to conform if they were to be deemed 'legitimate' – in particular, what Puchala (1972) describes as the 'EU concordance system': '[EU policy] conflict is regulated and [concordance] facilitated via institutionalised . . . precedential or . . . standardised, patterned procedures which all actors commit themselves to use and repeat' (ibid.: 279). This contrasts with the 'primitive confrontation politics' (ibid.: 280) of national life, including persistent confrontation between actors; disruptive behaviour leading to problem creation rather than problem resolution; institutional self-interest; and actor secrecy and deception. Collectively in the EU setting, these are characterized by Puchala (ibid.: 279) as 'rogue behaviour', recognized as the antithesis of 'legitimate' elite political practice.

In our view, the 2004 accession thus posed the following dilemma to CE elites: how to quash divisive sociospatial imaginaries associated with Eastness, while subscribing to the norms of EU spatial practice – that is, respecting concordance while not resorting to the 'rogue behaviours' associated with national politics. Before examining this process, we describe the methodological safeguards employed in this chapter.

Methodology

In order to shed light on elite spatializing political practice, research focused on the activities of senior officials (Ambassador and Deputy Ambassador level) within five CE Permanent Representations[4] to the European Union: the Czech Republic, Hungary, Latvia, Lithuania and Poland (hereafter CE-5). Though tremendously varied, with markedly different cultural affiliations and historical experiences, broadly all five states engaged with the 2004 accession via spatial imaginaries of belonging to, yet simultaneously being excluded from, the 'West' – namely, seeking to shed Eastness and enhance their Europeanness. Acting as diplomats and experts in management of negotiations between the EU Council of Ministers and the European Commission, we prioritized examination of Ambassador and Deputy Ambassador activities within EU Permanent Representations, as this diplomatic cadre were instrumental in the daily (re)working of EU sociospatialities (Lippert *et al.* 2001). Specifically, our analysis enabled consideration of how Europeanness and Eastness were transacted through elite actions and performativities (Kuus 2007c).

Twenty interviews were conducted over the twenty-six-month research period. Ambassadors and Deputy Ambassadors from each Permanent Representation were interviewed on a number of occasions between May 2004, June 2005 and June 2006. Data collection comprised interviews of, on average, two hours with respondents in offices within the five Permanent Representations, focusing upon their involvement in meetings of the Council of Ministers Committee of Permanent Representatives (COREPER I and II).[5]

Substantial methodological challenges confront any researcher analysing sociospatial concepts and their political animus, particularly when these fall within the purview of high-level diplomats. To minimize misunderstanding and ensure the veracity of interviewees's statements, wherever possible, explanations were validated by accounts from other respondents. In turn, these accounts were authenticated by analysis of secondary materials from Permanent Representations (both published and unpublished) and from sources within the European Commission's Directorate-General for External Relations. The length and detail of the interviews and the period over which empirical investigation took place enabled us to begin to pin down the fuzzy boundaries between spatializing rhetoric and pragmatic political practice of CE-5 Ambassadors and Deputy Ambassadors. Excavating spatializing political practice required us to be receptive to, and to interrogate carefully, the means by which CE-5 and EU diplomatic elites expressed ideas and concepts in high-level negotiating fora, and to be sensitive to the ways in which they used the intrinsic sociospatial registers of the European Union (such as multiscaled arenas and governance) to advance their negotiating goals.

Importantly, this work addresses crucial analytical avenues hitherto unexplored by researchers.[6] Thus, Kuus (2007a: 150) comments that the analytical 'challenge [in European geographies] is not to unearth a core meaning or location of the East, but the specific and often unremarkable processes by which Eastness is inscribed' by actors. As our analysis reveals, elite spatializing political practice among the CE-5 during 2004–06 comprised both these 'unremarkable', often banal, politics, punctuated by extraordinary events.

Probing spaces of Europeanization

Here we piece together how CE elites grappled with EU spatial practice and sought to play out its performative requirements through developing their own spatializing political practice. By doing so, these elites contributed to a refashioning of spaces of Europeanization. As discussed, to do so, CE elite practices mobilized imaginaries of belonging from representations of EU space, while striving to adhere to the performative norms and stipulations of EU spatial practice.

Our analysis identifies two types of EU spatialized political practice developed by CE elites (see Table 4.1). First was the explicit use of sociospatial concepts to evoke 'belonging'. To do so, CE elites consciously drew upon a plethora of sociospatial categories from representations of EU space (as Rumelili (2004: 40) comments, a central plank of the accession strategy was assertion of rooted territorial affiliations to Europe, with CE elites 'effectively push[ing] the cognitive boundaries of Europe to the East to group themselves with their Western neighbours. Their successful "identity-politics strategies" emphasised their common history and civilisation with Europe and the importance of developing the European identity'; Tunbridge and Ashworth 1996). As we show, this seems to have been used by elites in the immediate post-accession period to demonstrate 'EUropean' credentials and to open up new routeways within EU sociospatialities.

Second, confronted by the European Union's novel decision-making routeways, CE elites reappraised their lexicons of sociospatial concepts and began to develop new diplomatic tropes to meet the requirements of EU spatial practice. Over time, this saw the development of central and eastern Europe's own elite spatializing practices: variously multiscaled, networked and differently positioned modes of interaction. *Rhetorical* claims to the particular use of scales, spaces and territories were thus replaced over time by CE *political practices* that addressed the unique needs of EU governance.

Here we show how this dual strategy of peeling away Eastness while enhancing Europeanness was only partly successful for CE elites. For while many have, since 2004, very successfully emulated the requirements of EU

Table 4.1 Spatializing political practices adopted by elites of five central and eastern European countries

---

1: EXPLICIT USE OF SOCIOSPATIAL CONCEPTS AS

- a strategy for shedding 'eastness' through:
  - geographical repositioning/placemaking – 'pushing back' the eastern boundary
  - assertion of territorial propinquity – east and west as 'neighbours'
  - assertion of socio-cultural affiliations – shared sociospatial norms and beliefs between West and West
  - act of EU accession reuniting the European 'family'
- a strategy for opening up routeways in EU sociospatialities by:
  - affirming common understandings of sociospatial concepts to build networks of relations among the EU-25
  - establishing/deepening social relations among the EU-25: building consensus, trust, reciprocity
  - enhancing negotiating effectiveness with EU-25

2: MASTERING EU SPATIAL PRACTICE: ELITES' PERFORMANCE OF 'LICIT' SPATIALIZING POLITICAL PRACTICES BY

- adjusting to the EU as multi-scaled arena and the modes of interaction required in each institutional space (Council of Ministers, European Commission, European Parliament, European Court of Justice); in each territorial space (national, regional, local); as actors within networks of relations linking these spaces
- adjusting to intensive socialization
- interpreting, performing and practising norms of consensus and cooperation
- securing legitimacy of EU institutions with national arenas
- advancing national goals while respecting EU spatial practice
- mastering informal rules: working within/around rules; recognizing the value and importance of EU procedural 'routeways'
- mastering adversarial tactics/strategies, e.g. raising domestic thresholds for policy and political authorization
- coping with politics of hierarchy and difference within the EU

---

spatial practice, certain EU member states and some EU institutions have questioned their mastery of these practices. At the same time, CE elite interviewees alleged a double standard regarding their need to observe EU spatial practice, compared with the EU-15. As we show, following this probing of their spatializing practices, CE elites have resorted to the use of more robust diplomatic tactics in their dealings with the EU-15.

Explicit use by CE elites of sociospatial concepts to shed 'eastness'

In the wake of accession, CE elites sought to shed 'Eastness' by recoupling the 'East' with the 'West'. Importantly, these attempts were not simply confined to challenging rhetorics of marginalization and exclusion. From interviewees' testimonies, more common was to use repositioning as a vehicle for securing strategic goals, chiefly geo-economic or geopolitical ambitions. Thus, a senior Polish negotiator described how the collapse of the Soviet Union enhanced national feelings of Europeanness and significantly offered new national security possibilities:

> We weren't to know that in the late 1980s European geography and politics would alter completely. In a very short period of time, of several months, we became the neighbours of the Czech Republic, Slovakia, Ukraine, a united Germany, Belorussiya, Russia (Kaliningrad district) and Lithuania. And our attitudes, our needs, our feelings towards Europe, well, they were strengthened and deepened in ways I couldn't imagine. So, in my view, accession to Europe represents a decisive alternative to the past: in our case, a means of overcoming a bipolar Europe. I mean, in Poland, membership of the EU was definitely a political choice with a very strong security component – it's our best security option in over thirty centuries.

Here the collapse of Soviet territorial hegemony in 1989 and the subsequent redrawing of central and eastern Europe is characterized as presenting Poland (and other CE states) not only with the opportunity of geographical repositioning. More important were the implicit opportunities of opening new channels of engagement with EU sociospatialities, particularly as these related to political discourses and spatializing political practices of security, defence and foreign affairs.

At the same time, CE elites used their familiarity with European sociospatial imaginaries to underwrite their negotiating behaviours among the EU-15 – in a sense, using this knowledge to shine light on the elite spatializing political practices adopted by their counterparts around the negotiating tables they had so recently joined. Hence, for example, the Czech Ambassador's observation that

> Germans are 'long players', they stick to clear principles, they have a lot of passions, and know that because of the catastrophes they've had in the last century the only legitimate means for them to carry out their national interest is through Europe: through European categories, through Europeanization. And from my experience this is very deeply rooted in their political thinking and practice.

More general assertions of CE entitlements to Europeanness were also made in the immediate post-accession period, typified by remarks from André Plesçu (cited in Darnton 2004), former Romanian Foreign Minister, on the eve of the 2004 accession:

When we say 'Europe' in eastern Europe, we usually think about something in the past, something we lost and have to regain. It's like something in an old faded photograph, the world between the two world wars – a nostalgia, a longing. In the West, 'Europe' is now a project. In the East, it remains a strong memory.

Mobilization of sociospatial concepts thus played an important role, and not simply in concluding accession negotiations successfully, or in transacting eastness and boosting Europeanness. Important though these aims were, CE elites also used these concepts to secure strategic objectives, to provide valuable negotiating intelligence and to create openings and policy routeways within EU sociospatialities. However, soon after accession, CE use of sociospatial concepts gave way to experimenting with 'licit' spatialized forms of EU political practice – practices by and through which CE claims to legitimacy as EU political actors would be made. For CE elites needed to burnish their 'EUropean' credentials not only by embracing consensus and compromise, but also through playing out and performing these EU norms through their own spatializing political practice.

Mastering spaces of Europeanization? CE elites and 'licit' spatializing political practices

CE elites' immersion in the European Union's negotiating arenas provided many cues with which to fashion new spatializing political practices. In a formal sense, through their 'observer' status within the EU Council of Ministers (the European Union's principal decision-taking organ), CE elites were able to observe the EU-15's response to EU spatial practice at close quarters for two years prior to formal accession. Both informal prompts and this more formal induction enabled them to experiment with and to develop their own distinctive spatializing political practices.

All interviewees stressed how their EU Representations had changed national political practice to gain legitimacy and hence be perceived as bona fide EU elites – albeit with varying degrees of success. For what is clear is that, following the 2004 accession, detailed scrutiny took place of CE spatializing practices by EU-15 elites – most clearly in the EU Council of Ministers. This probing confirms the European Union as comprising differently empowered groupings (the EU-15, accession states, EU institutions) driven by differing opinions on the rights and entitlements of the acceding states to be considered 'EUropean', and exhibited variously in endorsement or scepticism among the EU-15 of CE elites' political practice.

One of the first tasks facing CE elites was to become familiarized with EU spatial practice as multiscaled interlinked decision-making arenas, totally unlike those of national political spaces. Thus, as the Czech Ambassador to the European Union recalled,

> *[A]fter* accession to the EU, we became part of a very complex, highly structured system of socialization – different kinds of relations and interrelations that were new, different. To become part of this whole structure, and to have the possibility to really influence the text and to present the position, the justified positions, to find the allies and to make the necessary alliances – well, these types of interrelations and socialization were new. It was a new element for me with no parallel in my time as diplomat. So, it's much more difficult, I would say, to work here, and you also have to combine the context of your government, your partners in COREPER, you have to deal with the European Commission representatives, so it's a much more structured and complex socialization.

The procedural novelties of EU spatial practice are here clearly set out, but equally important are its processual qualities – specifically, *how* norms of consensus and cooperation among EU elites are inculcated through a particular model of intensive routinized negotiation, creating a steep learning curve for CE representations:

> [T]he negotiation process here is a deeper experience [than in national settings] because you will be sitting in meetings for hours and hours – COREPER I, for example, is sitting two times a week usually; sometimes the meetings last ten or twelve hours, on many, many topics, with dossiers like this [shows doorstop dossier] – so if you are there, and are trying to reason how the Germans, how the Brits, how the Austrians defend their positions, and how to defend your own, then it's definitely a school for me.

For many interviewees, this novelty cannot be overestimated. It was not that respondents had not encountered norms of 'concordance'. Rather, what was novel was their customary use across all EU representational arenas (the Council and Commission principally), and the almost tangible sedimentation of years of concordance building:

> One of the first visits of the European Commission President, Jacques Santer, to Lithuania was, I think, in winter '93, to make a speech. And in this speech he'd made reference to all sorts of things – prospects, this and that – but one thing he did say was that as an applicant state it was important for us to develop and to learn 'working methods and habits of cooperation' – I remember this phrase very clearly. And I came back to

my office after the speech and I said to the guys, 'What is this? What did he mean by this?' And I didn't understand that phrase, those terms then, it didn't make sense to me then, but I can say now that there really are 'habits of cooperation' in the EU. 'Habits of cooperation' really was for me a striking phrase. I mean, there are obviously ways of cooperating nationally – we cooperate in Lithuania, I assure you! But the idea that you have to develop these *as a habit*, in a structured, systematic way, well, that's special, that's different.

However, tacit acceptance by CE elites of EU norms of consensus was insufficient to stake claims to legitimacy. Only through concrete political practice of these norms could change in quanta of Europeanness and Eastness be made. As Puchala notes, such concrete practice makes two requirements of elites: the first is to shed confrontational politics typically associated with national political arenas, and the second is to perform EU norms of concordance and reasoned negotiation.

Interviewees provided candid insights into the first of these sociospatial practices. Thus, for example, the Polish Ambassador to the European Union confided that

> sometimes even top-level politicians aren't willing to acknowledge this need for political compromise. I'll give you a very characteristic situation from several months ago. A summit had concluded and our Prime Minister was talking with me as we drove to the airport about how to present the result of this decision back home. And I said to him, 'You should just say, in public, "this result has been delivered by us striking a successful compromise with our partners"; that's an end in itself.' And he did. But what I was surprised at was that he was not thinking in these terms already. So in my view, Europeanization means exactly that: it's not about adapting to European law, or implementation of the *acquis communautaire* in member states, because it's easy to change the law, or to action policy. The real challenge is recognizing the way [to do so], finding the will to do [so].

Similarly, the Lithuanian Ambassador commented on the difficulty of practising consensus and cooperation:

> People are very angry in Vilnius – sometimes they're very angry with me – about the compromises: 'You personally and your Representation can never get a clear-cut, healthy yes or no from the Council, from the Commission, from other member states; there's no white or black, it's always unclear.' And then I have to say, 'Yes, but look: our main point

is there, there's another good piece we can use to our advantage here', to which they often reply 'OK, but why is this here? What's it mean to us?' So Europeanization's always a deal.

Following accession, therefore, a critical focus for CE elites was to articulate national interests effectively within the Union's complex sociospatialities. CE delegations approached this from different angles. The Polish Ambassador, for example, acknowledged that national styles of negotiation had to change:

> [F]or me, the basic problem from a managerial point of view – looking at Polish politics and how it's accommodated in the EU – the real issue is how to articulate our interests within this culture of compromise. I need to convince my staff that in debate, in negotiation, compromise is an asset – it's a very basic element of the Europeanized society and the Europeanized way of politics and of the Europeanized way of life.

The Czech Deputy Ambassador viewed EU spatial practice as a means of sharpening and refining state ideas and interests:

> [I]t helps really to clarify what your interests are. In other words, it has changed the ways that our national interests are put over. Because when you're thinking for yourself – when you're planning in your cosy Ministry room 'we'll do X, Y or Z on this' – that's one thing. But in Brussels, in Council, when you meet with your colleagues with their different experiences and political cultures, and they say, 'OK, you say this, but our experience is this', or 'our experience is that that doesn't work', that's very useful, it's a kind of feedback. So, it's this kind of constant circulation of ideas and interests on a whole range of topics, requiring compromising certainly, but still getting to a better end result than one would in isolation.

But despite these preparations, elite performativities could be ruthlessly exposed through ill-judged interventions. Thus, one interviewee spoke of how

> we sit together around the same table, but it is absurd to pretend that Slovenia has the same type of interest, the same scale of interest, as Great Britain or Germany or even Poland. And when the smallest country from the EU-10 – without naming names – speaks for fifteen minutes about doctors as a special profession, and the Presidency asks them, 'How many do you have?', and the reply is seven or eight of that particular type, and twenty-six people have had to listen for fifteen minutes, well . . .

Crucially, mastering EU spatial practice was viewed by all interviewees as *the* means for repositioning their states in European geopolitics and geographies, by shedding eastness. Hence, the Czech Ambassador opined:

> [H]opefully, when we do it right, our interventions change our country's perception among the large member states, they take us seriously, they recognize we are truly European. And it gives us a new understanding of the Czech Republic too: our position in Europe, our own self-image, changes.

Yet while CE elites had made strenuous efforts to conform with EU spatial practice, following accession, interviewees commented on scepticism being cast at their bona fides by some among the EU-15. Allegedly this was manifested in various ways. For example, the Hungarian Ambassador recalled an episode where his counterpart from one of the 'Big Four' EU states claimed Hungarian understandings of 'EUropean' norms to be naïve and unsophisticated:

> [W]e were talking about areas of collaboration, of common interest, et cetera, we'd had a very nice lunch, and after he'd been speaking for some time, my Antici[7] asked him, 'Mr Ambassador, how do your remarks relate to European ideals, the idea of Europe?' And he was, you know, *astonished* – astonished and confused. And then he said, very bluntly, 'Young lady, remember there is no European ideal, no European norms: there are just national interests.' And it wasn't just a shock for her: it was a shock for me as well. In my view (and referring particularly to debates in COREPER), we are twenty-five, twenty-seven with the observer states, Bulgaria and Romania, and I have to tell you the new member states have an impression that old member states are asserting their *own* national interests more forcibly, are fighting more, than the newcomers.

More damaging were interviewees' assertions that established parameters of EU power shaped EU sociospatialities to privilege the EU-15 over CE states; thus:

> I'll tell you what one of the highest EU officials told us some months ago: 'We have a problem with you regarding EU–Russian relations. For most of the EU – for most of the old member states – Russia is a strategic partner, but for you and for the Baltic States, Russia's still the enemy. You need, you must do something.' But from our perspective, in shaping an EU policy on Russia, the old member states take into account *their* national interest, yet they don't seem ready to recognize that we have *our* national interest.

Seemingly, this outbreak of discordant behaviours (Puchala 1972) was fuelled by representations of EU space that promoted marginalization and exclusion of 'East' from 'West'. And, according to interviewees, the use of these imaginaries of difference and hierarchy has not been confined to member states:

> Sometimes people *are* openly hostile. We have had a very important person from the Commission – it was not a Commissioner, but one of his high-level officials – the Commission DG dealing with enlargement. And I decided following accession to hold a dinner in his honour (he has since left the Commission and now has a very senior ambassadorial position). And I also invited the two former Polish chief negotiators, a representative of the Polish President, and the Ambassador to the EU of this person's own nationality. And during the lunch, after a few glasses of wine, he started to tell this story about why he and his colleagues in the Commissioner's *cabinet* generally didn't like Poland. An incredible situation for me! As host, I had to be silent, but the Ambassador of his country started apologizing profusely, and it ended in a scandal.

These issues of difference and hierarchy question not only the viability of Puchala's 'concordance system' but also the supposed role of the EU institutions as informal arbiters of EU spatial practice. Crucially, they demonstrate the dynamic and highly unstable nature of spaces of Europeanization. Two important corollaries flow from this, in our view. First, just as spatial imaginaries have shaped the performativities of CE elites during and immediately after accession, it implies that the accretion of CE spatialized practice since 2004 will have begun to reconfigure dominant 'western' sociospatial imaginaries of 'EUrope'. Thus, as one interviewee reflected:

> I now see Europeanization as [being] as much about adapting the Czech system, Czech standards, to Europe as it is about our partners learning from us. And maybe the enthusiasm for Europe from Prague has changed a little. Certainly we have changed the accent, the emphasis, so that the system of representing Czech interests is now stronger. And I think this is the case for all of us in the CEs, I think we are still in this learning process, this learning of Europe's ways.

The second is how CE elites have responded to the perceived challenge to their legitimacy as bona fide EU actors. Apparent disregard among some of the EU-15 for norms of EU spatial practice has clearly created ructions, reawakening older geographic divisions of Eastness and Europeanness that, as we have argued, were never far from the surface of EU spatializing politics.[8] Allegedly, since 2006 some of the CE-5 have contributed to this, through exhibiting 'Euroscepticism' (the Czech Republic) and 'obduracy' (Poland) in Council negotiations (Ross 2008: 407). To what extent this 'rogue behaviour' can be attributed to EU-15 and EU institutions' handling of CE accession remains a matter of speculation. But as recent events (such as the EU constitutional debacle) demonstrate, a systemic disruption of spatialized norms and, more pertinently, elite spatializing political practice has come about within the European Union. Even if the aftermath of the 2004 accession has not been the principal or even the main driver of this disruption, our analysis suggests it has been a significant contributory factor.

Building upon the last chapter, we have demonstrated here that spaces of Europeanization in the context of the 2004 accession comprised spatial norms and beliefs of Eastness and Europeanness, around and through which complex choreographies of elite spatializing political practice have been played out. Our findings confirm that the two constitutive elements, elite political practice and sociospatial concepts, cannot and should not be disentangled, as new institutionalist analyses suggest. Certainly this is borne out by the ways in which CE and EU-15 policy elites conceived, perceived and used sociospatial concepts in their political practice during and immediately after the 2004 accession. We have drawn on insights from the spatializing political literature to show why this is so: sociospatial concepts, and the complex imaginaries these concepts underwrite, suffuse political practice to create 'legitimate' modes of interaction. In the case of the EU's elite sociospatialities, conceived, perceived and lived spaces during accession proved permeable and indivisible, with the associated politics of each creating struggle within and between these spaces among CE-5, EU-15 and EU elites. We have identified some of the means by which these elite struggles – and the resultant refashioning of EU sociospatialities – came about. These included the assertion of particular sets of EU spatial norms; the challenge these norms posed to the pre-existing diplomatic performativities and practices of CE-5 elites, and their subsequent attempts to recalibrate these practices during accession; and, crucially, how this has contributed to the subsequent reconfiguration of spaces of Europeanization.

We therefore concur with Leitner *et al.*'s (2008: 158, 166) comment that 'geography matters to the imaginaries, practices and trajectories of contentious politics', and, while recognizing that 'differently positioned participants come together to challenge dominant systems of authority, in order to promote and enact alternative imaginaries', have shown that this is not by any means the only form of spatializing politics. For in this study, CE elites made explicit attempts to emulate, rather than compete with, hegemonic elite spatializing political practices. More pertinent for interviewees is Leitner *et al.*'s comment that actors 'draw on their experience and knowledge, crafting and intuiting strategies that they hope will succeed, and which simultaneously engage multiple spatialities'.

Importantly, our approach suggests that further research is needed to explore the temporal dimensions of sociospatial relations. As Brenner (2009: 134) notes, this remains a relatively neglected aspect, particularly exploration of the 'periodization' of particular suites of sociospatial relations. By tracking the use made of sociospatial concepts by particular groups of actors in longitudinal studies along the lines set out here, we believe highly valuable insights can be gained of the ways in which spatializing political practice and sociospatial concepts are juxtaposed and co-evolve. It is this unity of practice and rhetoric that is the real substance of spaces of Europeanization. In effect, spatializing political practice provides a valuable means of linking the microgeographies of political praxis with the geographical imaginaries of statecraft (Ó'Tuathail 1994). In the next chapter, we turn to these geographical imaginaries in the context of the promotion of Europeanization beyond Europe.

5 Discourses of Europeanization

The European Commission, European narratives and European Neighbourhood Policy

Introduction

Having examined spaces of Europeanization within the European Union – particularly the ways in which power relations configure norm building and norm acceptance among elites – in this chapter we turn our attention to Europeanization as a governance form and its projection beyond the Union's territorial boundaries. Developing this hitherto under-researched spatializing aspect of Europeanization, the chapter considers the Mediterranean neighbourhood as a geographical entity posing considerable difficulties to the European Commission in its recent efforts to 'Europeanize' non-EU space. This chapter therefore specifically addresses the lacuna observed by Lavenex (2007) on the extra-territorial impact of EU integration. The European Commission is at the centre of these Europeanization efforts through disseminating its market, democratic and governance norms beyond Europe's immediate territorial limits. These discursively based elite activities result in a complex, problematized space of agreements, concessions, diagnoses and actions. In this chapter, we reveal how European elites are pivotal to the (re)production of this space by animating the negotiating order between Europe and its socially constructed neighbourhood, critically affecting the ability of the European Union to promote Europeanization beyond EU borders.

In this context, the reach of Europeanization spaces into the global economy is reflected in a network of trading agreements and preferential concessions between the European Union and non-member countries, patterns of localized development aid and diverse forms of assistance, foreign and security diagnoses and actions, and mitigation of the impact on other states of EU efforts to create closer economic, political and social union within its own borders (Piening 1997). Here, projections of Europeanization spaces beyond the European Union's borders provide arenas through which the Union strives to gain meaning, actorness and presence internationally.

However, despite this widening reach of European geostrategic links to outside states and regions and the existence of institutional structures for the elaboration of common foreign and security, trade, and aid policies, this process of Europeanization and its achievements continues to be described in less than complimentary ways as either ambiguous (Collinson 1999), incomplete (Wallace and Wallace 1999), unsettled (Heritier 1999) or impotent (Carslnaes *et al.* 2004). Many of these writers argue that Europeanization is characterized by an ongoing internal tension and interplay between the drive to act collectively on the world stage and the desire by EU member states to retain national autonomy over foreign policy goals and actions. Importantly, this tension is seen as a key explanatory factor in the apparent success or failure of the Europeanization process. However, this is only part of the story. It is the contradictory demands of negotiating order at the 'internal' level and the 'external level', both operationally and normatively, that critically affect the ability of the European Union to produce policy outputs which obtain a desired policy outcome that accords the EU 'presence' and 'actorness' in international affairs (Ginsberg 1999).

The European Commission is at the centre of this internal–external Europeanization dynamic (Smith 2000), actively mediating between the contradictory demands of EU member states in search of European solutions to external events and problems and at the same time managing, negotiating and coordinating relations between the EU polity and a diverse range of global political spaces (Zielonka 2002). Crucially, the management of this two-way negotiation can be seen as central to Europeanization spaces 'beyond' the European Union since it affects the development of 'the European Union itself, the wider Europe and the world political economy', and while the European Commission remains 'at the heart of this process . . . the centrality and boundaries of its role will be contested both from within and without' (Smith 1997: 278). Europeanization spaces that intersect with the EU international policy arena thus comprise a number of important discursive and instrumental dimensions. One such dimension is that third countries seek concessions from the European Union and its member states beyond what they are prepared to concede. These concessions can disrupt resources and powers between EU states and have concrete effects upon domestic markets, producers and state roles. In addition, third countries seek concessions that can affect the ability of EU states to develop relations with other third countries. Internal tensions within the Union are also increased as EU states are forced to consider further delegation of roles and activities to the European Commission. This puts in sharp focus the preferences that the Commission may hold and their distinctiveness from those held by EU states.

Scholars have grappled with the issues of international negotiated order, most recently focusing upon discourse studies to illustrate how 'textual and social processes are intrinsically connected and to describe, in specific contexts, the implications of this connection for the way we think and act in the contemporary world' (George 1994). Given its position as one of the principal motors of Europeanization, projector of European solutions to international problems, and 'face' of the EU externally (Smith 2003), the European Commission's role in the external projection of Europeanization warrants further research. In particular, there has been little work focusing on the discourses, values and norms underpinning the external activities of the European Commission, especially in the emerging theoretical area of practical geopolitical reasoning as well as the growing area of discourse studies in international relations. In this chapter, we wish to address this by following the heuristic framework set out by Milliken (1999) and Ó'Tuathail (2002) for analysing practical geopolitical reasoning, a framework that includes problem categorization, storyline construction, geopolitical strategy and problem closure. For academic convenience, we group these into three components: discourse building, discourse performance and discourse survival. There are a number of reasons why this approach is of interest in this context. First, it enables a focus on the internal–external negotiating dynamic in which the European Commission occupies a central place in the projection of Europeanization spaces. Second, it enables emphasis to be placed on discursive processes underpinning EU international activities. Third, it emphasizes the significance of the European Commission to the external promotion of Europeanization spaces by recognizing that trade, aid and development, key areas of its business, are the core of the European Union's claim to international actorness. Moreover, it recognizes that Europeanization involves an intensive, continuous coordination of member state positions, in which the European Commission is pivotal. As Smith comments, the European Commission is 'a vital source of information, advice and initiatives alongside [EU] national governments' (1997). Additionally, the approach recognizes the complexities and artificialities of separating economic, political and security issues in the promotion of Europeanization.

Consequently, here we focus on the Commission's role in the discursive construction, performance and stabilization of Europeanization spaces. In particular, we examine events since 2000 and the Commission's role in projecting Europeanization towards the Arab states of the Mediterranean under the Euro-Mediterranean partnership (the Barcelona Process) and the European Neighbourhood Policy (ENP) (CEC 2003, 2006). Targeting many of the countries of the Mediterranean's southern and eastern littoral, EuroMed and the application of the ENP to this complex, fractured regional context has assumed great geopolitical importance recently by its addressing of foreign, security, defence and economic policies, as well as social and cultural affairs. Our analysis draws upon a comprehensive data set constructed between April 2003 and January 2006 comprising sixty-five interviews with state political and diplomatic representatives and EU political actors representing the key groups actively involved in the processes of Europeanization in the European 'neighbourhood'. Detailed semi-structured interviews were held with officials in the European Commission's Directorate for External Relations responsible for strategic policy development towards the Mediterranean. These officials included members of the Commissioner's cabinet, directors of specific policy units charged with formulating and coordinating policy initiatives, and those officials responsible for specific geographical areas of EU policy towards the Mediterranean, including relations with the Maghreb countries (Algeria, Tunisia and Morocco) and with the Mashreq countries (Egypt, Lebanon, Syria, Jordan and the Palestinian Authority). As has been reported elsewhere, this represents the largest empirical study of Europeanization and its discursive underpinnings conducted in political geography (Jones 2006).

Discourses, spaces of Europeanization and the European Commission

Milliken (1999: 229) identifies three components for the study of discourse in international policy. The first is discourses as systems of signification – that is, 'things do not mean, rather people construct the meaning of things'. Applied to the dynamics of Europeanization spaces, this would conceptualize them as arenas within which the relations between Europe and third countries are codified as a relation of power such that one element in the binary – that is, Europe – is privileged. This enables third countries to be differentiated from Europe, giving them 'taken for granted qualities and attributes', which are 'actualized in their regular use' by various modes of signification (ibid.: 231).

Milliken's second component emphasizes the production of discourses. Once again, applied to the establishment of Europeanization spaces, this renders logical and legitimate European interventions. As she explains, 'discourses make intelligible some ways of being in and acting towards the world, and of operationalizing a particular "regime of truth" while excluding other possible modes of identity and action' (ibid.: 229). In this way, discourses 'work to define and to enable, and also to silence and to exclude . . . [therefore] endorsing a certain common sense, but making other modes of categorizing and judging meaningless, impracticable, inadequate' (ibid.: 229). Applying this formulation to Europeanization, we can see how by this means Europeanization institutionalizes a social space premised on relational distinctions, power hierarchies and discursively based relationships.

The third component is the performance of discourse, which enables us to recognize that Europeanization spaces are fragile accomplishments that require strenuous efforts to communicate, coordinate and stabilize their contested knowledges and identities; this explains why Europeanization is changeable and historically contingent. The survival of Europeanization through these struggles is an under-researched aspect, especially efforts to retain its dominant meanings and discredit competitive interpretations. As Doty (1996: 6) explains, 'Any fixing of a discourse and the identities that are constructed by it can only be of a partial nature. It is the overflowing and incomplete nature of discourses that opens up spaces for change, discontinuity and variation.'

These components of Europeanization discourse are the 'product of an institutionalised negotiated process reflecting complex institutional relationships between EU member governments and EU institutions in EU international policy making' (Smith 1997: 259). We contend that the European Commission is critical to this process. It is responsible for building consensus among EU member states, positioned as it is at the interface of the internal–external negotiating dynamic, and has to coordinate and moderate the needs and interests of the member states without itself possessing a great deal of coercive power. It is therefore concurrently a negotiator, broker and enforcer. However, this is not to suggest that it does not have its own agenda or seek to manoeuvre, cajole or influence member states, as has been shown in a number of policy contexts. While the European Commission has legitimate functions externally (for example, it represents the European Union in external trade matters), it also articulates, projects and appeals through the Europeanization discourses. This involves the careful definition and delimitation of external situations for European intervention, the production of new systems of signification to render logical, meaningful and appropriate this intervention, and the deployment of a suite of tactics to ensure the survival of EU-brokered Europeanization discourses.

Our approach argues that the European Commission plays a substantive role in the assertion of agreed European interests, ideas and identities and in the delivery of EU policy narratives, norms, practices and procedures on terms that are favourable to Europe (Jones and Clark 1998). As Smith argues, 'The Community has established a major presence in the international arena, and the Commission is central to this presence' (1997: 270), though Smith concedes that there has been 'an increase in the scale, complexity and political sensitivity of what is being attempted [externally]' (ibid.: 282) and that this Europeanization process 'has both highlighted some long-standing problems and created some new ones for the role of the European Commission' (ibid.: 270). Likewise, Kelley (2006: 31) cites a Commission official on the specific case of the ENP:

[W]ith its plethora of rhetorical devices, the Council of Ministers may have appeared as the most influential arbitrator of EU foreign policy.

But when it came to 'real' foreign policy impact of the EU in the last decade, the power lay with the Commission. While one can debate the relative influence of Council and Commission foreign policy . . . [t]he Commission . . . conceptualized the ENP and will implement it.

In 1995, the European Union launched the Barcelona Process, hailed as the boldest design in European relations with the Mediterranean in the twentieth century (Jones 2006; Jones and Clark 2008; Jones 2009). It comprises a political and security partnership based on respect for human rights and democracy by the EU member states and the (originally twelve, now nine) third countries (Algeria, Egypt, Israel, Jordan, Lebanon, Morocco, the Palestinian Authority, Syria and Tunisia; Cyprus, Malta and Turkey have now acceded or have embarked on the accession process, and thus are no longer 'neighbours'), an economic and financial partnership through the progressive establishment of a free trade area accompanied by substantial EU aid, and a social-cultural partnership designed to promote greater understanding between cultures and rapprochement of the peoples in the Mediterranean.

The Barcelona Process is a clear attempt to instigate a space of Europeanization externally, in essence projecting the appeal of, and by, Europe. However, by the turn of the millennium Europe's first wave of Europeanization of the Mediterranean was receiving critical commentary, prompting the European Commission to issue a communication entitled 'Reinvigorating the Barcelona Process' (CEC 2000). This set out the difficulties encountered by Europe, a candid assessment of achievements, and future 'reinvigorating' proposals. This was addressed by the Commissioner for External Relations, Chris Patten, in a speech to the European Parliament in January 2001, which set out the revitalized process.

When I looked at the facts I found a certain dissatisfaction that more had not been done . . . my overriding approach has been to see how we could focus the [EU–Mediterranean] partnership on a clear set of short and medium term goals – ambitious but achievable – enabling those who want to go at a faster pace to do so.

(Patten 2001)

On the heels of this, Commission President Romano Prodi, in a speech on Europe and the Mediterranean at the Université Catholique de Louvain-la-Neuve on 26 November 2002 (Prodi 2002), flagged a change in the Europeanization discourse away from an emphasis on European security and bordered Europe to one emphasizing 'nearness', cooperation and friendship:

[R]elations between Europe and the Mediterranean are central to my concerns, my thoughts and my political actions. . . . At a time when we are building a new Europe . . . we must also develop our strategy towards the regions closest to Europe and, above all, we must be decisive in our Mediterranean policy. To build the new Europe but neglect the Mediterranean, Europe's cradle, would clearly be a grave mistake. . . . One thing is certain. . . . There is a human, social and historical reality called the Mediterranean – a reality that ever more urgently demands courageous, long-term action. We have two very different alternatives. The *first* involves viewing the Mediterranean primarily as a question of security. In this case, the Mediterranean becomes the southern border of the Union, where we must take up position to manage the flows of migrants, combat any forms of international terrorism there and encourage a development policy heavily geared towards cooperation in the fight against unlawful activities. The *second* option involves viewing the Mediterranean as a new area of cooperation, where a special relationship can be established within the context of a broader proximity policy which will need to address the whole band of regions around the Union, stretching from the Maghreb to Russia.

In 2003, Commissioner Patten and President Prodi articulated the task at hand for the European Commission in the external projection of this new Europeanization space. As Patten explained, 'For the coming decade we need to find new ways to export the stability, security and prosperity we have created within the enlarged EU. We should begin by agreeing on a clearer vision for relations with our neighbours.' As Prodi (2003) confirmed, '[Europeanization,] instead of trying to establish new dividing lines, [should] deep[en] integration between the EU and the ring of friends [which would] . . . accelerate our mutual political, economic and cultural dynamism'.

The outcome of these Commission interventions aimed at reinvigorating the Europeanization process was formalized in the ENP. This policy, launched by the European Union in February 2003, represents both the articulation of the limits of Europe's physical and legal space and, through a series of rewards for 'neighbourliness', an extension of the norms and discourses of 'Europeanness' beyond those limits (Pardo 2004). The Commission's DG Enlargement (charged with formulating neighbourhood policy) stated, 'The EU has a duty, not only towards its citizens and those of the new member states, but also towards its present and future neighbours to ensure continuing social cohesion and economic dynamism' (CEC 2003). The ENP is thus viewed by the Commission as 'a response to the practical issues posed by proximity and neighbourhood' (p. 5), with 'the premise of ENP [being] that the EU has a vital interest in seeing greater economic development and stability and better governance in its neighbourhood. The responsibility for [taking this forward] this lies primarily with the countries themselves' (CEC 2006).

There was much debate between the Commission and the member states over the terms, goals and membership of the European 'neighbourhood'. Initially, 'neighbourhood' was conceived by DG Enlargement as a primary way of addressing security concerns about cross-border criminal activities and illegal immigration in the east following the prospective largest wave of EU enlargement in May 2004 to include eight ex-communist central and eastern European countries. However, the outbreak of the second Intifada, the declared war on terrorism, and increasing disquiet among EU political elites over the limited achievements of the European Union's Mediterranean policy under the Barcelona process led to a re-evaluation of the Union's potential role as a normative force for good in the Mediterranean, and the adoption by DG External Relations of the neighbourhood concept. Under DG External Relations, the 'ring of friends' around the enlarged Union would thus include the Arab signatories to Barcelona (Algeria, Egypt, Jordan, Lebanon, Morocco, the Palestinian Authority, Syria and Tunisia, as well as Libya, with which the European Union's relations had been improving since its renouncement of support for international terrorism in the early 2000s). These countries, through their commitment to, and support for, the European projection of common values, the rule of law, good governance and respect for human rights, would secure economic and political rewards from the European Union. As the Commission reflected in 2003, 'the EU should act to reinforce and unite its existing neighbourhood policy . . . [and] to anchor the EU's offer of concrete benefits . . . within a differentiated framework which responds to progress made by the partner countries in political and economic reform' (CEC 2003).

In the following sections, we examine how DG External Relations constructed the principal elements of this new space for Europeanization and focused upon a new discourse to project a European identity in the Mediterranean and, finally, how it protects the hegemony of this discourse in European relations with third countries to ensure both EU actorness and EU presence.

The European Commission as discourse builder

The ENP represents a manifest effort by the European Union to structure European relations with a binary Mediterranean 'other' (Adler *et al.* 2006; Pace 2004). It is, as Smith (2004: 77) contends, a Europeanization that is designed to produce a 'Europe of boundaries in which a variety of geo-political, transactional, institutional and cultural forces create a world of separated spaces framing inclusions or exclusions. The resulting negotiations are focussed on inclusions and exclusions, across boundaries'. European-ization spaces are thus articulated and operationalized through the con-struction of systems of meaning and collective understandings of the neighbourhood in European political exchange. These, as Caporaso *et al.* (2001: 201) argue, lead to the creation of norms at the European level which serve as 'important focal points around which discourses and identities are fashioned'. Importantly, the construction of discourses for the external projection of Europeanization requires a careful negotiation between member states and the European Commission to achieve what Sedelmeier (2004: 129) describes as a 'reasoned consensus about which particular course of action is justified and appropriate to enact their collective identity as promoters of [Europeanization]'. Moreover, as he maintains (ibid.: 129), 'Agreement on a particular action reflects that all participants are persuaded of the normative validity of the arguments presented for such action.' These norms then become explicitly articulated, embedded and specified at the EU level.

The European Commission's centrality to the construction of the ENP discourse is supported by comments made by a senior source from within the institution. These comments demonstrate the ways in which the Commission considered how a concept of neighbourhood could be extended geographi-cally in order to include the Mediterranean third countries, assist the recovery of an ailing Barcelona Process and simultaneously project Europeanization:

> The discourse started off as something looking towards our eastern neighbours: 'My goodness, we've let in Poland and Slovakia; how are we going to keep Ukraine out?' So we thought, let's invent something where we can say, 'you can have this but you can't come in'. When we got a head of steam up on this, people here in the Commission realized that if there is a benefit to be getting out of this, it's for the Mediterranean partners. We could use it to push forward something that has already begun [the Barcelona Process] which hasn't gone very far in some areas. This would enable us to create a better dynamic.
>
> (Author's interview with senior official, DG External Relations)

The Commission's construction of neighbourhood was intended to facilitate an assertive projection of Europeanization into the European Union's 'near abroad' (Jones 2009). This projection beyond the Union's immediate geographical neighbourhood not only highlighted the geographical limits of the European project but also portrayed the neighbourhood as one in which some states, as Charillon (2004: 254) suggests, are 'invited to rejoin a Europe they once belonged to while Southern and Eastern Mediterranean countries are called upon to retrieve the spirit of the Mare Nostrum once shared with Europe'.

There was a geographical issue in these discourses. We talked about the European territory, but there was also a deep political concern; we cannot enlarge the EU up to China. We are playing with numbers now that come close to what is naturally going to be the final definition of the European Union, with the Balkans being a question mark. So the question is, what happens to the first ring of neighbours? Some wanted us to say to these Mediterranean neighbours, 'we want to do with you what we have done with the enlargement countries'. There's an obvious difference. With those enlargement countries we could sell them a lot, and we could go literally through their legislation because we were selling accession to them, and the massive economic benefits, investment, etc. that could change their country. That, for obvious reasons, is not going to be possible with the Mediterranean neighbours. So, we needed to look for an alternative model but we realized there were inherent dangers.

(Author's interview with senior official, DG External Relations)

There were concerns circulating within the Commission about the construction of a discourse based on neighbourhood to project Europeanization. In particular, Commission officials were worried about the vagueness in socio-cultural terms of European neighbourhood as a discursive construction. This is underlined by comments made by a well-placed Commission source:

Obviously, geography counts a lot, and it is easier to explain to an Italian citizen that the Mediterranean is an area of interest and that they are neighbours than it is to explain it to a Finnish citizen. I'm Spanish, and it takes me an intellectual effort to realize that Russia is a neighbour as well, so that happens regardless of whether it is the Mediterranean or not.

(Author's interview with senior official, DG External Relations)

Incorporating conditionality was vitally important to the Commission in the discursive construction. This conditionality would entail the linking of perceived benefits such as aid and trade concessions to neighbourhood countries in exchange for progress on democracy and human rights issues, and the progressive establishment of a liberal economic system. This exercise of 'soft' power in the projection of Europeanization is confirmed by a Commission source:

[We have] to be explicit about it, and to say clearly that we want certain things to happen if we are going to offer other things. That's the main change in the neighbourhood discourse. We have a something for something strategy. We had to get the member states to sign up to this.

(Author's interview with senior official, DG External Relations)

Building support for a neighbourhood discourse thus rested with the Commission, and success would critically depend upon its ability to bring together the disparate views of the member states into a common approach for EU intervention and, with it, the projection of Europeanization. While neighbourhood was conceived initially in the context of 'near abroad' in Eastern Europe (Hopf 1999), it was the External Relations Directorate of the Commission that saw the potential for a much larger geographical intervention for Europeanization spanning the South East and the South. Lengthy bilaterals were held between DG External Relations and southern member states concerning how the programme should be adapted to the Mediterranean context and which states should be included (Emerson and Noutcheva 2005), largely at the Commission's instigation, as a senior official in that Directorate reflected:

> [I]t was we who insisted on having Mediterranean countries in there; of course, Spain and southern states were very supportive of us in doing that, but we insisted on that ourselves, so that for us wider Europe – the new neighbourhood policy – is the vehicle for improving the Barcelona Process and making it more specific.
>
> (Author's interview with senior official, DG External Relations)

This Commission entrepreneurialism (Jones and Clark 2001) drew a large measure of respect from those member states such as France with long-standing historical engagements with the Mediterranean: 'We've found the Commission very supportive and we appreciate the difficulties that they faced in trying to balance not only a diverse range of views among Member States but also among Mediterranean partner states themselves' (Author's interview with French diplomat, Brussels). However, the Commission had to convince others less directly involved of the potential benefits of subscription to the discourse and, as it announced,

> change the sterile discourse into a virtuous one in a situation where different member states have different priorities and interests. Our goal was to get the member states together on this, and in our discussions with the UK, Nordic countries and Germany, it soon became clear to them and to us that the new neighbourhood policy was something that could be viewed quite positively as offering scope for delivering something. The idea then soon began to catch on.
>
> (Author's interview with senior official, DG External Relations)

Working within these bounded constraints, the Commission's role was to define and enable 'neighbourhood' in such a way as to facilitate its endorsement by member states as a legitimate means for projecting Europeanization, and as an appropriate political mechanism for European intervention. This process of accommodating often conflicting national interests was fraught with difficulties, as a UK diplomat involved in the discussions with the Commission explained:

> I would describe the Commission role [in the construction of this discourse] as really being an organization that was trying to manage conflicting expectations and priorities and take a balanced view without setting out its own view. It was more a case of it collating other member states' views, then coming to a decision that meets [them] halfway; a decision that no one is really pleased and no one is really upset about. A moderate organization trying to build consensus.
>
> (Author's interview, UK diplomat, London)

Specifically, to secure the discourse, the Commission had to broker an agreement between the member states that would allow the assertion of agreed European interests while not compromising established national ideals and identities towards the Mediterranean 'neighbourhood'. For example, some southern member states made clear their fears of uncontrolled immigration from Mediterranean 'neighbours', while others had anxieties about the potential infiltration of their national territories by Islamist terror networks in the wake of 9/11 (Del Sarto and Schumacher 2005). An indication of the amount of time and effort invested by the Commission in this brokerage is revealed in the comments made by a British diplomat involved in the United Kingdom's discussions with the Commission over the neighbourhood proposals:

> You had the Club Med countries who have strong views, although France and Spain were forced to recognize that it's not a question of pouring vast amounts of money into the region; there needs to be greater conditionality, with funding needing to be more focused upon priorities. The Spanish always consider EuroMed as their baby and this was evident in the discussions. Then you've got the Scandinavians, particularly the Swedes and Finns, who see human rights as their key priority, and then the UK, the Danes, the Dutch and Germans realize the importance of a more effective EuroMed instrument that can deliver the EU's reform agenda as set out in the strategic partnership. You'll get the likes of the French seeing their target countries like the Maghreb. But what was abundantly clear was that we've all got different domestic agendas.
>
> (Author's interview with diplomat, UK Foreign Office)

The tension within the European Union between the drive to act collectively in the projection of Europeanization and the desire by member states to retain autonomy over foreign policy goals and actions is summed up in the Commission's own evaluation of the construction of this discourse:

> I would say that the Commission at the time while preparing this discourse was more ambitious. We were more ambitious in terms of the size of the funding that was needed for helping with the economic reforms and maintaining social and economic stability during the restructuring period. We were also more ambitious in terms of trade. We were more ambitious; the member states toned us down.
>
> (Author's interview with senior official, DG External Relations)

There is an inherent tension evident here between the Commission's desire to fashion an effective supranational foreign policy space that subsumes member state interests and ideas in order to project normative European values across the Mediterranean, and its awareness that states inevitably view such policy as compromising long-standing domestic bilateral relations with these third countries (Pace 2006).

This section has shown how the Barcelona Process was recast as a 'neighbourly' space of Europeanization through the ENP, its application to the Mediterranean context, and the Commission's central role in fashioning agreement among member states over this process. In subsequent sections, we examine how, since 2003, the Commission has performed and sustained the discourse underpinning this space by focusing upon its efforts to communicate, coordinate and stabilize this discursive construction in its relations with the Mediterranean 'neighbours'.

The European Commission and the performance of the Europeanization discourse

According to the European Commission,

> In order to realise the vision of building an increasingly closer relationship with our neighbours, and a zone of stability, security and well-being for all, the EU and the partner country agree on reform objectives across a wide range of fields (from cooperation on political and security issues, to economic and trade matters, common environmental concerns, integration of transport and energy networks, scientific and cultural cooperation). The EU provides financial and technical assistance to support the implementation of these objectives.
>
> (DG External Relations website 2009)

The Commission is central to the instruments and methods used in the ENP, in effect setting the benchmarks for Europeanization through prescribed evolutionary stages for EU relations with specific neighbourhood partners. At the outset, the Commission prepares Country Reports assessing the political and economic situation as well as institutional and sectoral aspects, to assess when and how it is possible to deepen relations with the specific third country. Country Reports are submitted to the Council of Ministers, which decides whether to proceed to the next stage of relations.

This next stage is the development of an ENP Action Plan with the third country. These documents are negotiated with, and tailor-made for, each country, based on the country's needs and capacities, as well as its and the European Union's interests (see Table 5.1). The Action Plan in effect sets out a Europeanization agenda covering political dialogue and reform, economic and social cooperation and development, trade-related issues and market and regulatory reform, cooperation in justice and home affairs, sectors (such as transport, energy, information society, environment, research and development) and the human dimension (people-to-people contact, civil society). The incentives on offer to the third country, in return for 'Europeanization' progress, are greater integration into EU programmes and networks, increased assistance and enhanced market access. The Commission regularly monitors the Action Plans and produces periodic reports on progress and on areas requiring further development. According to the Commission, 'This is a dynamic process – when monitoring demonstrates significant progress in attaining the agreed objectives, the EU incentives on offer can be reviewed, or the Action Plans adapted, or further proposals made as regards future relations' (DG External Relations website, 2009).

This discourse for neighbourhood policy is shaped fundamentally by the bounded constraints of national interests imposed upon the Commission by member states. Operationalizing the neighbourhood discourse also involves the Commission negotiating with third countries in circumstances where member states may request hard bargaining of it and where the third countries conceive neighbourhood and their commitment to it in a multitude of ways and with varying degrees of eagerness. Thus, the contradictory demands of negotiating order at the internal and external level both operationally and normatively present the European Commission with real difficulties and produce a messiness in the projection of Europeanization in the neighbourhood.

The Commission is the key player in the performance of the neighbourhood discourse. It is responsible for negotiating trade aspects, implementing the aid programmes under MEDA (this was subsumed in October 2006 in the European Neighbourhood and Partnership Instrument, ENPI) and co-ordinating the schedule of meetings between the European Union and the neighbourhood third countries. It is at the front line in the projection of

Table 5.1 European Neighbourhood Policy: the 'third-country' situation, 2006

ENP partner country	Entry into force of contractual relations with the EC	ENP Country Report	ENP Action Plan	Adoption by EU	Adoption by partner country
Algeria	AA – 2005	Under development	–	–	–
Egypt	AA – June 2004	March 2005	Under development	–	–
Israel	AA – June 2000	May 2004	Agreed end 2004	21 February 2005	11 April 2005
Jordan	AA – May 2002	May 2004	Agreed end 2004	21 February 2005	11 April 2005
Lebanon	AA – imminent	March 2005	Under development	–	–
Libya	–	–	–	–	–
Morocco	AA – March 2000	May 2004	Agreed end 2004	21 February 2005	27 July 2005
Palestinian Authority	Interim AA – July 1997	May 2004	Agreed end 2004	21 February 2005	4 May 2005
Syria	AA pending ratification	–	–	–	–
Tunisia	AA – March 1998	May 2004	Agreed end 2004	21 February 2005	4 July 2005

Source: European Commission (2006).

Note: AA = Association Agreement.

Europeanization, though constantly under the watchful eye of the member states. This point is well made by a senior British diplomat:

> We tend to see the Commission as very much more than just another member state. They very much drive the agenda, drive the process and drive the direction of the new neighbourhood policy. Generally the UK doesn't have a problem with the general thrust in which the Commission wants to go, but yes, we do try to keep it in check if we think it's going too far or going too quickly or if we think their tactics are slightly off.
>
> (Author's interview with diplomat, UK Foreign Office)

While the Commission would acknowledge its pre-eminent role in the neighbourhood policy, it also is quick to point out the ways in which this role is hindered by the member states, particularly their reluctance to make concessions in certain critical areas. The promotion of Europeanization to third countries is consequently compromised. As a Commission official admitted,

> I think that it is very much the Commission driving the process because we do the day-to-day work. Obviously there are some member states who are very keen on this policy. I think one of the paradoxes and one of the problems of the neighbourhood policy is that the countries who are most interested in EuroMed relations – Spain, France, Italy and Greece – are the ones who are most defensive in certain areas like agriculture. Those countries press us for certain things, and when you come to test them as to whether they would be willing to liberalize more in Mediterranean agricultural products, they don't show much interest. So right now there is a combination of member states all with different goals. The Swedish, for example, are very supportive on the whole political and human rights reform but the one who really pushes the process forward, because we deal with day-to-day issues, is the Commission.
>
> (Author's interview with senior official, DG External Relations)

The Commission's growing frustration with the Mediterranean member states is scarcely hidden in comments made by one of the Commission's senior negotiators:

> We have to be clear about the countries that wish to push this forward. If Greece, Spain, Italy and France want to push Med policies by default, they are going to have to accept greater concessions for Med agriculture products, otherwise they can forget about the neighbourhood process. They will have to make this choice. We can't sell the wider Europe

process to our partner countries and then deliver nothing. Nobody's going to buy this. We can't avoid this question.

(Author's interview with senior official, DG External Relations)

While the Commission's frustration with the Mediterranean member states attracts some sympathy from UK diplomats involved in neighbourhood policy, there is much disquiet in Whitehall over the messiness of the internal EU situation and its resultant negative effects on the promotion of Europeanization:

> What we need from the Commission is a vision – how are we going to get there, what commitments should be expected, and benchmarks set out, and how these should be reflected in the European Neighbourhood Policy and action plans – and to achieve this we are going to need the following inputs from both the EU and the southern partners. We feel that since Barcelona we have lost this vision.
>
> (Author's interview with diplomat, UK Foreign Office)

Yet while the Commission may be regularly frustrated by the intransigence of some member states over agricultural concessions, it also recognizes that these same states have long-standing engagements in the neighbourhood and close relations with particular third countries there. The gradual shift from EuroMed to ENP thus potentially provides the Commission with both longer-term strategic gains (by enhancing its role as a global foreign policy actor) and important short- and medium-term tactical objectives (through increased *engrenage* – gearing, or alignment – of member states with this new policy, obliging states to make available tried and tested bilateral relations and contacts for EU political purposes). Consequently, the Commission has to temper its frustrations with the need to ensure good working relations with the member states, whose input is essential to the performance of the discourse. This skilful political calculus is set out by a Commission official in an interview:

> We try not to upset too many member states, especially those like France, who know what they are talking about in certain situations. But there are some areas where we disagree. But it is not a bad working combination. We try to listen to those who have a lot of contacts, intelligence, etc. We are not there to carry through complete consensus on every element all the time. I think that it works in practice. Nobody expects that there should be a rubber stamp before we say anything, but we try to be sensible.
>
> (Author's interview with senior official, DG External Relations)

The difficult negotiating position in which the Commission finds itself in the promotion of the Europeanization discourse also arises when it is forced to communicate to third countries hard messages over levels of progress. In these circumstances, member states are keen for the Commission to 'lead the charge' so that domestic fallout in the member state is kept to a minimum and national foreign policy not compromised. While at one level this enhances the role of the Commission in the external projection of Europeanization, the effectiveness of this can be quickly undermined when member states distance themselves from the Commission's stance. This is a worrying aspect of the internal–external negotiating dynamic, as testified by a well-placed Commission official and confirmed by a British diplomat:

> There are also some areas where the member states are happy to see us doing the 'dirty jobs', for example in the recent meeting with Tunisia. And then when the French talk bilaterally to the Tunisians – and this is a good example – they say very flowery things about them! We understand that this is part of our role and we are there to deliver the tough messages. We do not have the domestic consequences that member states have.
>
> (Author's interview with senior official, DG External Relations)

> There have been cases where the Commission has had to deliver strong messages which we have endorsed in Whitehall, but there have been cases where a member state has sidled up to a neighbourhood country and said, 'this isn't true', or that their position is different and it's X, Y or Z. And you normally get all hell breaking loose the following morning. It is very frustrating because it means the EU as a whole lacks any credibility if we are not really prepared to deliver tough messages to individual countries, and, by certain member states doing this, it obviously drives a wedge amongst ourselves.
>
> (Author's interview with diplomat, UK Foreign Office)

By 2009, in total seven action plans were in force with Mediterranean third countries: Egypt, Israel, Jordan, Lebanon, Morocco, the Palestinian Authority and Tunisia. EU progress with Syria is slow and an Association Agreement between itself and the European Union is still awaiting ratification at the time of writing. EU relations with Algeria have in the past two years shown some improvement, and an Association Agreement charting areas for mutual cooperation has been established.

The external projection of Europeanization requires the European Commission persuading Mediterranean third countries to accept a European project in which they occupy a position of asymmetrical dependence against the Union. As many argue, the 'neighbours' perceive a utility in closer links with Europe, given their economic dependence upon it and their geographic contiguity with it, and realize that they have very little choice in the matter. This obliges them to accept the European vision of a shared future, even if they may fear the consequences (Walters 2004).

Emerson (2004) contends that the Commission's task is made more difficult by the varying interpretations among the Mediterranean neighbours of European motivations for the ENP. He claims that the ENP is construed in one of three ways: as a modest, practical mechanism to mitigate the unfavourable effects of the enlargement on outside regions; as an attempt to motivate serious 'Europeanization' in the sense of political, economic and societal transformation of neighbouring states, albeit without foreseeable accession chances; and as a thin political gesture to try to placate the excluded. The Commission's position is summed up by two of its key officials for the ENP:

> We are not asking for change overnight in the Mediterranean neighbours. We are not saying that we do not understand the cultural specificities of these neighbours but there are some basic concepts in human rights and some basic international obligations that need to be respected.

> [T]he ENP is an offer. We are not imposing ENP. What we are saying is that if you wish to participate then we are happy to work with you. If you don't want to do so, you might as well go on, but you will see that others have jumped at the opportunity.
>
> (Author's interviews with senior officials, European Commission)

These revealing comments show the spectrum of interest behind the Commission's desire, on the one hand, to establish the European Union as a normative power exporting European identities and values to its Mediterranean neighbours, while on the other being aware of the potentially disruptive effect imposition of such values might have on domestic elite positions within these countries. As a number of well-informed analysts have shown, this dichotomy results in a gap between rhetoric on the ENP and the reality of EU policy action (Bicchi 2006; Diez 2005; Scheipers and Sicurelli 2007). Consequently, identifying and working closely with those most enthusiastic neighbours is central to the Commission's projection of Europeanization. As a Commission official explained, 'I hope that we can make enough progress with the Moroccans and the Jordanians in particular to prove to others how valuable ENP is.' Reflecting on the adoption of the ENP Action Plan by Morocco in July 2005, a Commission official proudly declared:

> [T]he agreement with Morocco went through very quickly, and the level of relations we have with Morocco – well, we have working groups, sub-groups working on each and every area you can possibly imagine *in detail*. The level of discussion we have in those meetings is completely different from the level we have, say, with Syria, with whom we haven't signed the agreement yet. That has taken years. We are not saying that countries can choose [Europeanization]. We are saying that maybe they take different time periods to go to the same objective at a different pace. We think that from our experience *the manner* in which to get everybody on board is to say, 'right, we are going to do it with those who really want to do it and we are going to prove to them all the benefits that this brings', and when Syria sees that we have concluded an Association Agreement with Lebanon, they become very interested about it. If that's what it takes.
>
> (Author's interviews with senior official, European Commission)

There are, however, certain implications for Mediterranean neighbours accepting the Europeanization discourse promoted by the Commission. For example, the acceptance of Europeanization by Moroccan state elites cooperating with the Commission produces specific anxieties over the effects upon other Mediterranean (Arab) neighbours, and exposes Europeanization as an inherently discriminatory discourse that not only isolates and pressurizes states to comply but weakens other forms of association. A senior Moroccan diplomatic source confirms these anxieties:

> I believe that if you can move or advance quickly, then normally you should do so. This doesn't mean other Arab states wouldn't do the same. Probably they would follow. We can't wait for the others. I don't see any problem with countries going faster within the EU but this doesn't mean that you are going to create a new organization or a kind of exclusive club. Maybe some people have ideas that this could be a way of excluding some states. You should be free to advance if you wish and the others should be given the opportunity to do so when they are ready and prepared. Look at Morocco: if you are advanced enough, then you should be able to have an advanced status with the EU but at the same time it should be open to others. We are not seeking a different role from the other Arab countries.
>
> (Author's interview with senior diplomatic source,
> Moroccan Embassy, London)

Accepting Europeanization does, however, bring benefits to Moroccan state elites in their drive to further state goals with the Commission and EU member states, though again there is a delicate balance to be struck between subscription to Europeanization and European intrusion into domestic affairs, as a Moroccan diplomat explained:

When you have a country that supports you within the EU, that's good, that's good for us, and we try to keep this support, and France is one of these countries. In our negotiations with the EU, France supports Moroccan requests, and we are thankful for that, and we would be thankful to Britain and Spain if [they] did the same. We share the [Europeanization] vision, but Europe has to remember that we are doing the reforms for ourselves. It's their right to follow where their money goes, but it must stop there. It can't be politically linked.

(Author's interview with Moroccan diplomat, London)

The Commission's promotion of Europeanization to Syria has been much less successful. The Association Agreement between the European Union and Syria under the Barcelona Process is still not implemented, and the Commission is continually confronted by state elites denying accusations of human right infringements. This, combined with a tardiness in Syrian economic reforms, has led to a rather bleak assessment by the Commission:

In Syria you have a lot of vested interests in maintaining the high level of central control, the corrupt form of management, the system of bribes for contract awarding, and you know it's going to hit people in the pocket when that disappears, when that changes, or as it changes. Syria is an extreme example of a virtual Soviet-type political and economic system still, and that's why the negotiations in Syria have taken so long. We still don't know when they are going to be finished. With Syria it has been the first time that we have gone hand in hand at negotiating the agreement and telling them, 'you'd better do this and that in terms of your domestic reforms'.

(Author's interview with senior official, European Commission)

The Syrian reaction to the Commission's more aggressive pursuit of reform has been strong. A Syrian diplomat gives a useful insight into the tone of the Commission's messages in its promotion of Europeanization to those less enthusiastic Arab neighbours:

Those in the Commission who talk of human rights in Syria are always accusing. Sometimes it's one instrument to put pressure on a country. I wish people would go to Syria before making these accusations. They would have a very positive impression. The government respects human rights. It's totally wrong that we don't respect human rights. We don't have any problems, we have democracy. If you have a law, you have to respect it, and if someone commits a crime, well . . .

(Author's interview, Syrian diplomatic source,
Syrian Embassy, London)

In the next section, we examine how the Commission has gone about protecting the hegemony of the Europeanization space and the discourses that define it in the face of growing frustration over progress among certain member states, and mounting difficulties in persuading neighbours to embark upon the wide-ranging political and economic reform agendas intrinsic to the neighbourhood policy.

The European Commission and the stabilization of the neighbourhood discourse

DG External Relations is critical in efforts to retain the dominant meanings of Europeanization spaces and their projection into the Mediterranean neighbourhood. The fixing of this discourse and the identities that are constructed by it, as we indicated earlier, are of a partial nature. DG External Relations has to protect the hegemony of these discourses while being confronted by considerable pressures for change, discontinuity and variation in interpretation among the member states and the neighbourhood partners themselves. Europeanization spaces are thus highly unstable and require continuous efforts by the Commission to stabilize their contested knowledges and identities. As Milliken (1999: 242) argues,

[D]iscourses require effort . . . in order to produce and reproduce them, and such efforts are not always successful. The open-endedness and instability of discourses mean that they are liable to slip and slide into new relationships via resistances that their articulation and operationalization may engender.

The persuasiveness of the Commission vis-à-vis the member states and the third countries in securing the hegemony of the Europeanization discourse in the Mediterranean neighbourhood is thus fundamental.

There are a number of state contestations and agitations that question the authority of Europeanization spaces and which create dissent. Within the European Union, these include: concerns over the capacity of the ENP to bring about Europeanization, leading to member state frustrations with progress and consequent pressures for new initiatives; arguments over the level and operation of European funding for the 'neighbourhood'; confusion over institutional roles in the delivery of Europeanization; and intra-institutional problems of coordination. Among the 'neighbours', there are concerns over the forcefulness of the Commission in its promotion of Europeanization, the rigidity of the European Union in the timetable for economic reform, the imposing and censorious approach concerning human rights and political change, the failure of France and Spain in particular to agree to the opening up of the EU market for Arab agricultural products, and the Union's unwillingness to underwrite socio-economic change in the Arab states or deal in a just way with the Palestinian situation (Nonneman 2004). Widening contradictory positions and conflicting multi-interpretability are thus emerging between Europe and the neighbourhood states over the Europeanization discourse.

The Commission has had to deal with these forms of discordance and discrediting resistance to the dominant meanings of Europeanization. It has responded in several ways in order to protect Europeanization spaces, not least through a vehement dismissal of the idea of policy change, tackling the bureaucratization within the Commission that has delayed aid programmes to the 'neighbours', greater vocalization by its key staff in promoting Europeanization, and emphasizing its distinctiveness and appeal over other competitive discursive representations and constructions.

Protecting Europeanization spaces from an unpicking by member states through enforcing their dominant intellectual and policy perspectives is a key responsibility of the Commission. This is observed in Commission efforts to exclude other policy practices and 'ways of thinking and doing' as either 'unworkable or improper' (Milliken 1999: 236). As a Commission official explained,

> I think that in foreign policy there has to be a lot of 'Since we are here, is it worth changing it now or are we going to create more damage?' My advice to the Commissioner has always been that there is no point in setting up new processes, but rather to try to improve the ones that you have. Otherwise you waste years.
>
> (Author's interview with member of the cabinet of the Commissioner for External Relations)

The Commission also discourages member states from taking initiatives that could be seen to weaken the collective foundations and dominant meanings of Europeanization. Enhanced cooperation between certain member states towards the 'neighbourhood' come in for a Commission rebuke, not least because it undermines the Commission's initiative functions and weakens the rationale for collective actions at a European level, as the following comments testify:

What member states shouldn't do is to drag that kind of thing into the European Community context because the other member states don't like it. There is nothing stopping any member state or group of member states from carrying out any discussion with whoever they want. They do it already. The question is that value is added when things are done together at an EU level. It is clear that in certain areas there is much greater potential [for promoting Europeanization] if EU member states act together rather than separately.

(Author's interview with senior official, European Commission)

A great deal of criticism has been directed at the Commission by the Mediterranean neighbours over its management of the development aid budget for the Mediterrranean (MEDA). The Arab states are critical of the length of time taken by the Commission to process grant approvals, especially given the urgency with which it seeks economic reforms in the neighbourhood countries. This animus has threatened the legitimacy of Europeanization and forced the Commission to address its own management problems in this area to protect its credibility and safeguard the Europeanization discourse from those who believe it is failing. This urgency on the part of the Commission to 'unmake this dissent' (Milliken 1999: 244) is shown by the following comments:

I think that MEDA is increasingly a success and is in my view one of the key elements of success of Commissioner Patten directly because he had to pick up this project, which was portrayed as the black sheep of our operation. Right now we have the best results of all our operations, much better than the Balkans, Latin America, Asia, etc. I think that has changed a lot because many of the Arab countries use MEDA as an excuse, saying, 'You tell us to do all this but why don't you get your act together with MEDA?' But now we have got our act together and we still cannot do some projects because the Arab states don't deliver on the conditions, or because they have so much bureaucracy that they take more than a year to do anything. Getting our act together on MEDA meant that it removed a whole 'discourse' on Europe among the Arab states.

(Author's interview with senior official, European Commission)

Concern over the capacity of the neighbourhood policy to bring about Europeanization may well have prompted a hardening of attitudes among Commission staff. But even with administrative reform of MEDA, realistically the balance of obligations on Mediterranean neighbours in relation to incentives offered under ENP is too unstable for the policy to achieve strategic leverage and the desired transformation towards better governance in these states (Emerson 2004). Recognition within DG External Relations that such change is likely to take years rather than months is evident in recent pronouncements from Benita Ferraro-Waldner, European Commissioner for External Relations and European Neighbourhood Policy. For example, in a speech at the Swedish Institute for International Affairs in Stockholm in March 2006 she explained that 'the impetus for meaningful reform must always come from within. If that desire is not there, no amount of external assistance or pressure will build sustainable reform. That is why the EU believes in encouraging, not imposing, reform'.

Yet what also emerges from this assertion is the Commission's representation of Europeanization as an extension of European order – that is, a distinctive space of political organization and governance for the Mediterranean neighbourhood (van Apeldoorn 2002). This distinctiveness makes 'intelligible some ways of being in and acting towards the world' (Milliken 1999: 229) and draws a contrast with other (potentially competitive) representations of the Mediterranean. For the Commission, the neighbourhood policy lies in contradistinction to that of the United States, and its promotion in the name of Europeanization is clearly central to EU identity formation, actorness and international presence (Youngs 2004). This is elucidated by a senior Commission official:

> We have to be realistic, though, as to where the US is right now in its relations with the Arab world, and they are playing things substantially different to what we are doing. They have had big announcements like they did on democracy for very little money and very little political commitment. There is a lot of animosity between the Arab world and the US and we don't like to be trapped in that fight. We have very valuable relations with many of these countries, valuable for these countries and valuable for the US also because we can play in between. They, for example, don't have any contact with Syria. So if there is anybody who has leverage on the Syrians and so on, then it's the EU. We have to balance all that. I don't think we should trap ourselves in a view of the Arab world that is not ours.
>
> (Author's interview with senior official, European Commission)

In this chapter, the emphasis has been placed on connecting the elaboration of new spaces of Europeanization, external to the European Union, with the underpinning discourses and actions of EU elites in order to demonstrate irrefutably its interactive processual nature. It has been shown how these Europeanization spaces are much more than simple unidirectional designations made by and for Europe. Our purpose has been to expose Europeanization spaces not as simple outcomes but, rather, as dynamic, socially constructed and contested processual arenas in which the European Commission is centrally placed. Europeanization has been portrayed as a discursive construction and the Mediterranean as a challenging subject of performative discursive practices and substantial European policy constructions.

We have identified three components of Europeanization spaces in the Mediterranean: first, a system of signification in which third countries are given taken-for-granted qualities and attributes which then become actualized in their regular use; second, a discourse production that renders logical and legitimate European interventions in the Mediterranean; and third, a discourse performance which recognizes that Europeanization is unstable and requires strenuous efforts to communicate, coordinate and stabilize its contested knowledges and identities.

We have demonstrated the European Commission's pivotal role in fashioning spaces of Europeanization outside and beyond Europe, focused chiefly on the ways in which it carefully defines and delimits external situations for European intervention, produces systems of signification to render meaningful and appropriate this intervention, and deploys a suite of tactics to ensure the survival of Europeanization spaces and their attendant discourses that it has brokered among EU member states. We have argued that the ENP now makes a critically important contribution as a space of Europeanization in the Mediterranean region. Within this, it is, of course, important to recognize that applying the European Neighbourhood Policy to the Mediterranean is still very much a new venture for the European Commission and member states alike, and, as demonstrated here, the use of neighbourhood in this specific geographical context is freighted with all manner of conflicting expectations among partners. These arise because of the Mediterranean's inherently unstable geopolitics.

Thus, the extent to which the Mediterranean can be characterized as a coherent geopolitical entity, the (in)compatibility of a potentially autonomous supranational policy directed towards this region with far longer-established national political goals and ambitions, particularly among southern member states, and the degree to which these states are prepared to subsume their own political ambitions within the novel construction of a EU Mediterranean 'neighbourhood' are all problematic issues. Such issues cannot easily be resolved, focusing as they do on ongoing debates about the European Union's role as a normative power capable of promoting genuine value change among member states versus depictions of the Union as an intergovernmental body, with the Commission fashioning policy from the interstices between the bounded interests of national states (Schimmelfennig 2005). But they do help explain why the 'export' of Europeanization to third countries produces a fuzziness and messiness in which the Mediterranean emerges as both a chaotic conception and a site of chaos. In doing so, Europeanization reveals the underlying unity and fragmentation not only of the Mediterranean, but also of Europe itself.

6 Territorial spaces of Europeanization

Narratives and politics of multifunctionality in English and French rural areas

Introduction

In the previous chapters, we have examined how Europeanization spaces both condition and are shaped by elite behaviours within the European Union (institutions and member states) and beyond (e.g. the European 'neighbourhood'). In this chapter, we develop this theme of Europeanization as mutable process by examining how these spaces transcend supranational, national and territorial scales, and the challenges facing elites seeking to recast Europeanization narratives from one purpose to another. Specifically, we analyse how a Europeanization narrative of multifunctionality, deployed originally by the European Union to coordinate the defence of agricultural policy entitlements within global trade fora and to communicate a new agricultural reform agenda within EU member states, has latterly been deployed as the pivotal organizing motif for implementing these reforms, creating a multiscaled interactive space of Europeanization. According to Bulmer (2007: 57), studies of the Europeanization of agriculture 'have received less attention' from researchers than other policy areas, hence our focus upon it as a case study here.

As previous chapters have shown, spaces of Europeanization are manifestly complex. Not only do they comprise scalar networks of negotiation, incorporating actors, institutions and agencies, but they also involve difficulties of 'translation', in the sense of embedding narratives supportive of Europeanization with elite constituencies at these different scales to ensure that they 'make sense' and have elite support and approval. Often, successful 'translation' is predicated on the interests and power relationalities of these elite constituencies. For as the case studies examined in this chapter make clear, Europeanization is habitually redefined by elites to ensure that its constitutive processes are realized in ways that uphold elite power positions (cf. Buller and Gamble 2002; Radaelli 2004). Nonetheless, we also demonstrate that Europeanization can be empowering in European rural areas.

Importantly, this challenges the portrayal of Europeanization as 'monolithic' externally imposed transformation of territories, so prevalent in 'first generation' studies (see Chapter 1). Instead we argue that Europeanization is more appropriately conceptualized as a continually evolving territorially mediated (rather than state-centric) process, comprising mosaics of projects with specific strategic goals and associated socialization and learning mechanisms, some elite-driven but others empowering.

The chapter proceeds as follows. First, we consider the origins of the Europeanization narrative of multifunctionality and outline some of the tensions between the European Commission and member states in promoting its coordinative and communicative aspects (this builds in part on the discussion in Chapter 5). We then show how its translation from global trade narrative to implementation template has come about in England and France. 'Translating' the narrative to suit state circumstances has been the responsibility of national elites, creating qualitatively different processes of Europeanization in national settings. In turn, we demonstrate how these states' own territories have developed their own distinctive tropes of socialization and learning around these national mediated narratives of Europeanization.

The French and English case studies of Europeanization reveal the complexities of policy translation, with nationally endorsed multifunctional interpretations accommodated regionally because the resources underwriting them are effectively state controlled. Crucially, however, the politics of these accommodations vary. Detailed empirical examination of these politics shows different organizational goals and aims for multifunctionality, creating tensions and rivalries – and, importantly, contradictions. Distinctive regional mobilizations around the Europeanization narrative of multifunctionality are thus apparent. In some cases, multifunctional narratives have merely 'mapped on' to local institutions and agricultural production discourses of the EU Common Agricultural Policy. Elsewhere, these mobilizations exhibit markedly different politics, encouraging greater participation by the full range of rural stakeholders, promoting forms of socialization among, across and between sectoral and territorial constituencies.

In the first section of the chapter, we consider the origins and development of multifunctionality within supranational spaces of Europeanization.

Supranational spaces of Europeanization: multifunctionality as politics and policy narrative

Although the antecedents of multifunctionality can be traced back to the origins of the European Union's Common Agricultural Policy in 1957 (see Louwes 1985; Rieger 2000; Tracy 1994), this concept was formally introduced only in the late 1980s as a means of denoting the multiple contributions that the EU agricultural sector could make to territorial economic development, the environmental management of farmed land, and the viability of rural communities (CEC 1988). Work by the OECD (2001: 12) has not provided a significantly clearer definition, noting 'Multifunctionality refers to the fact that an economic activity may have multiple outputs and, by virtue of this, may contribute to several societal objectives at once'.

Crucially, however, it was the inclusion in the late 1980s of agriculture as a single agenda item in the Uruguay Round of the General Agreement on Tariffs and Trade (GATT) that led to DG Agriculture seeking to develop multifunctionality as a distinctive Europeanization narrative (Fouilleux 2004). As Fouilleux notes, multifunctionality directly addressed the 'schizophrenic' position that the European Commission found itself in with regard to agricultural policy. That is, on the one hand the Commission had to coordinate member state positions into a coherent external position on global trade negotiations, which, as Fouilleux comments, more often than not meant presenting plausible reasons for *deferring* further CAP reform. On the other, the Commission was also responsible for promoting CAP restructuring within the European Union to *accelerate* these reforms by exerting pressure on member states: 'It forces the Commission into a two-sided discourse on CAP, arguing for conservative positions in the World Trade Organization, whilst pushing for reforms internally on the other' (Fouilleux 2004: 246).

The multifunctional narrative assumed increasing importance from the mid- to late-1990s as the Commission used it to defend agriculture's historic policy entitlements within GATT and, latterly, the WTO. This defence was based on the contention that agriculture was exceptional compared to other industrial sectors, in that it in addition to creating tradeable (marketable) commodities it also generates untradeable (public or collective) goods not valued through market mechanisms. Multifunctionality's status as a Europeanization narrative is clearly seen in the then EU Agriculture Commissioner Franz Fischler's assertion in 2002 that

> [i]f asked to define the 'European model' of agriculture in a nutshell, I would stress the multifunctional role that EU agriculture plays, and its underlying objectives, which are: the promotion of a competitive agricultural sector and of production methods that protect the environment and supply quality products, the support of rural communities, and simplicity and subsidiarity in agricultural policy.

Similarly, ex-EU Trade Commissioner Pascal Lamy characterized the substance and importance of the multifunctional narrative in the same year:

Agriculture is not coal. Yes, there is a European agricultural model, and there is indeed an agricultural project specific to Europe. What is it? It starts from a principled position anchored in our history and culture: agriculture is an economic sector which cannot be left to the vagaries of market capitalism. The reason is clear: the choice of constantly producing more at lower costs has intolerable consequences for our communities. This is because the volatility of prices undermines the stability of farmers' incomes; because the market does not recompense services to the community by farming in terms of protection of the environment or rural life. And finally, this is because if agriculture were subject to the international division of labour – that is, were we to allow the consumer to choose, in a globalized market, the most efficiently produced goods – the six million farms in Europe would be reduced to one million. This is not sustainable and contrary to our choice for European civilization. In short, the shortcomings of the market, in this domain as in some others, demand regulation by way of public policy. In other words, agriculture is not coal. Our farmers will not be the miners of the twenty-first century. This basic point distinguishes Europe from those who would like to apply to agriculture the economic laws of the market.

At the same time as asserting European agriculture's exceptional status and manifest multifunctional attributes, however, the Commission also had to convince member states of the need to reform their agriculture sectors in the face of growing international condemnation of the CAP. Alongside the pressing need to reform the policy to redress distortions in global commodity markets, these were addressed in the so-called MacSharry reforms (named after the then European Commissioner for Agriculture, Ray MacSharry) of 1992; the *Agenda 2000* reforms of 1997; the CAP Mid-Term Review (2003); and, more recently, in the European Commission's 'Health Check of the CAP' (2008), which proposed a range of measures to allow a better response to the new challenges and opportunities faced by European agriculture, including global climate change, the need for better water management, the protection of biodiversity and the production of green energy.

Multifunctionality's 'translation' from a high-level Europeanization negotiating discourse to a Europeanization narrative of territorial engagement is apparent over the course of these four reforms. In particular, the link between agriculture and territorial concerns was addressed explicitly in 1996 through the European Commission's proposal for an 'integrated rural development policy' for the European Union (CEC 1996: 2), of which agriculture would form a part. Once again, multifunctionality was deployed by EU policymakers as the basis for connecting these disparate territorial issues to agriculture, and hence as the principal means of developing the new policy approach. Under the Irish presidency of the European Union, a conference convened at Cork between 7 and 9 November 1996 discussed the implications for an integrated rural policy and, among other conclusions, noted:

> The integrated rural development policy must be multidisciplinary in concept, multifunctional in effect, with a clear territorial dimension. It must apply to all rural areas in the Union. . . . It must be based on an integrated approach, encompassing within the same legal and policy framework: agricultural adjustment and development, economic diversification . . . the management of natural resources, the enhancement of environmental functions, and the promotion of culture, tourism and recreation.
>
> (CEC 1996: 2)

Moreover, the importance of public policy in promoting this new direction for agriculture was foreseen in the conference's pronouncement that

> the shift from price support to direct support will continue; the CAP and the agricultural sector will have to adjust accordingly, and farmers must be helped in the adjustment process and given clear indicators for the future [through the integrated rural development policy].
>
> (CEC 1996: 1)

However, in refashioning multifunctionality as a Europeanization narrative of territorial engagement, the Commission has had to contend with the disparate viewpoints of member states. A subsequent meeting of the Agriculture Council in Dublin saw this endorsement of a new territorial vocation decisively rejected, chiefly through the actions of French and German delegates, both with entrenched and vociferous agricultural lobbies (Lowe *et al.* 1996). But continued pressure exerted on the CAP during the late 1990s by global trade blocs through the World Trade Organization (WTO), and growing recognition that the eastward enlargement of the European Union would require a policy approach that integrated rural and agricultural concerns more directly, kept up the impetus for reform. At the same time, the European Commission ensured the preservation of the new policy emphasis: that of a multifunctional agriculture with an explicit territorial dimension. Thus, EU Commissioner Fischler argued in April 1997 that

> [r]ural development and agricultural policy are often still two separate entities. What we need is for them to be intertwined more effectively . . . we need an integrated approach enabling us to take advantage of

synergy effects [between agriculture and rural development], an integrated policy design that increases agricultural competitiveness and diversifies [territorial] economic activity.

(Fischler 1997: 3)

This aspect was given concrete form in the European Commission's comprehensive *Agenda 2000* reform package of the CAP, introduced in March 1999 to facilitate the enlargement process, through the introduction of the Rural Development Regulation (RDR) (EC 1257/99; CEC 1999a), which drew together in a single policy instrument the three MacSharry 'accompanying measures' and a wide range of other CAP structural aids. According to a Commission press release issued shortly after the Agriculture Council had ratified *Agenda 2000*, this Regulation sought to

promote a competitive, multifunctional agricultural sector in the context of a comprehensive integrated strategy for rural development and hence become the 'second pillar' of the CAP. The new policy explicitly recognises that farming should play a number of roles including the creation of alternative sources of income and employment opportunities as an integral part of rural development policy.

(CEC 1999b: 1)

Similarly, the preamble to the RDR stated that

for almost two decades, attempts have been made to integrate agricultural . . . policy into the wider economic and social context of rural areas . . . agriculture will have to adapt to new realities and further changes in terms of market evolution, consumer demand and preferences . . . these changes will affect not only agricultural markets but also local economies in rural areas in general.

(CEC 1999a: 1)

Clearly, therefore, ratification of the RDR by the Agriculture Council not only marked member states' acceptance that agriculture's exclusive emphasis on commodity production was no longer desirable but also acknowledged for the first time that, through the multifunctional narrative, a new policy mandate for the sector lay in elaborating a constructive engagement with disparate territorial development needs, be they economic, social or environmental. Another innovative feature of the Regulation was the way in which this engagement was to be fostered – preferably at territorial rather than national scale, through the Regulation's implementation via Rural Development Programmes (RDPs). As Commissioner Fischler explained,

'This change in the architecture of the CAP will bring about major improve-ments. We must give all rural areas within the Union the chance to build up their own coherent development strategy [through RDPs]' (2000: 3). Likewise, the Agriculture Directorate of the European Commission noted in connection with the implementation of measures under the RDR:

> There will be greater flexibility of implementation [with these mea-sures]. They are in line with the principle of subsidiarity; all the mea-sures will be put into effect in a decentralised way at the appropriate level determined by Member States . . . Member States should select those programmes that are best suited to resolving the particular rural difficulties of each rural area.
>
> (CEC 1998: 111–12)

Since 1999, member states have chosen to implement the RDR, and with it the concept of multifunctional agriculture, in distinctively different ways. However, a common feature is that territorial actors and organizations are directly involved in promoting new multifunctional policy goals to agri-cultural businesses to create greater engagement between them and the territories in which they are situated.

During the late 1990s and early 2000s, therefore, a multitude of different interventions were made by actors within this elite-driven supranational Europeanization space. These interventions and the resulting spatialized politics revolved around attempts by actors to shape an interpretation of multifunctionality to suit their aims and ambitions. Thus, the European Commission's DG Agriculture and Rural Development sought a vision of multifunctional agriculture that would unlock the unbending and inflexible politics of agricultural policy reform, allowing new scalar relationalities to be fashioned with the European Union's global trading partners while imparting a new strategic direction for this sector to member states that would contrast strongly with the decades-old productivist ethos of the CAP. So, multifunctionality was badged by DG Agriculture and Rural Development as a Europeanization narrative capable of unleashing new territorial develop-ment opportunities in rural areas. For their part, dependent on their national and territorial politics, member states variously enthusiastically embraced (Ireland, Italy) or challenged and contested this position (France, Germany). In order to examine in more detail these national and territorial politics of Europeanization and their spatial manifestations, we next consider national spaces of Europeanization in England and France.

National spaces of Europeanization: the development of multifunctionality in England

To understand how multifunctionality was translated in England to become an organizing motif for agricultural policy reform, reference needs to be made to two state projects instigated by the New Labour Government in the late 1990s and early 2000s. The first was UK constitutional reform focused on devolution and regionalization, while the second, undertaken in the wake of the catastrophic 2001 foot-and-mouth epidemic, was to find new ways of reinserting agriculture into territorial economic development and to reshape its monolithic policy frameworks to assist rural economies. Both heightened and provided a focus for politics of Europeanization nationally and regionally.

The 1997 UK constitutional reforms created the Welsh National Assembly and reinstated the Stormont (Northern Ireland) and Scottish Parliaments. In England, changes were less dramatic; a new regionalization agenda was, however, apparent with the introduction of new governance structures in the nine Government Regions (GRs), the most important being the creation in 1999 of Regional Development Agencies (RDAs) to ensure 'a dynamic local economy and vibrant communities able to respond to changes in traditional industries and to contribute positively to the regional and national economy' (DETR and MAFF 2000: 82). Change was also evident in the fabric of agricultural governance, with the Department of Environment, Food and Rural Affairs (DEFRA, established in 2001 in the aftermath of the foot-and-mouth epidemic) channelling all its territorial operations through Government Offices for the Regions (GOs), unlike its predecessor, the Ministry of Agriculture, Fisheries and Food (MAFF). At the same time, implementing the RDR was geared to the specific needs of GRs via territorially distinct 'chapters' of the England Rural Development Programme (ERDP). These 'chapters' granted some policy discretion to territorial agencies in shaping the three 'rural economy' schemes (DEFRA 2002: 2) designed to integrate agricultural businesses in territorial economic development. These schemes were administered via the Rural Development Service (RDS), a DEFRA Executive Agency, with another DEFRA Executive Agency, the Countryside Agency, having responsibilities for socio-economic development. In effect, a whole tier of English governance now had direct or indirect interest in promoting multifunctional objectives encouraging greater agricultural engagement in territorial economic development (Clark 2006; Clark and Jones 2007).

Second, prompted by a succession of rural policy crises, the New Labour Government made a concerted attempt to reintegrate English agriculture into territorial economic development and to reshape the decades-old policy frameworks of the CAP to assist rural economies. Foot-and-mouth, BSE, the classical swine fever and bovine tuberculosis outbreaks had all raised public awareness of the failures of the 'productivist' agricultural model, and, more specifically, the historic separation of agriculture from territorial economies. Consequently, when the New Labour Government took office in 1997, it made a major push to increase regional capacity to shape agricultural policy. As the then Agriculture Minister, Jack Cunningham MP, commented,

> With my European colleagues, I want to establish a more defensible Community framework that encourages farmers to be rural entrepreneurs, to become more competitive so as to create wealth and provide jobs in rural areas. . . . Within such a framework, regions should be able to develop their own [agricultural] policies to meet their own individual requirements.
>
> (Cunningham 1997: 2)

The Agricultural Advisory Group, a think tank established by Cunningham and chaired by him until July 1998, played an important role in elaborating how multifunctionality might advance territorial aspirations within national agricultural policy. Reporting in 1999, the Group noted:

> The concept of multifunctionality, if used in the sense of policy instruments targeted upon the achievement of . . . rural goals, can play an important role in the process of CAP reform. . . . The Group recommends that the Government should develop the multifunctionality concept so that it supports a wider vision of the positive role of agriculture in the rural economy [through] the introduction of pilot schemes and approaches designed by way of regional partnerships to target specific rural . . . objectives.
>
> (AAG 1999: 30–34)

This recommendation was given greater impetus by a succession of government policy commissions and inquiries – hence the Performance and Innovation Unit's assertion in 1999 that '[r]ural England needs a vibrant and competitive agriculture industry . . . as a source of employment and wealth' (PIU 1999: 12); the 2000 Rural White Paper's exhortation to farmers to 'make the character of the countryside an economic as well as an environmental asset' (DETR and MAFF 2000: 5, 11); and the Farming and Food Commission's (FFC) trenchant recommendation that agriculture must be 'reconnected' with viable markets and the rest of the food supply chain and that '[t]o stay in profit . . . the industry will have to be more dynamic. It will have to be multifunctional' (FFC 2002: 60). Importantly, this statement endorsed the government's advocacy of a multifunctional approach nationally, made in its 'Strategy for Agriculture':

> 'For the past year, Government has been working in partnership . . . to deliver long-term strategy for the agriculture industry. . . . The strategy is a framework of opportunities to help the farming industry become more competitive, diverse, flexible, responsive to consumer wishes, environmentally responsible *and an integral part of the rural and wider economy.* . . . The new Rural Development Programmes, implementing the Rural Development Regulation . . . are key vehicles for [its] delivery.
> (MAFF 2000: 5; emphasis added)

Together, these regionalization and reintegration imperatives shaped politics within the national Europeanization space – specifically, by focusing and sharpening debate on the shortcomings of the CAP's monolithic regulatory structures for territorial development and rural economies. By doing so, these debates forged closer relations between scalar politics of the national and the territorial. Thus, national goals for multifunctionality have been to 'reconnect' agriculture with territorial economies by exhorting farm businesses to diversify, with appropriate diversification activities in each GR identified by 'regional partnerships' of actors and organizations and promoted through regional 'chapters' of the England RDP. Government foresaw an important role for territorial governance in implementing these regionally appropriate multifunctionality strategies – albeit kept within tight nationally imposed financial limits.

Equally, for territorial actors these new politics of Europeanization offered a range of strategic possibilities and opportunities. 'Rural development is . . . becoming Europeanized as a common European framework [the RDR] guides the direction of support in countryside management, agricultural structures and rural development measures across the member states' (Ward and Lowe 2004: 132). Importantly, the new pulse of Europeanization ushered in by the RDR offered financial resources and new sanctions and powers to territorial actors such as GOs: 'Ongoing reform of the EU's CAP in favour of more inclusive rural development, with increased funding earmarked for a range of measures identified in regional plans, meant that the GOs took on a range of new functions in the rural policy sphere' (Burch and Gomez 2004: 13). GOs and RDAs were not slow to 'use Europe' to augment and improve their own modest powers and resources. Significantly, too, the socialization and learning processes engendered by Europeanization were 'focused on a regional perspective rather than local or national ones' (ibid.: 7), giving territorial politics of Europeanization new dynamism, direction and purpose. We examine these emergent politics in the context of the English East Midlands later, but first consider French national spaces of Europeanization.

National spaces of Europeanization: the development of multifunctionality in France

An overriding concern from the national French perspective was to ensure that multifunctional narratives legitimized the continuation of the post-war policy support arrangements for agriculture. More specifically, multifunctionality was viewed as a strategic opportunity; first, to maintain the vibrancy of farming communities; second, to stall the decline in numbers of farmers; and only third, to connect agricultural production with local economic and environmental objectives.

The French government's response was to introduce the *loi d'orientation agricole* (LOA) in July 1999 and a strategic plan for agriculture and rural development for the period 2000 to 2006 (*Plan de développement rural national*, PDRN). This established a set of six priorities around which new and existing measures were combined into major implementing programmes, as follows:

1   the promotion of sustainable, multifunctional agriculture via the *contrat territorial d'exploitation* (CTE);
2   the occupation of territory by farmers and foresters, to help manage the process of structural change in rural land management and to support marginal areas in danger of abandonment;
3   to encourage value-added primary production in rural areas;
4   to maintain forest resources;
5   to meet ecological requirements – particularly France's obligations with regard to *Natura 2000* sites; and
6   training of farmers and foresters.

Combined, they contribute to the fashioning of a new strategic and financial template for French rural policy for the twenty-first century. Intrinsic to this strategic plan was the CTE. This measure recognized specifically the multifunctionality of agriculture and the need to promote contractual relations between French authorities and the farming community to develop '*une emploi activité agricole bien conduite qui contribue en même temps, à la production agricole, à la création de valeur ajoutée mais aussi à la protection et au renouvellement des ressources naturelles, à l'équilibre du territoire et à l'emploi*' (a well-managed agricultural activity that contributes to agricultural production, adds economic value and also protects and renews natural resources in line with territorial and employment goals) (Ministère de l'Agriculture 2000: 4).

The CTE was a voluntary farm management contract bringing together the three goals of improving the economic, social and environmental contribution of agriculture to rural development. Significantly, each CTE contract was designed by territorial agencies, including agricultural businesses, local civic interests (conservation, recreation, amenity, etc.), state authorities and local economic concerns through the forum of local Agricultural Steering Groups (*Commissions départementales d'orientation agricole*, CDOAs).

CTEs comprised two axes: first, a socio-economic axis, the main goal of which was to secure the economic development of businesses through diversification of on-farm activities, and alteration of existing on-farm practices; and second, an environmental and social axis, which incorporated existing schemes established under the agri-environment Regulation (EC 2078/92; CEC 1992), as well as other rural development measures. Participating farm businesses had to undertake activities from both axes as part of their contractual obligations. The precise activities offered to farm businesses varied with the economic, environmental and social needs of specific *départements*. By 2001, €152 million had been allocated to the CTE programmes by the French state, and this amount was supplemented by a further €150 million from the European Union. By mid-November 2001, 20,304 contracts had been signed between French farmers and the state under CTE programmes, with the goal of creating a more sustainable and multifunctional agricultural sector in France. Each CTE contract covered the entire farm holding, committing farmers to produce food with due regard for the protection and renewal of environment and natural resources, and, importantly, the need to maintain as well as create rural jobs.

The French approach to multifunctionality thus prioritized *equally* the concept's economic, environmental and social aspects, with the specific aim of supporting agricultural businesses by creating new partnerships between farmers, territorial actors and an already well developed subnational government structure. By contrast, in developing the multifunctional concept in England, the emphasis was placed on encouraging agricultural business diversification to support territorial economic development efforts by bringing together a new tranche of subnational agencies introduced as part of the government's 'regionalization' programme (Keating 1997) with the operation of traditional agricultural extension services. In other words, the significance in the French case was still very much on supporting the farm; in the English case, it was to reorientate farm businesses to support the rural economy more generally (see Lowe *et al.* 2002). We next examine how these national Europeanization spaces and their animating politics have invested territorial spaces of Europeanization in the two focal countries.

From national to territorial spaces of Europeanization: the English East Midlands

The English East Midlands GR comprises the counties of Derbyshire, Leicestershire, Lincolnshire, Northamptonshire, Nottinghamshire and Rutland (Figure 6.1), and has a diverse agricultural sector comprising arable, mixed arable–livestock and livestock farming systems.

Catalysed by recognition of how the new 'pulse' of Europeanization differed from post-war sectoral arrangements in agriculture, territorial politics here were based around elite attempts to direct and steer the English

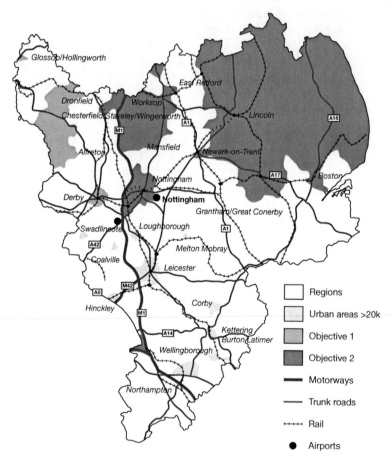

Figure 6.1 The English East Midlands.

Source: Department for Transport, Local Government and the Regions

multifunctional narrative to suit territorial strategic goals. Not surprisingly, perhaps, the perception of regional elites in agricultural organizations was to view the national multifunctional narrative with misgivings, seeing its promotion as a direct consequence of agriculture's declining economic fortunes. Among them there was noticeable hesitancy over whether a regionally appropriate multifunctional narrative for the East Midlands could be implemented. Hence, reflecting on the emergence of national priorities for multifunctionality, DEFRA's senior representative in the Government Office for the East Midlands (GOEM) commented:

> [I]n 1997, this government wanted to look at rurality as a whole and not just the industry's interests, and consequently farming has had to change, it has had to become more multifunctional, because the world has changed, what society expects of the sector has changed. So what we're looking for is for farms in the region to become more market oriented, more them helping themselves, and more their efforts benefiting rural economies. I think what we're seeking through promoting the multifunctional model is better integration [of agriculture] with the rural economy and social fabric of the region as a whole.
>
> (Author's interview, 16 May 2001)

This confirms that the national narrative of multifunctionality – namely, a new sectoral mandate seeking to 'reconnect' agriculture with wider territorial economic development (FFC 2002) – has been accommodated in GOEM (unsurprisingly, as GOEM represents state bodies within regions). However turning this narrative into a coherent strategy sensitive to regional concerns provoked much greater uncertainty, with this respondent admitting that substantial reorientation of agricultural norms and ethos would be needed. Asked to elaborate how the new Europeanizing narrative of multifunctionality might conflict with the region's production-oriented goals, this respondent replied:

> Well, in the glory days of MAFF, there was this massive national policy: what we're about is increasing self-sufficiency, and you could see projects that furthered that goal marching across the countryside. In the 1960s and 1970s, the drainage contractors would just draw a line on their maps and proceed to drain every field: single tender, drain everything in sight. And then in the late 1990s we take that imperative away, but we leave the price structure sort of intact. . . . British agriculture doesn't have that overriding mission any more, and I think it'll take a while yet for multifunctionality to fill the gap. Even the most enlightened farmer is grappling with its meaning: I mean, it's easy to say it's about producing

new goods and services unconnected with commodity production, but for many of them that's *precisely* what they've done all their lives. The new mission needs to be couched straightforwardly: 'the countryside is still 80 per cent agricultural, we should maintain it as it is'. And at the moment, production support is still underlying the old production message. Ninety per cent goes on CAP spending, just 10 per cent goes on the Rural Development Regulation. Massive amounts of money needs to be swapped over. There's a danger there, I think, of multifunctional farm businesses being left in limbo.

(Author's interview, 16 May 2001)

Crucially, this reveals a territorial politics of Europeanization emerging, in the respondent's questioning of the practicalities of multifunction-ality endorsed in his earlier remarks. Implicitly, this politics is based on territorial concerns of lack of national preparatory planning – specifically, how the narrative should be presented to the agricultural community; and the inadequacy of resources available regionally to support putative multi-functional businesses. Yet despite the sense of resignation and of problems to be confronted, the interviewee acknowledges the need for East Midlands agriculture to embrace multifunctionality. This opinion was shared by other elite respondents within agricultural organizations, and was clearest among land agents and consultancies working closely with agricultural businesses. Thus, asked about the importance of promoting multifunctionality in the East Midlands, an agricultural consultant with many years' experience stated:

I think it's fundamental. If you want jobs and people living and working in what is still predominately a rural region, their cash circulating within rural areas, there must be a move towards a multifunctional agriculture. It's difficult to see what is still largely a farming economy such as that in the East Midlands, in the aftermath of CAP reform, contributing to the region's development otherwise. I mean, farm incomes in the region are down 14 per cent on ten years ago. But multifunctionality to my mind is very broad. You can still be farming, but it might be different crops, non-subsidized crops; equally, you can be providing non-agricultural services.

(Author's interview, 5 December 2002)

The absolute necessity of promoting the multifunctional narrative regionally is confirmed here. And again there is recognition that the aim of this new strategy for agriculture should be to provide more direct support for territorial economic development. Implicitly, there is also a revision of the national narrative though, in the respondent's intimation that multifunctional activities should remain *agricultural*, rather than embracing genuinely *territorial* enterprises. In effect, the national interpretation of the multifunctional narrative is being reinterpreted in such a way as to support the goals and interests of regional actors and organizations involved in its promotion.

Certainly there was also a strong consensus among non-sectoral organizations within the region on the need to accommodate the national multifunctional narrative. Thus, in the opinion of GOEM's Regional Director:

> Those of us at the top attach a great deal of importance to it; because agriculture, despite the recession, is still a major industry, and the multifunctional vocation, shall we say, provides a plausible means of bringing this major industry back into engagement with the rural economy; to use Sir Don Curry's [Chairman of the Policy Commission on Farming and Food, which reported in January 2002] overused phrase, for 'reconnecting' the industry with territorial concerns. I mean, even if it's gone down the dip a bit since 1999, I guess regional income is still of the order of £1 billion. And, admittedly locally, it's still a major employer. In parts of south Holland [in Lincolnshire], you've still got 19, 20 per cent of the workforce employed in the sector, and that's not taking account of upstream and downstream industries. And when you link this sector in with the food industry, it's of massive importance regionally – it's one of our most important economic sectors. Yes, we're still pretty big in engineering, but that's all relative. Textiles has gone down the dip, and coal mining's all but disappeared. And while farming's suffering, you've still got 80 per cent of the region under agriculture, a bigger percentage live in this region in rural areas than probably any other part of the country . . . therefore you can't ignore its economic contribution, I think it'd be criminal to ignore it in any assessment of how to instil greater economic growth regionally in future.
>
> (Author's interview, 19 July 2002)

While this is a categorical endorsement from the region's leading civil servant of the need to accommodate the national multifunctional narrative, there are notable contrasts here with preceding respondents from agricultural organizations. First, for the Regional Director the aim of the narrative is seen very much on national terms – that is, to reconnect agriculture with the regional economy, and to use a multifunctional conception of agriculture as a means of generating 'greater economic growth regionally'. This conflicts directly with the agrarian vision from the previous respondent. Clearly, therefore, the territorial politics of Europeanization are coloured by pre-existing organizational roles and responsibilities, with the national multi-functional narrative viewed through the prism of particular pre-existing rural mobilizations, some sectoral, some territorial, allowing the national narrative to be recast and justified or legitimized along various axes of territorial power as 'in the regional interest'.

From these responses from territorial elites, it is evident that the English narrative of multifunctionality has had a formative influence on territorial development debates in the East Midlands. Territorial politics have evolved chiefly by placing subtly different emphases on its goals, purposes and orientation. Nonetheless, subsequent fieldwork demonstrated that these minor differences of opinion were exacerbated when 'mapped on' to existing territorial politics and organizational relationalities. In particular, in projecting a consistent message to agricultural businesses on multifunctionality, much depended upon high levels of trust and interdependency *between* agricultural and non-sectoral agencies, for working in a genuinely non-partisan way is essential to promoting multifunctional goals to farmers. We examine these prevailing territorial politics of Europeanization in the East Midlands later. First we consider the interrelations between the national and territorial Europeanization spaces in France.

From national to territorial spaces of Europeanization: the Languedoc

As in England, the RDR acted as a catalyst in France for new forms of territorial engagement through the PDRN's six priorities. While channelling forms of Europeanization into particular categories, therefore, the PDRN also offered considerable latitude to territorial elites at regional and *département* scale to fashion multifunctionality in ways that were sensitive to local circumstances. The mechanism of the CTE was pivotal to delivering this local sensitivity and to fashioning new forms of territorial political engagement. Thus, within territorial spaces of *départements*, local state elites, agricultural leaders and environmental interests were responsible for agreeing a template setting out territorial economic and environmental needs, within which farmers could broker individual CTEs. Importantly, this could result in new territorial politics reflecting the different production systems and landscape types, so strengthening territorial distinctiveness.

In many cases, the creation of these CTE schemes in *départements* resulted from the actions of dynamic territorial groups, eager to further disparate production, environmental and socio-economic goals. Indeed, as Lucbert (2000: 11) claims, 'the task is to anchor the CTE in collective initiatives which develop territorial approaches'. These collective interests often included economic groups (e.g. cooperatives), representatives from private–public institutional partnerships (e.g. in environmental management), and members of agricultural organizations working either alone or in conjunction with other local institutions. CTEs were drawn up by these groups following discussions, and presented to the CDOA. Each CTE presented to the CDOA identified the individual actors and organizations responsible for its drafting, their motivations and aspirations, and links with existing policies of the *département*, as well as their available resources to implement and oversee the specific CTE. CTEs also set the territorial parameters: area covered, physiographic description, socio-economic and historical unity, number of farmers involved, key farm business characteristics, and the potential of the CTE to meet the stated socio-economic and environmental objectives.

This territorial diagnostic of the CTE mechanism provided the key template for evolving territorial politics of Europeanization by giving the impetus for any shift from the hard-wired *filière* politics typical in so many *départements* to the *territoire* approach sought for an integrated French agricultural and rural policy. (The shift is one from an approach based on commodity production in agriculture to one based on diversified farming activities and greater consideration of agriculture's contribution to rural development.) The

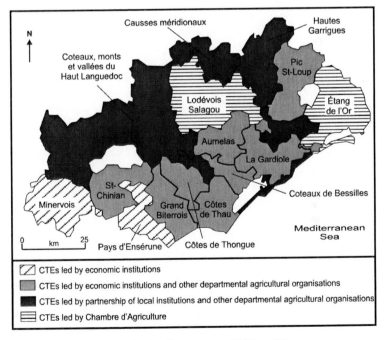

Figure 6.2 CTE schemes in the *département* of L'Herault.\

Source: Ministère de L'Agriculture, Languedoc-Roussillon, 2003

nature of these all-important territorial politics therefore would shape enthusiasm nationally towards the CTE idea and the multifunctional narratives embedded in it, evidenced by the number of CTE programmes set up and, importantly, the reaction to them from the agricultural community. As Figure 6.2 shows, farmers in the South-west and in the Massif Central led the process of CTE enrolment. Almost one-fifth of those enrolled in the CTE nationally farmed the country's mountainous areas, with farmers in the *départements* of Loire, Aveyron, Isère and Tarn heading the list.

The Languedoc region of southern France provides an instructive example of these evolving territorial politics of Europeanization. Here, territorial politics were expected by elites to foster innovative efforts to combine agriculture diversification with environmental objectives and to generate productive links between farming and the region's burgeoning tourist industry. However, the integration of a territorial dimension into existing deeply embedded viticultural politics through the vehicle of the CTE was not without its problems, not least the different perceptions and definitions of *territoire* held by local farmers and local policy elites, which affected scheme design, delivery and, ultimately, its uptake by farmers.

Each Languedoc *département* was requested to draw up CTEs relating to specific farming systems and territorial, environmental and economic preoccupations. Over 1,240 farmers signed CTE contracts, representing some 6 per cent of the total number of farmers enrolled in this programme nationally. There was considerable variation between Languedoc *départements* over the take-up of contracts by farmers, with the highest figures being recorded in Aude, where, as one policy official explained, political support for CTE initiatives was warmest. By mid-November 2001, 218 farmers in l'Hérault had signed contracts under one of the fifteen CTEs in existence in the *département*. These are shown in Figure 6.3. The initiative for these CTEs came from one of three types of institutional elite: the *chambre d'agriculture*, a *cave coopérative* or a *syndicat de cru*. The traditional dependence of the *département* upon the *filière viticole* and the importance of the cooperative movement within this *filière* account for the large proportion of the CTEs in the *département* initiated by wine institutions.

The CTEs in the Hérault *département* are either top-down initiatives on the part of the *chambre d'agriculture*, such as the CTE *l'Étang de l'Or*, or those inspired by locally based actors (often in the viticulture sector) working either independently of, or in conjunction with, other local institutions, for example the CTE *Pays d'Ensérune*. Here we examine local elite involvement in the fashioning of territorial politics in the CTE *l'Étang de l'Or* (EDO).

This scheme was spearheaded by the *chambre d'agriculture* and was established in June 1999. Mindful of the high profile of viticulture in other CTEs across Languedoc, in this case the *chambre* was eager to introduce a

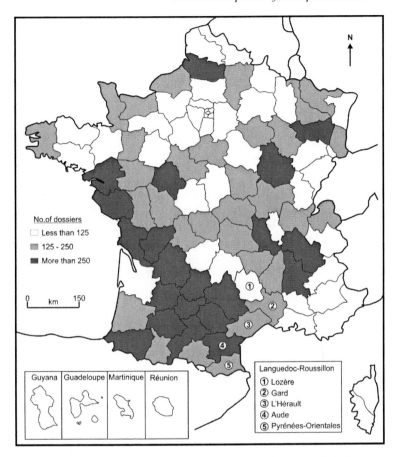

Figure 6.3 Contracts signed with France under CTE schemes by 2001 by
    département.

Source: Ministère de L'Agriculture, Languedoc-Roussillon, 2003

programme that embraced aims and objectives and which encompassed more
than simply vine growing. In essence, the EDO scheme represents a broad-
based top-down, elite-driven initiative hinged on the twin goals of tackling
water pollution and the problems facing the fruit sector (*filière arboricole*) in
the east of the *département*, particularly in the *cantons* of Lunel and Mauguio
to the east of Montpellier.

The CTE *l'Étang de l'Or* covers forty-six *communes* in Lunel and
Mauguio, a vast area displaying a considerable variety of geographical
conditions and problems. The *Étang de l'Or* itself is a lagoon, surrounded by
salt-water marshland. It is ranked the fifth largest wetland in the Languedoc

region and designated not only as a site for bird protection, but also one of generally high ecological interest and value. The surrounding marshland has also been identified for biotope protection, while the entire area has been classified by the regional authorities as vulnerable to nitrate pollution from agricultural practices. The EDO area, with its sensitive environmental balance, is confronted by growing tourism, residential and agricultural pressures.

The area's proximity to Montpellier and the presence of major coastal resorts, such as Carnon, La Grande Motte, and Palavas-les-Flots creates considerable summer tourist pressures. In recent years, for example, the *commune* of Carnon, with fewer than 2,000 inhabitants, has witnessed the arrival of 40,000 tourists each year. The expansion of Montpellier has itself resulted in numerous land-use pressures in the EDO area. Recent population census figures record that the area has witnessed the highest population growth rates in the Languedoc over the past twenty-five years. For example, the market town of Mauguio had only 4,000 inhabitants in the early 1980s, but by the early 2000s its population had grown to 16,000.

The EDO area is also important agriculturally. Farmers in Hérault were at the forefront of efforts to diversify production away from vine growing, capitalizing on irrigation water provision by the *Compagnie nationale Bas-Rhône Languedoc* and the close proximity of Montpellier as a marketplace. These efforts were given renewed impetus as a result of tumbling wine prices, the adoption by the European Union of a tougher stance on lower-quality wine production, and the sponsorship by the French state of measures to encourage Languedoc farmers to diversify. Consequently, the number of *vignerons* and vineyard area in the EDO area decreased greatly over the period 1988–2000. There were 397 *vignerons* in 1988 and only 200 in 2000, a fall of 49 per cent. Similarly, the vineyard area fell from 1,957 hectares in 1988 to 1,214 hectares in 2000, a decrease of 38 per cent. Some *communes* in the area suffered disproportionately. For example, Mudaison lost almost one-third of its *vignerons* and almost half of its vineyards over this period.

Consequently, the *chambre* decided to draw up plans for two CTEs, one focused upon livestock rearing in the upland areas and another centred upon what a senior *chambre* official describes as 'a complex diversification of productions' based on the coastal plain. The serious environmental and economic development pressures in the *Étang de l'Or* area placed it in a leading position for inclusion under the CTE programme. As an official from the *chambre* explained,

We began the process by identifying the area to the east of Montpellier, then drew up a possible list of members for the *comité de pilotage* in the first instance drawn from the various *filières* present there. Since we had already been working on pollution control in the *Étang de l'Or*, it was thought appropriate that water management should be the central focus for the CTE.

Elites in the *chambre* worked on the preparation of the CTE for the EDO area from June 1999. As this was the first CTE in the *département* to be prepared by the *chamber*, it was imperative that all interested parties were involved in its elaboration and that a sound cooperative management structure was put in place. Of particular importance was the need to bring together officials from the fruit, environment and land-management divisions of the *chambre*. In September 1999, *chambre* elites agreed that the proposed CTE for the area would comprise four priority objectives: ameliorating water quality, improving the quality of agricultural products, organizing territorial management and promoting rural employment. These were demanding goals, given the geographical diversity and competitive economic pressures in the area. This was reflected in the long political process surrounding the formulation of the CTE for this area. So, while the proposal was passed to the CDOA of the *département* in December 1999, there followed a further five months of discussion within the *chambre* over the proposed aims, resulting in a revised proposal being delivered to the CDOA in May 2000. Difficulties of reconciling the different sectoral objectives (e.g. viticulture and fruit growing) and problems of transforming the attitudes of local elites, from narrow *filière* goals to broader territorial objectives, accounted for this protracted institutional deliberation. As one well-placed official from the *chambre* explained,

> The lack of dynamism and the plodding attitude delayed the CTE's progress. It was a top-down programme, and therefore not led nor widely supported by local farmers. We were faced with locals who were not at all sensitive to the purpose of the CTE. The problem was compounded by the fact that they were unaccustomed to working together. The net result was delays and disinterest.

Given this geographical diversity in the CTE EDO, it was difficult for *chambre* elites to engender a sense of *territoire* among local actors, particularly since they were unaccustomed to working collaboratively with actors outside their particular *filière* associations. This lack of dynamism and accompanying stagnant politics did not bode well for a policy that placed *territoire* as its central concept. By early 2002, therefore, not a single farmer living in the area covered by the CTE had enrolled in the scheme. This prompted lengthy discussions among the *département*'s key institutions as to why France's latest rural development tool for promoting multifunctional agriculture had failed to encourage farmers in the *Étang de l'Or* to participate.

As one senior representative of the Ministry of Agriculture confessed, 'I am very embarrassed to speak about this because it's a CTE that just hasn't taken off, and there are several reasons for this.'

Strong leadership, categorical endorsement of the CTE's aims by the farming community through its subscription to the principle, meaning and personal significance of *territoire*, combined with clear institutional goals and responsibilities, were essential for the successful implementation of a CTE. Several of these components were absent in the CTE *Étang de l'Or*. As an official from the *chambre* explained, this scheme was unsuccessful because

> of conflicts between policy makers over its content, and also because of a lack of motivation to make the CTE work. It's a scheme that has really dragged its heels, and is still progressing only very slowly. In addition, there have been a certain number of disillusioned farmers who haven't really taken the time or effort to understand the purpose of the CTE and have failed to appreciate that this is a new way of tackling rural problems.

The politics of Europeanization within territorial spaces: the East Midlands

Overall, interviews confirmed a relatively supportive territorial politics among agencies involved in developing multifunctionality. However, responses also demonstrated problems in building the 'new politics' needed to structure relations between organizations with sectoral and territorial affiliations where working cultures, procedures, norms and routines were often dissimilar.

An exhaustive interview with the Chairman of the East Midlands Development Agency (EMDA) provided valuable insights into these issues. Asked whether there was a pervasive working culture in the region that favoured collaboration between organizations, the Chairman commented:

> [O]ne of the particularly strong features of the East Midlands region is the willingness among extension groups and lead organizations, such as my own, to work together. All the agencies in the East Midlands rural scene work very closely; we don't stand on ceremony, we're not turf-protective, we muck in and help each other out, despite some political differences at the heart of our organizations. [By political differences] I mean our agenda is a regional one, very clearly; the Countryside Agency's agenda is a national one, yet here in the region we couldn't be closer. I know in other English regions the same is not so true. So, yes, there's obviously been learning among us, on agriculture and on a whole range of different sectors, but there's been a willingness to learn, to bend, to flex on the part of different organizations. I can honestly say that I

don't think there's a single organization that doesn't want to be a part of the team.

(Author's interview, 14 May 2001)

This response emphasized positive political engagement among agencies. But it also suggested the respondent may have glossed over deeper tensions and rivalries among agricultural and territorial organizations, resulting in some agencies selectively promoting those elements of the national multifunctional narrative that accorded with their own organizational goals.

Certainly problems surfaced in developing 'joined-up' arrangements for regional multifunctionality. For example, the Farm Business Advisory Service (FBAS) Operations Manager commented as follows on the difference in working cultures among private- and public-sector organizations:

> I mean, it's just some of these agencies we're working with are very bureaucratic, while we're trying to come at it from a business angle. The important thing is trying to get the needs and the wants of the farmers through to the policy administrators . . . farmers can't expect it on a plate, but administrators also can't expect a huge uptake of grants and support without making the process easier to follow. And we're just trying to be the linking body in between.

(Author's interview, 3 January 2002)

Moreover, interviews confirmed that orchestrating a regional multifunctional narrative had prompted a variety of *new* inter-organizational tensions and rivalries. Partly these had arisen from attempts to develop a 'joined-up' communications strategy encompassing agricultural and territorial agencies for promotional purposes. Tensions had also emerged as a result of structural changes in English regionalization, requiring realignment of organizational roles and resources. Thus, the introduction of the FBAS in April 2000 saw policy responsibilities for agricultural training and enterprise – originally held by county councils – being transferred to this organization. This prompted a senior official from Nottinghamshire County Council to comment:

> I thought it was a strange move when they put the advisory function with the Small Business Service [the Small Business Service is the FBAS's 'parent' organization]. It was previously with the Nottinghamshire TEC [Nottinghamshire Training and Enterprise Council, a Nottinghamshire County Council agency]. I mean, OK, it's a new body, and maybe the government was hoping that as a new body it would be perceived to be different, and let's just hope it works, but I wonder if that's going to happen. It's a difficult period, because we've just been through the foot-

and-mouth crisis when the SBS couldn't go out to farms. So they're immediately starting on the back foot, because they've not got the proper track record that they should have had by now, really.

(Author's interview, 4 Jauary 2002)

The FBAS was defensive on this issue:

At the end of the day, DEFRA was saying there needs to be a business oriented organization fronting this service, and that's why it came through to the SBS; it wasn't on some whim, you know, 'let's give the Small Business Service something to do'.

(Author's interview, 3 January 2002)

DEFRA's creation in June 2001 also precipitated change in territorial politics of Europeanization, with the resulting shake-up of departmental responsibilities giving one DEFRA Executive Agency, the Rural Development Service, control of the England RDP, the most important policy programme for encouraging multifunctionality – which a second DEFRA Executive Agency, the Countryside Agency, had played an instrumental role in developing. Plainly, this has led to antagonism between regional elites in the two organizations. As an influential figure in the Countryside Agency commented ruefully,

The intra-departmental relations between various bits of DEFRA I still perceive as being strained on occasion. I wish they'd given us the ERDP to run – personally, I think that if the schemes it comprises are meant to work as an integrated programme, then the agency to do it would be us. But existing mechanisms have to be accommodated. But the one weakness in our network of communication is with the running of the ERDP. When you're looking at a package that's supposed to embrace multifunctionality – that is, it relates to the rural community and rural services, and the cultural heritage and tourism – the fact that such activity does not involve the Agency grates with us. It would be better if RDS accepted the proffered assistance from the three statutory agencies. . . . We have got expertise to bring to the table, and then they could set up a more balanced form of project appraisal. Because at the moment, that Assessment Panel does not involve the outside agencies, it's just GOEM and RDS. The lack of integration in the programme is a real source of frustration in the system. I mean, we've offered, but RDS has never come and asked us what we think. And in the portfolios of projects being approved for RDP funding, there is little or no integration across and between measures, and the thematic spread is concentrated on the socio-economic. I don't know where this exclusion of outside agencies from the approvals process is coming from, I don't know what the politics are behind it. If the rural agencies are to join up their thinking and their spending, then we've got to have a mechanism for seeing what's going on in the ERDP. And that's the big weakness in the system at the moment, as far as I'm concerned. . . . So that's the worst bit of the rural–agricultural link in the region.

(Author's interview, 20 August 2001)

When asked to comment on this point, the RDS's Senior Policy Adviser stated:

[O]ne of the difficulties you're always going to get – and it's something that we're working on all the time – you've got to stop organizations fighting their own corner. Some see the ERDP as something that's going to further their aims and objectives, and not those of the intended beneficiaries. Well, at the end of the day, the beneficiary is not organizations, it's the farmer, and the rural economy, and the countryside. So it's a different culture to get over to all the support organizations as much as to farmers. I mean, we do get some agencies saying 'well, we want the ERDP to follow our organizational line'; they haven't said that in as many words, but they certainly do try to use moneys to achieve their agency aims rather than the stated aims of the programme. But I think they've failed to a certain extent because they're now beginning to realize this is all private-sector focus. They've woken up to the fact that this money has to go to the private sector, it doesn't actually go to public bodies.

(Author's interview, 5 December 2001)

Hence, although territorial politics were strongly positive among actors developing and promoting regional multifunctionality, analysis revealed underlying organizational tensions and rivalries. These remain acute around the old divisions between agricultural and territorial interests – precisely the division the new Europeanizing discourse of multifunctionality sought to address. In particular, the joint organizational working required to develop a multifunctional approach has meant reallocation of resources and organizational responsibilities among regional agencies, bringing these long-standing tensions to the fore. However, territorial politics of Europeanization were not simply about the reinscription of old territorial political–rural mobilization power struggles into new narratives. Increasingly, multifunctionality is beginning to challenge these old sectoral factions through introducing new working procedures. Before examining this aspect, we consider the Languedoc's territorial politics.

The politics of Europeanization within territorial spaces: the Languedoc

In the Languedoc, a deeply traditional area of France, forging new territorial politics bringing together *filière* and *territoire* required nothing less than reversing the mindset of farmers. Clearly, such a task is fraught with problems (Jones 2003; Jones and Clark 2000, 2003). Crucially, a key difficulty for the successful development of the CTE in the *Étang de l'Or* area was that the institutional mosaic for farming was founded on various production *filières*. Despite the tremendous changes that have taken place within the *filières* in the post-war period, this institutional base remained largely unmodified.

Certainly, within the CTE *Étang de l'Or*, *filière* rather than *territoire* politics continued to preoccupy institutional actors, be they from the *filière*'s sectoral institutions (such as wine or fruit cooperatives), or elites employed in the *département*'s political institutions. With the fruit sector in the Languedoc experiencing serious economic crisis in the early 2000s due to falling prices, overproduction and changing consumer preference in northern Europe, few, if any, of its representatives in the EDO area believed that solutions to these problems lay in the CTE schemes. Dispirited fruit growers in this area appeared little interested in vague, subjective notions of *territoire* when their incomes were falling. Moreover, given their bitter experience of agricultural policy, having invested heavily in fruit production, only later to be encouraged to grub up their fruit trees, they were deeply suspicious of yet more government-backed schemes that, in their view, promised much but delivered little. Strong, committed leadership was clearly lacking from local *filière* elites to ensure that the CTE prospered in any way under these conditions. Promoting active interest among an already beleaguered farming population was without doubt an unenviable task for any leadership.

Such leadership was also required to drive forward new forms of territorial political engagement bringing together *filière* and *territoire*. Key in this respect was the role of the *comité de pilotage* steering each CTE. Each *comité* comprised representatives from the key *filières*, environmental groups and other interested territorial partners. *Comités des pilotage* were charged with three key responsibilities. The first was to set out the key objectives for the CTE and ensure that participating farmers abided by them; the second was a supervisory role, overseeing project implementation and advising farmers on best practices; and the third was responsibility for ensuring that there was coherence to all the various actions contained within the CTE programme.

The *comité de pilotage* for the *Étang de l'Or* CTE thus comprised a diverse group of actors. The *chambre* was acutely aware that it needed to have representatives not only from the key *filières* of fruit growing, market gardening and of course viticulture, but also actors with specific nature conservation and environmental interests. However, the *comité*'s eventual composition reflected the importance of sectoral interests rather than broader concerns. Since the *chambre* clearly wished the CTE in the area to be focused on the fruit sector and water quality issues, and not on viticultural concerns, it selected as president of the *comité* a prominent figure from the region's horticultural sector. The *chambre* expected the president to play a *dirigiste* role in setting the CTE's objectives, promoting them among the farming community and ensuring their effective implementation.

However, the selection of the president from a specific *filière* undoubtedly weakened the drive to achieve a truly *territoire* programme. As an official from the *chambre* confirmed,

> The president is steeped in *filière* thinking, and the apple sector at the moment is confronted by major difficulties, which greatly overshadow any interest in the CTE initiative. In my view this explains why the implementation of CTE in the *Étang de l'Or* is progressing so slowly.

There were other factors too that explained the poor performance of the CTE in the *Étang de l'Or*. Principally, they related to elite decisions to emphasize the fruit sector in the CTE's overall objectives, and by implication downplay the significance of viticulture. As it turned out, this decision came at high political cost. As many writers have remarked, the vine imposes its traditions and folklore across the Languedoc, indelibly stamping the countryside and rural ways of life, as well as fashioning social and economic relations. The EDO region was no exception to this. In particular, the wine cooperatives in the area were an important repository of local knowledge and social networks, vital to any broader promotion of the CTE locally. Moreover, the region's wine sector included a number of innovative *vignerons* keen to put in place schemes under the CTE to improve the quality of their wine production, using more environmentally sound production methods.

In effect, the viticultural legacy and its associated productivist discourses have exerted a deadening influence on new forms of territorial politics in the EDO. Elite decision making has strongly favoured existing sectoral interests, and efforts to engage new constituencies – and to exhort and inform farmers – have been fragmentary. Ironically, however, the negligible engagement by farmers with elite-sponsored multifunctional projects stimulated grassroots initiatives in the region. We discuss these after examining new territorial politics in the English East Midlands.

New territorial politics and the promotion of multifunctionality: the East Midlands

Despite the organizational tensions reported, insertion of the national multifunctional narrative into territorial spaces has also catalysed new forms of territorial politics based on new patterns of regional working and collaboration. Two collaborative structures were particularly important in facilitating this 'joined-up' working on multifunctionality. The first was the Regional Planning Group (RPG) and its associated fora, promoting the ERDP regionally. The ERDP offers three 'rural economy' schemes whose main purpose is to reintegrate agriculture with territorial economic development. These schemes are the Rural Enterprise Scheme (RES), the Processing and Marketing Grants Scheme (PMG) and the Vocational Training Scheme (VTS). Each seeks to encourage agricultural business managers to diversify their activities from commodity production towards the adoption and implementation of alternative enterprises that directly benefit the rural economy. While the establishment of the RPG is thus a response to the second 'pulse' of Europeanization (namely, the obligatory introduction by the UK government of EU Regulation 1257/99), its constituent actors and organizations are wholly responsible for decision making on these 'rural economy' schemes (financial budgets for the ERDP are, however, settled at the national and supranational scales). Specifically, the RPG canvassed the opinions of territorial actors and organizations to provide a regionally appropriate focus for the three schemes, as well as approving or rejecting individual scheme applications submitted by farmers.

The second coordination structure is the East Midlands Rural Affairs Forum (EMRAF), set up as part of the 2000 Rural White Paper to marshal opinion on national proposals affecting rural areas. Increasingly in the East Midlands, EMRAF is 'providing a forum for sharing information, issues and initiatives affecting rural areas' and identifying 'issues of concern to rural people and businesses' (EMRAF 2002: 14), both of which are directly relevant to the promotion of multifunctionality to the region's farmers. This is reflected in EMRAF's wide membership, embracing both agricultural *and* territorial interests.

Hence, while the RPG's and EMRAF's roles are complementary, their focus is quite distinct. Discussions within the RPG centre on the three 'rural economy' schemes, and results in the disbursal of funds. By contrast, EMRAF's brief is much wider and, without having specific resource allocation functions, is essentially discursive. In both cases, participation and decision-making in these governance structures is tiered. Clearly, part of the explanation for the adoption of this structure lies in the need to expedite regional decision making (particularly on ERDP scheme approval), but equally important would appear to be a desire (on the part of DEFRA and GOEM respectively) to maximize participation in these new structures of rural governance.

The ERDP's regional decision making relies on consultation and partnership working. Its focus is the RPG, chaired by DEFRA's senior official in GOEM and composed of representatives from the Local Government Association, the Countryside Agency, the Environment Agency, the Rural Development Service, English Heritage and the Forestry Commission. The RPG meets four times a year to assess the delivery of the three 'rural economy' schemes, so providing strategic direction and enabling linkages to be made with other territorial economic development initiatives. The aim is to ensure that benefits from financial spend under the ERDP are maximized. In the words of an RDS official, the RPG provides the ERDP with its 'core organizational representation . . . the RPG takes action' (Authors' interview, 5 December 2001) on issues proposed or highlighted by its two supporting fora. Clearly, therefore, the RPG's role is highly significant in coordinating joint organizational working to promote multifunctionality in the East Midlands. As one panellist commented,

> [Y]ou're trying all the time to control the process, to guide farmers down this new route, to move the industry in a direction it's not moved in before and, with the best will in the world, may well not move *en masse*, anyway.
> (Author's interview, 3 December 2001)

Implicit in these comments is the enormous difficulty of trying to instil a new relational logic within a sector that has been wedded to productivist agricultural ideologies. To overturn this embedded institutional structure is clearly a massive undertaking.

By contrast, EMRAF's wide-ranging agenda permits a 'longer view' and a more strategic level of discussion on multifunctionality than the RPG, as its Chairman described in interview:

> [T]he management committee of EMRAF actually consists of representatives from the main farm sectors, plus the main agencies [the Countryside Agency, EMDA, the East Midlands Regional Assembly, GOEM], the county councils, education and outreach services, so in some respects what EMRAF is doing is helping to identify what multifunctionality means in the region, what role the different organizations can play in its promotion, and what direction we all take, through ensuring consensus, through securing support and input from others. That's the aim, but obviously working through a forum like ours, the actual mechanism for achieving these goals can be difficult.
> (Author's interview, 23 August 2002)

These comments suggest that EMRAF was beginning to address the 'silo mentality' in English rural areas of distinct (and seldom interacting) agricultural and territorial policy communities. New socialization patterns were being created which, in turn, might lead to new learning repertoires among regional actors. Undoubtedly, EMRAF's contribution to 'identify[ing] what multifunctionality means in the region' has been substantial (see Box 6.1).

Both ERDP and EMRAF decision making rely heavily on partnership working, which is a novel development for many of the organizations involved and has proved difficult to implement, as GOEM's Regional Director confided:

> Partnership working is never easy; you have to work at it. At the end of the day, sometimes you just have to agree to differ. And I think one of the real problems about partnerships is that most organizations have a

---

Box 6.1   EMRAF's role in developing the East Midlands' multifunctional narrative

EMRAF has been instrumental in developing the East Midlands' multifunctional agenda. It has done so by providing an arena within which different actors and organizations have networked and negotiated over possible future directions for multifunctional agriculture in the East Midlands. As a representative from the East Midlands Learning and Skills Council commented in interview, 'I sit on a couple of EMRAF's new panels and committees [and] it's helped us to get better known. So I find it's good. On the EMRARG, there's about fifty of us in it and we network – everyone there does – you should have seen yesterday after the meeting, everyone's talking to each other. I mean, next week I have a meeting scheduled with DEFRA and the NFU [National Farmers Union], and the CLA's [Country Land & Business Association] rep spoke to me to ask if he could come along. Well, together we'll see whether we can raise how local communities can become more involved in this new agriculture. I think if you put people together that are used to these sorts of forums and groups, if they're brought together now and again, they can help shape the multifunctional agenda and push it forward. You can use Any Other Business, or introduce an agenda item. So the EMRARG [East Midlands Rural Affairs Reference Group] is much more than a talking shop – it's a useful basis for forging partnerships.'

Source: Author's interviews, 1999–2002.

---

vested interest; you see it especially in European funding. Everyone's pointing a finger, you know. You have to live with that. If you take the rural element, take dealing with the ERDP, you get these interests sharply defined in terms of a sectoral or functional basis. So you'll get English Nature coming along; they want everything to be environmentally checked and tested. And they want us to spend more money on environmental aspects of the ERDP. Then you've got the Countryside Agency, who'd like you to spend more on villages and things like that, and you've got others who see it primarily as being a farmers' programme, see it as money to help farmers out. And English Heritage, who are always short of money, are looking for someone to do something for the built environment. So there are always these demands and you're always getting conflicts over how the resources should be spent. And in the end you have to come to some kind of consensus. And I think GOEM's role tends to be in the end, I suppose cynically, you'll never get agreement between all the partners, so at the end we make up our mind what the consensus is and the decision is taken.

(Author's interview, 11 June 2001)

These comments illustrate how territorial politics underwrite the second 'pulse' of Europeanization. These politics are now transacted through formal coordination mechanisms in the East Midlands, namely the RPG and EMRAF, and appear to be playing a significant role in dampening down potential conflicts between organizations over developing regional multifunctionality, and in clarifying the need for specific promotional activities – for example, 'strategic' roles, such as the identification of new sources of information and knowledge, or more 'tactical' functions, such as developing communication mechanisms between subnational agencies and agricultural businesses. But these comments also indicate the institutional *limits* of partnership working – that is, the point where achieving consensus can be made only at the cost of 'sclerosis' in decision making. In such situations, GOEM seemingly adopts an hierarchical role by 'mak[ing] up [its] own mind what the consensus is and the decision is taken'.

This examination of the operation of new decision-making and decision-taking fora in the East Midlands demonstrates the crucial role of territorial spaces in developing and promoting regional multifunctionality. Formal coordination mechanisms *have* been introduced regionally, namely ERDP and EMRAF decision-making structures, and, more pertinently, these structures are shaping the development of regional multifunctional narratives – for example: in terms of EMRAF's promotion of 'quality' foodstuffs; exhorting business managers to network with other elements of the food chain; and through the Forum's role in focusing attention on the institutional constraints on multifunctionality imposed by structures such as the local planning system. Most pertinently, it emphasizes the complex, territorially configured nature of the Europeanization of rural areas in the twenty-first century. Multifunctionality represents a major departure in English rural policy, and it is vitally important that territorial elites relay this to the farming community in a way that offers an exciting prospect for individual farm businesses. This excitement will quickly fade if farmers are faced with complicated application procedures and time-consuming paperwork which many of them would complain of as being their experience of previous EU policy initiatives in agriculture.

New territorial politics and the promotion of multifunctionality: the Languedoc

Ironically, in the Languedoc this breakdown of an elite-sponsored form of multifunctional engagement has encouraged a grassroots territorial politics, albeit one anchored in the viticultural *filière*. An emerging politics led by viticultural interests has seen groups of farmers working in conjunction with local wine institutions and other organizations. Such initiatives include schemes to promote wine sales, maintain viticultural landscapes and conserve specific species of fauna or flora. For example, in the *commune* of Saint-Christol, as a *chambre* official explained,

> *Vignerons* have decided to set up a CTE within the overall CTE of the *Étang de l'Or*. They have managed to assemble various interests from within the viticultural *filière* and hold productive dialogue with nature conservationists and botanists, as well as securing the backing of the local mayor. The *vignerons* intend to use the CTE as a vehicle not only to promote the economic development of the *commune* but also to identify important conservation goals.

There are a number of important lessons to be learned from this case study of the territorial politics of Europeanization focused on the formulation and implementation of this CTE in the Languedoc. The CTE was an attempt to engender a genuinely multifunctional response among farmers by shifting the policy emphasis from a productivist viticultural ethos to a territorial approach in which farmers were encouraged to link environmentally sound agricultural production with broader rural development objectives. Clearly, the importance of developing this territorial politics has not been understood or appreciated by the local agricultural community or by elites within particular production *filières*. For that to happen, there has to be a much greater degree of dissemination of information to farmers about multifunctionality, if there is to be any active interest or participation in policies such as the CTE which sponsor this new form of territorial engagement.

There are several ways in which this dissemination could take place. From the case study, it is evident that the *filières* are central to successful rural development generally. The *filière*, as we have seen in the case of viticulture, operates on the basis of established rules, procedures, information channels and highly networked social relations. These furnish an important means by which the message of multifunctionality can be transmitted to the agricultural community. Again from the case study, it is clear that the key to success in implementing any new form of territorial engagement is to build on the efforts of local dynamic actors, eager to promote multifunctional objectives and engender enthusiasm for new policy programmes, and willing to foster collaborative links between wider assemblies of actors in the rural domain. Much as in the English case, therefore, there is now a pressing need for territorial elites to build new constituencies of interest within farming if the innovative prospects of multifunctionality are to be captured by farm businesses.

Though profoundly different in significant ways (most clearly in the political-administrative arrangements of the two case-study regions), the English and French experience of developing multifunctional narratives within spaces of Europeanization confirms how networks of actors have sought to promote meanings and concepts of Europe to rural constituencies for their own purposes. As we have shown, these 'uses' of Europe provide an increasingly potent resource for these actors within European political geographies, in both a discursive and an instrumental sense.

Underpinning both case examples are tremendously varied Europeanization politics. Nonetheless, important cross-cutting themes are evident in these manifestations of the Europeanization of territoriality. For example, politics in both study regions 'map on' very closely to existing organizational templates – even if these are largely locally driven in France, and state- and regionally driven in England. Long-standing differences in local territorial and agrarian politics have also acted as focal points for contrasting allegiances towards multifunctionality – some supportive, others ambiguous or actively antagonistic. More particularly in England, there seems to be incompatibility between private- and public-sector organizational modi operandi, creating another source of contentious multifunctional politics. The resulting complex, messy political debates have been further riven by the reallocation of financial and authoritarian resources, with Europeanization spaces becoming increasingly the arenas within which mediation of finance, authority and organizational responsibilities are shaped and reassigned under the imprint of Europe. We have therefore been able to confirm Roederer-Rynning's (2007: 219–20) observation that '[m]onolithic representation of agricultural policy in Europe is obviously problematic. . . . Analysing and explaining contrasting patterns of change in both time and space are important tasks for any future research'.

Most importantly, the chapter has shown how territorial spaces of multifunctionality are fragile political accomplishments, prone to be easily undermined by the disparate and often competitive interests at play in French and English rural space economies. Transforming the deeply ingrained views and attitudes of sectoral actors to wider territorial considerations continues to be a major challenge in both the Languedoc and the East Midlands. Of equal difficulty is convincing farmers in both regions that the long-term future stability of businesses and the livelihoods of families depend upon a funda-mental change of emphasis away from commodity production. Certainly, generating innovative working partnerships between bureaucrats, farmers and local politicians through the medium of multifunctional schemes and projects is critical to ensure the success of what some have suggested might be a model for future EU agricultural policy. Yet while agricultural policy in England and France is now seeking to grapple with broad rural development objectives in which employment creation, improving food quality and security, and protecting the natural environment are given greater priority, escalating prices for agricultural commodities on global markets are now threatening to derail this consensus building. Recent attempts by the English and French states to appease and placate agricultural lobbies during this difficult period do not bode well for the piecing together of durable and robust multifunctional policies in these two states.

7 The spatialities of Europeanization

Power, governance and territory in EUrope

Introduction

In this book, we have argued that Europeanization comprises continually evolving processes of socialization and learning among elites, focused on temporally contingent constructs of Europe that are both discursive and instrumental in nature. We have conceptualized these elite-led processes taking place within overlapping, intersecting spaces, played out variously as rhetorical positioning, collaborative actions and carefully choreographed sets of political practices that, taken together, promote a mosaic of possible spatializing outcomes – some representative of the identities and values embodied in 'normative Europe', others asserting diverse national, community, organizational, and even individual, ideas and interests.

Previous chapters have shown how these Europeanization outcomes are the product of highly dynamic processes that until recently were shaped largely by the hegemonic narrative of European integration focused upon state-based politics and phenomena. However, we have argued that this narrative is waning in importance, and is likely to diminish further to give way to wider territorial and popular expressions of what constitutes Europeanization – with, in our opinion, substantive consequences for future modalities of governance and power across Europe. Consequently, the mainstream view (in political science especially) of Europeanization as monolithic and transformative – most notably as the 'domestic impact' of Europe upon and within its member states – is, we believe, an increasingly questionable formulation.

By focusing upon the triptych of power–governance–territory, we have been able to examine the ways in which Europeanization unfolds in different spaces at particular times. One of the key attractions and strengths of this approach is how it facilitates what we have termed the spatializing political practices of elite actors – practices that are often conducted at a variety of geographic scales – thereby furnishing new insights into Europeanization as process. Specifically, we argue, spaces of Europeanization comprise discursive and essentialist components that are (re)produced through mediations and intersections between different actors' practices – whether 'EUropean', member state or 'third country' in origin – with such practices given purpose and meaning by the territorially defined norms and beliefs of elites relating to what it means to be 'EUropean'.

We have used the power–governance–territory triptych to examine four longitudinal case studies, in adherence with our original aims of providing an empirically based, theoretically driven account of Europeanization's complex, multifaceted character, which, crucially, builds upon contemporary literatures within the social sciences. These empirical analyses have yielded a variety of novel perspectives. *Conceptually*, they demonstrate Europeanization's intrinsically social, territorial and political basis, lodged in place-based and temporally contingent mores; *ideologically*, they show its close affinity to and with prevailing hegemonic discourses of power – most recently, that of the guiding narrative of European integration, an elite formulation and relic of post-war Europe; and *cartographically and thematically*, they show the complexity of this process set in the sense of 'mapping' its operational extent in varied territorial, public policy and scalar domains.

These empirical analyses provide 'fresh insights' (Lehmkuhl 2007: 352) into the processual basis of Europeanization and, more specifically, offer a valuable basis for revisiting and in some cases revising existing conventions on Europeanization in the social sciences. In effect, our analyses present Europeanization as a 'living concept' (ibid.: 340) that reflects the ebb and flow of European integration and the exigencies of EU policymaking.

At the outset of this volume, we identified recent work on Europeanization from a variety of disciplinary perspectives. One of these recent works, undertaken by Paulo Graziano and Maarten Vink (2007), assembled a team of scholars to explore this research terrain. Their work considered Europeanization from conceptual, theoretical and methodological standpoints, affording some important insights into recent debates and academic positioning. In the light of our empirical analyses, it is worthwhile revisiting the findings of Graziano and Vink to assess possible complementarities – and, equally, points of departure.

From their own disciplinary perspective, Graziano and Vink (2007) adduce the most salient characteristics of contemporary Europeanization to be as follows. First, they argue that there is 'nothing necessarily top-down' about mainstream research (ibid.: 8) – a point with which we certainly agree. However, since these authors do not clarify *why* this is so, this continues to be the *de facto* position of much political science scholarship. Indeed, in the same edited collection, Caporaso (2007: 26–27; our emphases) comments that Europeanization studies 'ask novel questions about cross-level relationships – not only from the Member States to the EU, but also *from the centers of the EU back to the Member States. This latter set of questions is associated with the Europeanization focus*', noting later that 'Europeanization turns the causal arrow around to ask how European integration and everyday policymaking affect domestic structures *[as well as] refer[ring] to the processes by which domestic structures adapt to European integration*'. Both statements implicitly endorse a top-down approach. More generally, political science's widely used notions of 'goodness of fit', 'fit' and 'misfit' to scrutinize Europeanization presuppose an 'ideal type' of the EU state in a Europe of astonishing geographical, cultural, social and political diversity.

Our findings, by contrast, show *why* Europeanization remains a stubborn and unruly process – heterarchical rather than hierarchically driven in its origins, approach and effects. In Chapter 6, for example, we show how spaces of Europeanization reflect the fragility of local-level political agreements that can be easily sundered by competitive interests. In the French and English case studies presented, we demonstrated how local, deeply ingrained views and attitudes exert a pivotal influence on Europeanization by shaping political discourses and resultant actions and outcomes locally and regionally.

Second, Graziano and Vink maintain that Europeanization research needs to be cognisant of 'direct effects . . . as well as indirect effects' (2007: 8). In our opinion, this imposes a rather mechanistic division on the canon of contemporary Europeanization research, perpetuating the widespread binary of 'EU-ization' and 'Europeanization' which we considered in Chapters 1 and 2. We argued there instead that these two categories are mutually constitutive – that is, that 'EU-ization' is merely a contemporary inflexion of a much older, continent-wide suite of Europeanization processes, the political geographies of which researchers have barely begun to explore. Thus, political science studies express surprise at the continuing 'diversity' and 'variety' of Europeanization outcomes and the 'resilience' of domestic institutions in the face of a fifty-year integration process, but until recently had failed to engage with the profoundly geographical notions that might explain this variability of territory, territoriality, cultural differentiation or geographical propinquity. As we have argued throughout, this points to the need for a wider disciplinary engagement among political scientists, geographers, sociologists and anthropologists with the *political geographies* of Europeanization, rather than the polity–policy–politics focus of so many contemporary studies.

In Chapter 4, we offered one promising means of engaging with these geographies by providing a longitudinal study of the spatializing political practices of central and east European elites. Here a blending of territorial associations, place-based affiliations and credentials and scaled loyalties seems to have been used to assert 'Europeanness', demonstrating the importance of historic and cultural mores in Europeanization at the 'sharp end' of high-level diplomatic negotiation. Undoubtedly, therefore, profoundly geographical variables are at play in the fashioning of contemporary Europeanization dynamics.

Third, and closely related to this last point, Graziano and Vink assert that Europeanization outcomes 'should not be restricted to uniform impact . . . but should allow for differential impact' (2007: 8). We concur that research should not presuppose outcomes. Indeed, our approach places this 'differential impact' at the heart of analysis by emphasizing the place- and scale-based politics of Europeanization rather than the often artificial foregrounding of policies, politics and the workings of states. What might be termed the 'state fetish' may have been suitable for analysis of European integration-led Europeanization. Yet, as preceding chapters have shown, it limits capacity for projecting where 'EUrope' and Europeanization might be heading in the twenty-first century, as this process spills out beyond elite and polity confines. It disregards the very considerable geographical variation in Europeanization patterns already apparent across Europe, even among the 'old' EU-15. And, ultimately, it relegates Europeanization largely to the status of an elite managerial tool, rather than a potentially empowering academic exploratory focus. The European Neighbourhood Policy proposed by the European Commission in 2003 reflects the differentiated geographies of implementating a multi-state-based approach to Europeanization. In Chapter 5, we examined the place- and scale-based problematic confronting the Commission in its efforts to grapple with this new policy, and its efforts as a non-state-based organization to overcome the conflicting positions articulated by state actors on the Mediterranean 'neighbourhood'. This chapter confirms that much is missed in Europeanization studies that have an exclusive state-based focus; arguably, this should now be set aside.

Fourth, Graziano and Vink (2007: 9) contend that Europeanization research should now be broadened to permit wider consideration of the 'traditional levels of a political regime'. However, it is our contention that this broadening should offer more than another round of impact-type studies. For, as we have shown, 'impact' is a problematic notion. Most clearly, however it is gainsaid, it results in gradations of 'transformation' in the analytical categories (often polity, politics and policy processes) under scrutiny, whereas, as we have shown, Europeanization is more appropriately conceptualized as arising from the cross-cutting scalar activities of actors, variously linked and/or opposed. We have contended that it is only through the analysis of the politics arising from these cross-cutting activities that a grounded processual understanding can be attained. Through the notion of spaces of Europeanization discussed here, we have offered an analytical means by which the broadening of Europeanization research can take place, allowing scale, territorial, and historical-cultural fractions to be encompassed in analysis.

Finally, Graziano and Vink (2007: 17) argue for a 'more explicit and transparent use of interviews, and qualitative work more generally'. This they see 'could be of great use to Europeanization research', which would constitute 'a major source of information and may be plausibly used to trace motivations for certain actions'. We agree wth this view, and in the preceding chapters we have drawn on a rich vein of detailed interview materials conducted over a lengthy period to examine how Europeanization unfolds in different spaces at particular times.

Consequently, we are firmly of the view that spaces of Europeanization provide a constructive means to interrogate underlying processes. Such spaces provide a means to engage in the examination of the spatialities of Europeanization, namely:

- the division of space by Europeanization's constitutive processes (be they territorially based processes, power-laden discourses or governance driven);
- the fundamental interconnection between these constitutive processes;
- the means by which these processes aggregate to create particular kinds of spatialized political practice (and, at higher geographic scale, spatialities of acquiescence, adaption, facilitation and resistance); and
- the active ways in which these practices and spatialities fashion the spaces and scales of Europeanization.

We discuss these spatialities in more detail in the next section.

The division of space by Europeanization's constitutive processes

Europeanization has significant spatial implications. We have argued that these implications can be considered in terms of power, governance and territory. Perhaps the least well covered of these in contemporary literatures is territory, which has often been depicted as a passive backdrop over which Europeanization politics and political actions are played out – a setting, rather than a dynamic quantity in its own right. Thus, Goetz (2006: 1) comments that 'territory has received little attention in Europeanization research'. Similarly, Radaelli notes 'the idea of [supranational] impact' of Europeanization on the national 'is somewhat static and mechanistic . . . real-world processes of Europeanization provide [domestic actors with] considerable opportunities for creative [territorial] uses of Europe' (2004: 3; cf. Buller and Gamble 2002; Méndez *et al.* 2006). By contrast, we have shown how territory may be monopolized by state actors as a device to control, contain and discipline Europeanization processes and outcomes (see the work of political geographers in other spheres, for example Agnew 2005; Cox 2003; Gilbert 2007; Jessop *et al.* 2008; cf. Sack 1986). This continual (re)production of territory through individual, societal and state activities and interaction is, we believe, a fruitful avenue for future research, with political geographical concepts such as territoriality providing a potentially powerful analytical lens for scrutinizing Europeanization dynamics in the twenty-first century. Indeed, territoriality could prove to be a pivotal notion in future research, as popular expressions of Europeanness begin to weaken and undermine the state's hold on Europeanization.

The fundamental interconnection between these constitutive processes

Spaces of Europeanization are predicated upon constitutive processes of power, governance and territory. Our analysis has confirmed that these quantities and their associated (largely political) processes are animated through the actions and discursive practices of numerous individuals, organizations and a plethora of formal and informal institutions. Critically, these actors are not simply state-based, or even necessarily state-related. In turn, this suggests that greater academic attention be given in Europeanization analyses to the interconnections between these constitutive processes, focused upon *identity*. An important starting point for such analyses is the ways in which identities have hitherto been framed within academic literatures on the European Union. Thus, as demonstrated in Chapters 3 and 4, partly because of the dominance of functionalist accounts centred on federal and inter-governmental approaches to the Union, Europeanization is often character-ized as opaque, a binary distinction between member state and EU identities, denying the reality that EU political elites continually shift within and between 'national', 'EU', 'organizational' and 'individual' agendas and objectives depending on their decision-making context (cf. Clark and Jones 1999; Jones and Clark 2001, 2002; Ruggie 1993). Most clearly, personnel in the EU institutions, including the European Commission and European Parliament, are drawn from the European Union's twenty-seven member states and are, in effect, obliged to hold 'multiple' identities. Again this omission within Europeanization studies is puzzling, as recent excellent analyses have been conducted within the political science and political soci-ology of the relationalities underpinning the 'bleeding together' of national and supranational identities (e.g. Beck and Grande 2007; Etzioni 2007; Hooghe 2005; Soysal 2002; Stråth 2002). Yet application to Europeanization continues to be of a rather standardized kind, where survey data on identity tends to impose 'a conceptual unity on extremely diverse sets of political processes that mean different things in different contexts. . . . Indeed, survey questions may create the attitudes they report' (Checkel and Katzenstein 2009: 14). Hence, studies consider the process as a product of 'either'/'or' actions and reactions between the European Union and national governments, rather than the complex commingling of identities among elite actors within the Union shown in Chapters 3–6. For as Jerneck (2000: 42) notes, elite 'EU politics is conducted . . . without it being possible to determine with certainty what are national preparatory processes and what are EU level negotiations'. Interrogating the 'identity complex' of actors involved in Europeanization potentially offers a wealth of new insights into Europeanization's malleability and durability, in particular its capacity over time to be commandeered and redefined through different political ideologies.

The ways in which power, governance and territorial processes aggregate to create particular kinds of spatialized political practice

The empirical studies in the preceding chapters have provided new insights into the complex reworking of Europeanization through existing, and emergent, spatialized political practices variously deployed by emergent territorial interests, community and stakeholder groups, and social factions and individual elites at local, national and supranational scales. This resonates with recent work attesting to the interrelations between territory and identity and their appropriation by geographical sites of authority, which is absent from many Europeanization studies (see, for example, Heeg and Ossenbrugge 2002; Paasi 2001, 2005; Painter 1995, 2001, 2005; Rodríguez-Pose 2002; Scott 2002, 2005; Smith 2002; Western 2007). Where these political practices service particular state-based interests, it may result in the 'uploading' of national political preferences to the EU level (see Howell 2004; Radaelli 2004). Europeanization's frequent invocation as 'impact' of the European Union upon national political life and its consequent transformation overlooks the capacity of states for selective acquiescence in this process through spatialized political practice, a characteristic enabling national political elites to steer Europeanization in their territories on terms that buttress existing state orders (see Chapter 6's elucidation of these processes in the context of rural France and England; see Buller and Gamble 2002). Again this aspect has been largely neglected by Europeanization scholarship and would, we contend, benefit from detailed empirical research.

The active ways in which these practices and spatialities change the scales of Europeanization

We have argued that elite and everyday practices, struggles and discourses over varied uses of Europe as a discursive and instrumental resource are becoming increasingly commonplace, in order to fashion Europeanization outcomes to favour particular interests. Inevitably, this multidirectional process is resulting in a multiplication of cross-scale and multilevelled activities and interactions, creating growing interdependence among actors at different scales in the (re)production of Europe. Key drivers of this growing interdependence are socialization and learning among these actors in, on and around Europe, resulting in dissolution of scales and increased spatial 'reach'.

We realize that making a claim for growing interdependencies might seem improbable in the current era of intergovernmental retrenchment and 'rowing back' against 'Brussels'. Yet there are clear historical precedents of Europeanization changing scalar metrics irrespective of prevailing attitudes towards the 'European project'. In particular, since the 1980s, existing territorial scalar rhetorics have been reimagined and reconceptualized through the European Union's structural funds as Europeanized 'spaces of development' (Leitner 2003), creating entirely new repertoires of political engagement between EU political elites and territorial groups, and a new European cartography of networked power that arguably has contributed to the 'decentring' (Low 2003: 626) of EU member states as empirical foci for research. The effects of this decentring have extended to the trappings of the nation-state, as boundaries, places and state sovereignties across the Union become increasingly 'fuzzy' (see Markusen 1999), arguably providing less explanatory purchase than they once did.

Even more ambitious and far-reaching is the recent manifestation of Europeanization processes at the scale of the individual. The original text of the rejected EU Constitution (CEC 2003) devoted almost one-fifth of its content to defining and delimiting *personal* political geographies by setting out the fundamental rights and entitlements for a new European citizenry (Part II, Titles I–V). Undoubtedly this represented the most insidious and sweeping political strategy of territoriality to date – effectively an attempt to create a standardized political geography of mind–body–self for half a billion people. As the French political commentator Dominique Moisi observed, the French '*non*' to the Constitution indicated that such micro-managed political geographies were unacceptable to twenty-first-century Europeans.

Such upscaling and downscaling of Europeanization shows little sign of abating. There are, for example, clear indications of the dynamism and increasingly popularist substance of Europeanization spaces. Thus, while the European Union's stability and longevity have been anchored in its multiple layers and spaces of political engagement, there is growing evidence that these can be populated by novel political permutations (alliances of far right, far left and Communists in France and the Netherlands campaigned for a 'no' in the 2005 Constitution referenda, for example) to thwart, as well as support, this project. The recent rejection by the Irish of the successor to the

Constitution, the Lisbon Treaty, in summer 2008 is indicative. Similarly, the formation in June 2009 of a new right-of-centre European Parliament political grouping, the European Conservatives and Reformists, by UK, Polish and Czech conservatives was made ostensibly on grounds of greater popular representation. Yet this has not stopped political opponents characterizing the new grouping as 'a bizarre cabal of ultra-Catholics from Poland and ultra-Calvinists from the Netherlands', while others have branded it a party of 'racists, fascists and climate-change deniers' (Taylor 2009: 3).

Certainly, Europeanization spaces redound of a generalized anomie to 'building Europe' in the twenty-first century, based upon a perceived politico-geographical distanciation/'remoteness' between EU political elites and publics within the twenty-seven member states; a public bafflement at the complexity of the national–supranational political process and people's place within it; and widespread disillusion, most frequently expressed in the need to correct a 'democratic deficit' – that is, make the EU institutions more transparent and accountable to national populations, and to ensure that popular opinion, when solicited, is not circumvented (as has been the case with national referenda to ratify previous EU treaties in member states including Ireland, Italy and Denmark). At its most fundamental, the roots of this anomie are visceral, though rarely articulated: how should existing political geographies of Europeanization be recast, where should popular democratic power reside, and how should European powers be exercised, by whom, and for what purpose?

Such questions require us to envisage what a more empowering Europeanization might be like in the twenty-first century. For within the next decade, we anticipate Europeanization spilling out beyond the conventional confines of elite and state-based metrics fashioned as part of the post-Second World War consensus and becoming a genuinely societal-wide set of processes once more – much as it was prior to its subjugation by nation-states in the seventeenth century (see Chapter 2). And, following the logic of the arguments presented in previous chapters, it is likely to affect territories and peoples not presently considered 'European' today: as Jacques Attali (1993) presciently noted:

> Remember: in twenty years time there will be two billion Chinese and one and a half billion Americans, north and south – but still only three hundred million Europeans. . . . If Europe can do with Africa and the Maghreb what the US is now doing with South America, then the configuration of the 21st century will have been established.

At the least, to study and conceptualize such a geographically and societally wide set of processes will, we submit, need a much broader palette of

Table 7.1 Spaces of Europeanization: future research directions

---

- Europeanization should be analysed as a suite of processes – not as an output or an 'impact'.
- These processes are manifested as territorially differentiated socialization and learning activities.
- These socialization and learning activities are configured by institutional, discursive and governance arrangements, which are heavily influenced by territoriality.
- The 'effect' of Europeanization's socialization and learning processes is dependent on sequencing in time and space.
- Europeanization as process has scalar dimensions: for example, at individual (actor) scale, socialization and learning can occur through passive observation, reflection, deliberate instruction, network creation and informal networking.
- At community scale, Europeanization involves the establishment of collective understandings (intersubjective meaning structures) of 'EUrope' by and among political and policy elites and stakeholder groupings for communal advantage.
- Europeanization among political elites is guided by a variety of cross-cutting decision-making logics: appropriateness, consequentiality and justification.
- While Europeanization can mean the assimilation by actors of new rules, norms and practices, it can also result in the retrenchment of existing national, territorial, organizational or careerist norms, habits and practices.
- Where the socialization of elites into European norms occurs, processes of persuasion and learning of new political practices, social roles and behaviours are often significant drivers of processual change.
- Europeanization through socialization may prompt elites to re-evaluate their interests and identities.
- Europeanization can expose 'inappropriate' positions, practices and habits, prompting further re-evaluation through socialization and learning.
- Europeanization may be promoted by 'norm entrepreneurs'.
- Europeanization can be driven by the existence of consensus-building institutions.
- Europeanization is sustained by a process of discourse hegemony and discrediting of competitive discourses.

---

analytical colours than we have presently. Indeed, as Europeanization constitutes a suite of quotidian processes infiltrating and dissolving geographic scales, linking what goes on in territories with purposive action to influence the content of these territories – that is, as a dynamic that links territory with territoriality – no single social science approach will be sufficient to unpack its spatializing bases and manifestations.

The approach to Europeanization set out here will of course need further development. Specifically, from the analysis we have conducted, we identify key propositions worthy of additional empirical scrutiny through the varied politics of spaces of Europeanization (see Table 7.1).

The pursuit of these propositions should enable a more holistic under-standing of Europeanization's complex dynamics to emerge, one that will place what we judge to be the correct emphasis on process, rather than output or outcomes. In doing so, we anticipate a new wave of studies arising in which power, governance and territory are foregrounded, enabling a more liberating form of Europeanization to be unleashed.

Notes

1 Europeanization: a critical stocktaking

1   An increasingly influential term used in the social science literature on the European Union, with its roots in John Ruggie's (1993: 140) characterization of the European Union as the world's 'first truly postmodern international political form'.

2   Compare with Radaelli's (2004: 8) comment that 'the strategy of political leaders [is often used] to disguise globalisation or domestic politics under a discourse of Europeanisation – either by blame-shifting strategies or by using the appeal of Europe to add legitimacy to choices at home'.

4 Spaces of Europeanization: central and eastern European elites and the 2004 accession

1   Defined here as elites' use of sociospatial concepts and associated diplomatic practices for political effect, and/or adaptation of these sociospatial concepts and practices to suit new spatializing political contexts.

2   As Kuus (2007a: 98) observes, 'Central Europe is a malleable term. In the early 1990s, it denoted the three Visegrad states. Over the decade, common usage of the term gradually expanded to all former satellite states of the Soviet Union. Today, Central Europe connotes the east-central European states that acceded into either the EU or NATO in 2004. To use the category of Central Europe is not to downplay the marked differences within the region.'

3   Bulgaria, the Czech Republic, Estonia, Hungary, Latvia, Lithuania, Poland, Romania, Slovakia and Slovenia. Empirical work in this chapter focused on the Czech Republic, Hungary, Latvia, Lithuania and Poland.

4   Each EU member state has its own Permanent Representation or diplomatic mission, with offices based in Brussels. The head of each Representation is typically both a Permanent Representative and an Ambassador.

5   Our focus is on the EU Council of Ministers and its constituent fora, COREPER I and II, the most significant of the EU decision-making and decision-taking arenas. COREPER, from the French *Comité des Représentants Permanents*, is the Committee of Permanent Representatives in the European Union, made up of the head or deputy head of mission from the EU member states in Brussels. COREPER I consists of heads of mission and deals largely with political, financial and foreign policy issues, COREPER II of deputy heads of mission, dealing largely with social and economic issues.

6   Research offered a snapshot of the unfolding drivers and processes of elite spatializing political practice among the EU-25, and represented to our knowledge one of the first empirically grounded accounts of the use of Europeanness and eastness narratives within EU decision making. All quotations retain interviewees' original emphasis.

7   Assistants to Ambassadors to Permanent Representations. The ANTICI Group is responsible for deciding on the organization of Council meetings. ANTICI Group meetings usually take place on the afternoon before full sessions of Council involving Ambassadors (COREPER I). Typically, ANTICI also take notes of the discussions by heads of government at European Councils.

8   Thus, as Jaskułowski (2006), notes, '[Poland and Germany] have different (and quite often very different) interests both within and outside the EU. Mutual distrust and prejudices are still visible in their societies. Thus, it was an error to expect that after the breakthrough of 1989 and later after Poland's accession to the EU, bilateral relations would be free from conflicts.'

References

AAG (1999) *Europe's Agriculture: The Case for Change*, London: Agricultural Advisory Group, Ministry of Agriculture, Fisheries and Food.

Abélès, M. (1992) *La vie quotidienne au Parlement Européen*, Paris: Hachette.

Adler, E. (2002) 'Constructivism and international relations', in W, Carlsnaes (ed,) *Handbook of International Relations*, London: Sage.

Adler, E., Bicchi, F., Crawford, B. and Del Sarto, R. (eds) (2006) *The Convergence of Civilizations: Constructing the Mediterranean Region*, Toronto: University of Toronto Press.

Adshead, M. (2005) 'Europeanization and changing patterns of governance in Ireland', *Public Administration*, 83: 159–78.

Agnew, J. (1995) 'The rhetoric of regionalism: the Northern League in Italian politics, 1983–94', *Transactions of the Institute of British Geographers*, 20: 156–72.

—— (2001) 'How many Europes? The European Union, eastward enlargement and uneven development', *European Urban and Regional Studies*, 8: 29–38.

—— (2005) 'Bounding the European project', *Geopolitics*, 10: 575–80.

Agnew, J. and Corbridge, S. (1995) *Mastering Space: Hegemony, Territory and International Political Economy*, London: Routledge.

Albrecht-Carrié, R. (1965) *The Unity of Europe: An Historical Survey*, London: Secker & Warburg.

Allen, J. (2004) 'The whereabouts of power: politics, government and space', *Geografiska Annaler B*, 86: 19–32.

Attali, J. (1993) 'Asia's doing it, America's doing it. Let's do it here too', *The European*, 26 November – 2 December.

Bache, I. (2003) 'Europeanization: a governance approach', paper presented at the EUSA Eighth International Biennial Conference, Nashville, TN, March.

—— (2006) 'The Europeanization of higher education: markets, politics and learning?', *Journal of Common Market Studies*, 44 (2): 231–48.

Bærenholdt, J. O. and Simonsen, K. (2004) *Space Odysseys: Spatiality and Social Relations in the 21st Century*, Farnham, UK: Ashgate.

Barraclough, G. (1963) *European Unity in Thought and Action*, Oxford: Basil Blackwell.

Barzini, L. (1984) *The Europeans*, London: Penguin.

Baun, M., Durr, J., Marek, D. and Saradin, P. (2006) 'The Europeanization of Czech politics: the political parties and the EU referendum', *Journal of Common Market Studies*, 44: 249–80.

Beck, U. and Grande, E. (2007) 'Cosmopolitanism: Europe's way out of crisis', *European Journal of Social Theory*, 10: 67–85.

Beloff, M. (1957) *Europe and the Europeans: An International Discussion*, London: Chatto & Windus.

Bendor, J. B., Glazer, A. and Hammond, T. (2001) 'Theories of delegation', *Annual Review of Political Science*, 4: 235–69.

Beyers, J. (2004) 'The Europeanization of intergovernmental cooperation and conflict resolution in Belgium', *Perspectives on European Politics and Society*, 5: 103–34.

—— (2005) 'Multiple embeddedness and socialization in Europe: the case of Council officials', *International Organization*, 59: 899–936.

Beyers, J. and Dierickx, G. (1997) 'Nationality and European negotiations: the working groups of the Council of Ministers', *European Journal of International Relations*, 3 (4): 435–72.

Bialasiewicz, L. (2008) 'The uncertain state(s) of Europe', *European Urban and Regional Studies*, 15: 71–82.

Bialasiewicz, L. and Minca, C. (2005) 'Old Europe, New Europe: for a geopolitics of translation', *Area*, 37 (4): 365–72.

Bialasiewicz, L., Elden, S. and Painter, J. (2005) 'The best defence of our security lies in the spread of our values: Europe, America and the question of values', *Environment and Planning D: Society and Space*, 23: 159–70.

Bicchi, F. (2006) 'Our size fits all: normative power Europe and the Mediterranean', *Journal of European Public Policy*, 13: 286–303.

Borneman, J. and Fowler, N. (1997) 'Europeanization', *Annual Review of Anthropology*, 26: 487–514.

Börzel, T. (2005) 'Coping with accession: New modes and EU enlargement', in G. Schuppert (ed.) *Europeanization of Governance: The Challenge of Accession*, Baden-Baden, Germany: Nomos-Verlag.

Bourdieu, P. (1977) *Outline of a Theory of Practice*, Cambridge: Cambridge University Press.

Brenner, N. (2004) *New State Spaces: Urban Governance and the Rescaling of Statehood*, Oxford: Oxford University Press.

—— (2009) 'Open questions on state rescaling', *Cambridge Journal of Regions, Economy and Society*, 2: 123–39.

Brenner, N., Jessop, B., Jones, M. and MacLeod, G. (eds) (2003) *State/Space: A Reader*, Oxford: Blackwell.

Brown, M. (2000) *Closet Space: Geographies of Metaphor from the Body to the Globe*, London: Routledge.

Buller, J. and Gamble, A. (2002) 'Conceptualising Europeanisation', unpublished paper, Department of Political Science, University of York. Copy available from the authors.

Bulmer, S. (2007) 'Theorizing Europeanization', in P. Graziano and M. Vink (eds) *Europeanization: New Research Agendas*, Basingstoke, UK: Palgrave Macmillan.

Bulmer, S. and Burch, M. (1998) 'Organizing for Europe: Whitehall, the British state and the European Union', *Public Administration*, 76: 601–28.

Bulmer, S. and Lequesne, C. (eds) (2005) *The Member States of the European Union*, Oxford: Oxford University Press.

Bulmer, S. and Radaelli, C. (2005) 'The Europeanization of national policy', in S. Bulmer and C. Lequesne (eds) *The Member States of the European Union*, Oxford: Oxford University Press.

Burch, M. and Gomez, R. (2004) 'Europeanisation and the English regions', University of Sheffield, Department of Politics, ESRC/UACES Series of Working Papers 2004-07-16.

Bursens, P. and Deforche, J. (2008) 'Europeanization of subnational polities: The impact of domestic factors on regional adaptation to European integration', *Regional and Federal Studies*, 18 (1): 1–18.

Bychkov, T. J. and Bychkova-Jordan, B. (2002) *The European Culture Area: A Systematic Geography*, Lanham, MD: Rowman & Littlefield.

Byrnes, T. A. and Katzenstein, P. J. (eds) (2006) *Religion in an Expanding Europe*, Cambridge: Cambridge University Press.

Caporaso, J. (2007) 'The three worlds of regional integration theory'. in P. Graziano and M. Vink (eds) *Europeanization: New Research Agendas*, Basingstoke, UK: Palgrave Macmillan.

Caporaso, J. and Jupille, J. (1999) 'Institutionalism and the European Union: beyond international relations and comparative politics', *Annual Review of Political Science*, 2: 429–44.

Caporaso, J., Checkel, J. T. and Jupille, J. (eds) (2003) 'Integrating institutions: rationalism, constructivism and the study of the European Union', Special issue of *Comparative Political Studies*, 36 (1): 5–231.

Caporaso, J., Cowles, M. and Risse, T. (eds) (2001) *Transforming Europe: Europeanization and Domestic Change*, New York: Cornell University Press.

Carlsnaes, W., Sjursen, H. and White, B. (2004) *Contemporary European Foreign Policy*, London: Sage.

CEC (1988) *The Future of Rural Society*, COM(1988) 601, Brussels: Commission of the European Communities.

—— (1992) 'Council Regulation EEC Number 2078/92 of 30 June 1992 on agricultural production methods compatible with the requirements of the protection of the environment and the maintenance of the countryside', *Official Journal*, L215: 85–90.

—— (1996) 'The Cork Declaration: A Living Countryside', European Conference on Rural Development, Cork, Ireland, 7–9 November. Brussels: Commission of the European Communities.

—— (1998) *The Agricultural Situation in the EU*, Brussels: Commission of the European Communities.

—— (1999a) Council Regulation (EC) 1257/99 of 17 May 1999 on 'Support for Rural Development from the European Agricultural Guidance and Guarantee Fund (EAGGF) and Amending and Repealing Certain Regulations', Brussels: Commission of the European Communities.

—— (1999b) 'The new rural development policy. Elements of the political agreement of the Agriculture Council, 22 February – 11 March 1999', DGAgri Press Notice, 11 March. Brussels: Commission of the European Communities.

—— (2000) *Reinvigorating the Barcelona Process*, COM(2000) 497 final, Brussels, 6 September.

—— (2003) Communication from the Commission to the Council and the European Parliament, *Wider Europe – Neighbourhood: A New Framework for Relations with our Eastern and Southern Neighbours*, COM(2003) 104 final, Brussels, 11 March.

—— (2004) *European Neighbourhood Policy – Strategy Paper*, Communication from the Commission, COM(2004) 373 final, 12 May, Brussels.

—— (2006) Communication from the Commission to the Council and the European Parliament, *Strengthening the European Neighbourhood Policy*, COM(2006) 726 final, Brussels, 4 December.

Chabod, F. (1947) 'L'idea di Europa', *La Rassegna d'Italia*, 2: 3–37.

Charillon, F. (2004) 'Sovereignty and intervention: EU's intervention in its near abroad', in W. Carlsnaes, H. Sjursen and B. White (eds) *Contemporary European Foreign Policy*, London: Sage.

Checkel, J. T. (1999) 'Norms, institutions, and national identity in contemporary Europe', *International Studies Quarterly*, 43: 83–114.

—— (2001) 'Why comply? Social learning and European identity change', *International Organization*, 55 (3): 553–88.

—— (2003) 'Going native in Europe? Theorizing social interaction in European institutions', *Comparative Political Studies*, 36: 209–31.

—— (2004) 'Social constructivism in global and European politics: a review essay', *Review of International Studies*, 30 (2): 229–44.

—— (2005) 'International institutions and socialization in Europe: introduction and framework', *International Organization*, 59: 801–26.

—— (2007) 'Whither Europeanization?', *International Studies Review*, 9: 307–09.

Checkel, J. T. and Katzenstein, P. (eds) (2009) *European Identity*, Cambridge: Cambridge University Press.

Clark, J. R. A. (2006) 'The institutional limits to multifunctional agriculture: Sub-national governance and regional systems of innovation', *Environment and Planning C: Government and Policy*, 24: 331–49.

Clark, J. R. A. and Jones, A. (1999) 'From policy insider to policy outcast? Comité des Organisations Professionelles Agricoles, EU policymaking, and the EU's "agri-environment" regulation', *Environment and Planning C: Government and Policy*, 17: 637–53.

—— (2007) 'Diversification, networks and English rural futures', in H. Clout (ed.) *Contemporary Rural Geographies: Land, Property and Resources in Britain. Essays in Honour of Richard Munton*, London: Routledge.

—— (2008) 'The spatialities of Europeanization: territory, power and governance in Europe', *Transactions of the Institute of British Geographers*, 33: 300–18.

Collinson, S. (1999) 'Issue-systems, multi-level games and the analysis of the EU's external commercial and associated policies: a research agenda', *Journal of European Public Policy*, 6 (2): 206–24.

Cox, K. (2003) 'Political geography and the territorial', *Political Geography*, 22: 607–10.

Cunningham, J. (1997) 'CAP reform can help create an integrated rural policy', Speech to the Farmers Club, London, 27 October.

Dahl, M. and Giacomello, G. (2000) 'Simulating Europe: a role play simulation of the EU Council of Ministers'. *EUI Working Paper 2000/1*, Florence: European University Institute.

Darnton, J. (2004) 'Union but not unanimity, as Europe's East joins West', *New York Times*, 11 March. Online, available at: http://www.nytimes.com/2004/03 /11/world/union-but-not-unanimity-as-europe-s-east-joins-west.html?page wanted=1.

Davies, N. (1990) *Europe: A History*, Oxford: Oxford University Press.

DEFRA (2002) 'Activity under the English Rural Development Programme in 2001', *ERDP Bulletin*, London: Department for Environment, Food and Rural Affairs.

Del Sarto, R. and Schumacher, T. (2005) 'From EMP to ENP: what's at stake with the European Neighbourhood Policy towards the southern Mediterranean?', *European Foreign Affairs Review*, 10: 17–38.

Delanty, G. and Rumford, C. (2005) *Rethinking Europe: Social Theory and the Implications of Europeanization*, London, UK: Routledge.

DETR and MAFF (2000) *Our Countryside: The Future – A Fair Deal for Rural England*, Department of the Environment, Transport and the Regions and Ministry of Agriculture, London: Department of Environment, Food and Rural Affairs.

Dicken, P. (2004) 'Geographers and "globalization": (Yet) another missed boat?', *Transactions of the Institute of British Geographers*, 29: 5–26.

Diez, T. (2005) 'Constructing the self and changing others: reconsidering "normative power Europe"', *Millennium: Journal of International Studies*, 33: 615–36.

Doty, R. (1996) *Imperial Encounters*, Minneapolis: University of Minnesota Press.

Dyson, K. and Goetz, K. (2003) *Germany, Europe and the Politics of Constraint*, Oxford: Oxford University Press.

Egeberg, M. (ed.) (2006) *Multilevel Union Administration: The Transformation of Executive Politics in Europe*, Basingstoke, UK: Palgrave.

Elden, S. (2004) *Understanding Henri Lefebvre: Theory and the Possible,* London: Continuum.

Emerson, M. (2004) *The Wider Europe Matrix*, Brussels: Centre for European Policy Studies.

Emerson, M. and Noutcheva, G. (2005) *From Barcelona Process to Neighbourhood Policy: Assessments and Open Issues*, Brussels: Centre for European Policy Studies.

EMRAF (East Midlands Rural Affairs Forum) (2002) *East Midlands Rural Affairs Forum and East Midlands Rural Affairs Reference Group: Terms of Reference*, Nottingham: Government Office for the East Midlands.

Eriksen, E. O. (1999) 'Towards a logic of justification: on the possibility of postnational solidarity', in M. Egeberg and P. Lægreid (eds) *Organizing Political Institutions: Essays for Johan P. Olsen*, Oslo: Scandinavian University Press.

Eriksen, E. O. and Fossum, J. E. (2003) 'Europe in search of its legitimacy: assessing strategies of legitimation', in E. O. Eriksen, C. Joerges and J. Neyer (eds) *European Governance, Deliberation and the Quest for Democratisation*, Oslo: ARENA.

Ethington, P. and McDaniel, J. (2007) 'Political places and institutional spaces: The intersection of political science and political geography', *Annual Review of Political Science*, 10: 127–42.

Etzioni, A. (2007) 'The community deficit', *Journal of Common Market Studies*, 45: 23–42.

Exadaktylos, T. and Radaelli, C. (2009) 'Research design in European studies: the case of Europeanization', *Journal of Common Market Studies*, 47 (3): 507–30.

Falkner, G. (2003) 'Comparing Europeanisation effects: from metaphor to operationalisation', *European Integration Online Papers* 7 (13).

Faulconbridge, J. (2007) 'Relational networks of knowledge production in transnational law firms', *Geoforum*, 38 (5): 925–40.

Feakins, M. and Bialasiewicz, L. (2006) '"Trouble in the East": the new entrants and challenges to the European ideal', *Eurasian Geography and Economics*, 47 (6): 647–61.

Featherstone, K. (2003) 'In the name of "Europe"', in K. Featherstone and C. M. Radaelli (eds) *The Politics of Europeanization*, Oxford: Oxford University Press.

Featherstone, K. and Radaelli, C. M. (2003) *The Politics of Europeanization*, Oxford: Oxford University Press.

Feldman, G. (2005) 'Estranged states: diplomacy and containment of national minorities in Europe', *Anthropological Theory*, 5 (3): 219–45.

FFC (Farming and Food Commission) (2002) *Farming and Food: A Sustainable Future*, London: The Stationery Office.

Fischler, F. (1997) 'Sustainable rural development in support of a sustained cohesion policy', speech to the Cohesion Forum, Brussels, 28–30 April.

—— (2000) 'Future evolution of the Common Agricultural Policy', speech to the Oxford Farming Conference, Oxford, 7 January.

—— (2002) 'European agricultural model in the global economy', speech to the Second International Conference on Globalization, University of Leuven, 26 November.

Fossum, J. E. (2000) 'Constitution making in the European Union', in E. O. Eriksen and J. E. Fossum (eds) *Democracy in the European Union: Integration through Deliberation?* London: Routledge.

Foucault, M. (1972) *The Archaeology of Knowledge*, London: Tavistock.

Fouilleux, E. (2004) 'CAP reforms and multilateral trade negotiations: Another view on discourse efficiency', *West European Politics*, 27: 235–55.

George, J. (1994) *Discourses of Global Politics: A Critical (Re)introduction to International Relations*, Boulder, CO: Lynne Rienner.

Geyer, M. (2007) 'The subject(s) of Europe', in K. H. Jarausch and T. Lindenberger (eds) *Conflicted Memories: Europeanizing Contemporary Histories*, Oxford: Berghahn.

Gilbert, E. (2007) 'Money, citizenship, territoriality and the proposals for North American monetary union', *Political Geography*, 26: 141–58.

Ginsberg, R. H. (1999) 'Conceptualizing the European Union as an international actor: narrowing the theoretical capability–expectations gap', *Journal of Common Market Studies*, 37 (3): 429–54.

Goetz, K. H. (2001) 'Making sense of post-Communist central administration: modernization, Europeanization or Latinization?', *Journal of European Public Policy*, 8 (6): 1032–51.

—— (2006) 'Territory, temporality and clustered Europeanization', *Reihe Politikwissenschaft 109*, Vienna: Institut für Höhere Studien (IHS).

—— (2007) 'Territory and Europeanization', in P. Graziano and M. Vink (eds) *Europeanization: New Research Agendas*, Basingstoke, UK: Palgrave Macmillan.

Goetz, K. H. and Hix, S. (eds) (2001) *Europeanised Politics? European Integration and National Political Systems*, London: Frank Cass.

Goldmann, K. (2005) 'Appropriateness and consequences: the logic of neo-institutionalism', *Governance: An International Journal of Policy, Administration and Institutions*, 18 (1) 35–52.

Goldsmith, M. (2003) 'Variable geometry, multi-level governance: European integration and sub-national government in the new millennium', in K. Featherstone and C. M. Radaell (eds) *The Politics of Europeanization*, Oxford: Oxford University Press.

Gollwitzer, H. (1951) *Europabild und Europagedanke*, Munich: C. H. Beck.

Grande, E. (1996) 'The state and interest groups in a framework of multi-level decision-making: the case of the European Union', *Journal of European Public Policy*, 3 (3): 318–38.

Graziano, P. and Vink, M. P. (2007) *Europeanization: New Research Agendas*, Basingstoke, UK: Palgrave Macmillan.

Green Cowles, M., Caporaso, J. and Risse, T. (2001) (eds) *Transforming Europe: Europeanization and Domestic Change*, Ithaca, NY: Cornell University Press.

Grossman, E. (2006) 'Europeanization as an interactive process: German public banks meet EU state aid policy', *Journal of Common Market Studies*, 44: 325–48.

Gualini, E. (2003) 'Europeanisation in comparative perspective: institutional fit and national adaptation', in K. Featherstone and C. M. Radaelli (eds) *The Politics of Europeanization*, Oxford: Oxford University Press.

Haas, E. B. (1958) *The Uniting of Europe: Political, Social, and Economic Forces, 1950–1957*, Stanford, CA: Stanford University Press.

Habermas, J. (1996) *Between Facts and Norms: Contributions to a Discourse Theory of Law and Democracy*, Cambridge, MA: MIT Press.

Harvey, D. (1982) *The Limits to Capital*, Oxford: Basil Blackwell.

—— (1990) 'Between space and time: reflections on the geographical imagination', *Annals of the Association of American Geographers*, 80 (3): 418–34.

Haverland, M. (2003) 'Methodological issues in Europeanization research: the no variation problem', paper prepared for the session 'Europeanisation: Challenges of a New Research Agenda', ECPR Conference, Marburg, 18–21 September.

—— (2005) 'Does the EU cause domestic developments? The problem of case selection in Europeanization research', *European Integration Online Papers*, 9 (2). Online, available at: http://eiop.or.at/eiop/texte/2005-002a.htm.

—— (2007) 'Methodology', in P. Graziano and M. P. Vink (eds) *Europeanization: New Research Agendas*, Basingstoke, UK: Palgrave Macmillan.

Hay, D. (1968) *Europe: The Emergence of an Idea*, Edinburgh: Edinburgh University Press.

Hayes-Renshaw, F. and Wallace, H. (1997) *The Council of Ministers*, Basingstoke, UK: Macmillan.

Heath, J. (2001) *Communicative Action and Rational Choice*, Cambridge, MA: MIT Press.

Heeg, S. and Ossenbrugge, J. (2002) 'State formation and territoriality in the European Union', *Geopolitics*, 7: 75–88.

Heffernan, M. (1998) *The Meaning of Europe*, London: Arnold.

Held, D., McGrew, A., Goldblatt, D. and Perraton, J. (1999) *Global Transformations: Politics, Economics, and Culture*, Stanford, CA: Stanford University Press.

Herbert, S. (1996) 'Normative ordering of police territoriality', *Annals of the Association of American Geographers*, 86: 567–83.

Heritier, A.(1999) *Policy Making and Diversity in Europe: Escape from Deadlock*, Cambridge: Cambridge University Press.

Herod, A. (2009) *Geographies of Globalization: A Critical Introduction*, Chichester, UK: Wiley.

Hix, S. (1999) 'Dimensions and alignments in European Union politics: cognitive constraints and partisan responses', *European Journal of Political Research*, 35: 69–106.

Hooghe, L. (2001) *The European Commission and the Integration of Europe*, Cambridge: Cambridge University Press.

—— (2005) 'Several roads lead to international norms, but few via international socialization: A case study of the European Commission', *International Organization*, 59: 861–98.

Hopf, T. (1999) *Understandings of Russian Foreign Policy*, Philadelphia: Pennsylvania State University Press.

Howell, K. (2004) 'Developing conceptualisations of Europeanisation: synthesising methodological approaches', *Queen's Papers on Europeanisation* 3, Queen's University Belfast.

Hudson, R. (2003) 'European integration and new forms of uneven development', *European Urban and Regional Studies*, 10: 49–67.

—— (2004) 'Thinking through the geographies of the new Europe in the new millennium: dialectics of circuits, flows and spaces', *European Urban and Regional Studies*, 11: 99–102.

Hughes, J., Sasse, G. and Gordon, C. (2004) *Europeanization and Regionalization in the EU's Enlargement to Central and Eastern Europe: The Myth of Conditionality*, Basingstoke, UK: Palgrave Macmillan.

Huntington, S. P. (1993) 'The clash of civilizations?', *Foreign Affairs*, 72: 22–49.

Imig, D. R. and Tarrow, S. G. (2001) *Contentious Europeans: Protest and Politics in an Emerging Polity,* Lanham, MD: Rowman & Littlefield.

Jachtenfuchs, M. (2001) 'The governance approach to European integration', *Journal of Common Market Studies*, 39 (2): 245–64.

Jaskułowski, T. (2006) 'Poland's relations with Germany', *Yearbook of Polish Foreign Policy*, 1: 89–99.

Jerneck, M. (2000) 'Europeanization, territoriality and political time', *Yearbook of European Studies*, 14: 27–41.

Jessop, B. (2005) 'The political economy of scale and European governance', *Tijdschrift voor Economische en Sociale Geografie*, 96: 225–30.

Jessop, B. and Sum, N.-L. (2006) *Beyond the Regulation Approach*, Cheltenham, UK: Edward Elgar.

Jessop, B., Brenner, N. and Jones, M. (2008) 'Theorizing sociospatial relations', *Environment and Planning D: Society and Space*, 26: 389–401.

Jones, A. R. (2003) 'Power in place: viticultural spatialities of globalization and community empowerment in Languedoc', *Transactions of the Institute of British Geographers*, 28: 11–29.

—— (2006) 'Narrative-based production of state spaces for international region building: Europeanization and the Mediterranean', *Annals of the Association of American Geographers*, 96: 415–31.

—— (2009) 'Questionable actorness and presence: projecting "EU"rope in the Mediterranean', *Political Geography*, 28: 79–90.

Jones, A. R. and Clark, J. R. A. (1998) 'The agri-environment Regulation EC 2078/92: the role of the European Commission in policy shaping and setting', *Environment and Planning C: Government and Policy*, 16: 51–68.

—— (2000) 'Of vines and policy vignettes: sectoral evolution and institutional thickness in the Languedoc', *Transactions of the Institute of British Geographers*, 25: 333–57.

—— (2001) *The Modalities of European Union Governance: New Institutionalist Explanations of EU Agri-environment Policy*, Oxford: Oxford University Press.

—— (2002) 'D'accord or discord? New institutionalism, concordance and the EU's Agriculture Council', *Environment and Planning C: Government and Policy*, 20: 113–29.

—— (2003) 'From *filière* to *territoire*: Changing rural policy in the Languedoc', *Modern and Contemporary France*, 11: 335–47.

—— (2008) 'Europeanization and discourse building: the European Commission, European narratives and the European neighbourhood policy', *Geopolitics*, 13 (3): 1–27.

Jones, M. and Jones, R. (2004) 'Nation states, ideological power and globalization: can geographers catch the boat?', *Geoforum*, 35: 409–24.

Juncos, A. and Pomorska, K. (2006) 'Playing the Brussels game: strategic socialisation in the CFSP Council Working Groups', *European Integration Online Papers*, 10. Online, available at: http://eiop.or.at/eiop/index.php/eiop/article/view/2006_011a/33.

Keating, M. (1997) 'The invention of regions: Political restructuring and territorial government in Western Europe', *Environment and Planning C: Government and Policy*, 15: 383–98.

Kelley, J. (2006) 'New wine in old wineskins: promoting political reforms through the new European Neighbourhood Policy', *Journal of Common Market Studies*, 44 (1): 29–55.

Knill, C. (2001) *The Europeanization of National Administrations: Patterns of Institutional Change and Persistence*, Cambridge: Cambridge University Press.

Kohler-Koch, B. (1999) 'The evolution and transformation of European governance', in B. Kohler-Koch and R. Eising (eds) *The Transformation of Governance in the European Union*, London: Routledge.

Kratochwil, F. V. (1989) *Rules, Norms and Decisions: On the Conditions of Practical and Legal Reasoning in International Relations and Domestic Affairs*, Cambridge: Cambridge University Press.

Kuus, M. (2007a) 'Something old, something new: Eastness in European Union enlargement', *Journal of International Relations and Development*, 10: 150–67.

—— (2007b) 'Intellectuals and geopolitics: the "cultural politicians" of Central Europe', *Geoforum*, 38: 241–51.

Ladrech, R. (1994) 'Europeanization of domestic politics and institutions: the case of France', *Journal of Common Market Studies*, 32: 69–88.

—— (2002) 'Europeanization and political parties: towards a framework for analysis', *Party Politics*, 8: 389–403.

Laegrid, P., Steinthorsson, R. S. and Thorhallsson, B. (2004) 'Europeanization of central government administration in the Nordic states', *Journal of Common Market Studies*, 42 (2): 347–70.

Laffan, B. (2007) 'Core executives', in P. Graziano and M. P. Vink (eds) *Europeanization: New Research Agendas*, Basingstoke, UK: Palgrave Macmillan.

Laffan, B., O'Donnell, R. and Smith, M. (1999) *Europe's Experimental Union: Rethinking Integration*, London: Routledge.

Lamy, P. (2002) Speech/02/451, Conférence-débat, *The Economist*, Paris, 3 October. (No English version.)

—— (2005) Interview, *Newsnight*, BBC 2 television, 29 May.

Lavenex, S. (2004) 'EU external governance in "wider Europe"', *Journal of European Public Policy*, 11: 680–700.

Law, J. and Hetherington, K. (2000) 'Materialities, spatialities, globalities', in J. Bryson, P. Daniels and J. Pollard (eds) *Knowledge, Space, Economy*, London: Routledge.

Lefebvre, H. (1974) *La production de l'espace*, Paris: Anthropos.

—— (1991) *The Production of Space*, trans. D. Nicholson-Smith, Oxford: Blackwell.

Lehmkuhl, D. (2007) 'Some promises and pitfalls of Europeanization research', in P. Graziano and M. P. Vink (eds) *Europeanization: New Research Agendas*, Basingstoke, UK: Palgrave Macmillan.

Leitner, H. (2003) 'The politics of scale and networks of spatial connectivity: transnational interurban networks and rescaling of political governance in Europe', in R. McMaster and E. Sheppard (eds) *Scale and Geographic Inquiry: Nature, Society and Method*, Oxford: Blackwell.

Leitner, H., Pavlik, C. and Sheppard, E. (2002) 'Networks, governance and the politics of scale: inter-urban networks and the European Union', in A. Herod and M. Wright (eds) *Geographies of Power: Placing Scale*, Oxford: Blackwell.

Leitner, H., Sheppard, E. and Sziarto, K. (2008) 'The spatialities of contentious politics', *Transactions of the Institute of British Geographers*, 33: 157–72.

Lewis, J. (2005) 'The Janus face of Brussels: socialization and everyday decision making in the European Union', *International Organization*, 59: 937–71.

Louwes, S. (1985) 'Squeezing structural agricultural policy: From the Mansholt Plan to a mini-policy', in J. Pelkmans (ed.) *Can the CAP Be Reformed?*, Paris: Institut Européen d'Administration Publique.

Low, M. (2003) 'Political geography in question', *Political Geography*, 22: 625–31.

Lowe, P. D., Buller, H. and Ward, N. (2002) 'Setting the next agenda? British and French approaches to the second pillar of the Common Agricultural Policy', *Journal of Rural Studies*, 18: 1–17.

Lucbert, A.-K. (2000) *Le territoire dans les CTE : une analyse comparée des projets collectifs de l'Hérault*, Montpellier: INRA (Institut national de recherche agronomique).

McAdam, D., Tarrow, S. G. and Tilly, C. (2001) *Dynamics of Contention*, Cambridge: Cambridge University Press.

McMaster, R. and Sheppard, E. (eds) (2003) *Scale and Geographic Inquiry: Nature, Society and Method*, Oxford: Blackwell.

MAFF (2000) *Strategy for Agriculture*, London: Ministry of Agriculture, Fisheries and Food.

Majone, G. (1989) *Evidence, Argument and Persuasion in the Policy Process*, New Haven, CT: Yale University Press.

Major, C. and Pomorska, K. (2005) 'Europeanisation – framework or fashion?', presentation to the FORNET Plenary Conference, Brussels, 23 April.

March, J. G. and Olsen, J. P. (1984) 'The new institutionalism: Organizational factors in political life', *American Political Science Review*, 78; 734–49.

—— (1989) *Rediscovering Institutions: The Organizational Basis of Politics*, New York: Free Press.

—— (1998) 'The institutional dynamics of international political orders', *International Organization*, 52 (4): 943–68.

—— (2002) 'The logic of appropriateness', *Arena Working Papers 04/09*, Centre for European Studies, University of Oslo.

—— (2005) 'Elaborating the "new institutionalism"', ARENA Working Paper 11, Centre for European Studies, University of Oslo.

Marks, G. (1993) 'Structural policy and multi-level governance in the EC', in A. W. Cafruny and G. G. Rosenthal (eds) *The State of the European Community*, vol. 2: *The Maastricht Debates and Beyond*, Boulder, CO: Lynne Rienner.

Markusen, A. (1999) 'Fuzzy concepts, scanty evidence, policy distance: the case for rigour and policy relevance in critical regional studies', *Regional Studies*, 33: 869–84.

Martin, D. and Miller, B. (2003) 'Space and contentious politics', *Mobilization: An International Journal*, 8: 143–56.

Martin, R. (2004) 'Geography: making a difference in a globalizing world', *Transactions of the Institute of British Geographers*, 29: 147–50.

Massey, A. (2004) 'Modernisation as Europeanisation: the impact of the European Union on public administration', *Policy Studies*, 25: 19–35.

Massey, D. (1992) 'Politics and space/time', *New Left Review*, 196: 65–84.

—— (1994) *Space, Place and Gender*, Cambridge: Polity Press.

—— (1999) 'Spaces of politics', in D. Massey, J. Allen and P. Sarre (eds) *Human Geography Today*, Cambridge: Polity Press.

—— (2005) *For Space*, London: Sage.

Mattila, M. (2004) 'Contested decisions: empirical analysis of voting in the European Union Council of Ministers', *European Journal of Political Research*, 43: 29–50.

Méndez, C., Wishlade, F. and Yuill, D. (2006) 'Conditioning and fine-tuning Europeanization: negotiating regional policy maps under the EU's competition and cohesion policies', *Journal of Common Market Studies*, 44: 581–605.

Milliken, J. (1999) 'The study of discourse in international relations: a critique of research and methods', *European Journal of International Relations*, 5 (2): 225–54.

Milward, A. S. (1992) *The European Rescue of the Nation-State*, London: Routledge.

Ministère de l'Agriculture et de la Pêche (2000) 'La viticulture en 2000 en Languedoc-Roussillon – avril 2000', Paris: MAF.

Mittelman, J. H. (2004) 'What is critical globalization studies?', *International Studies Perspectives*, 5: 219–30.

Moravcsik, A. (1998) *The Choice for Europe: Social Purpose and State Power from Messina to Maastricht*, Ithaca, NY: Cornell University Press.

—— (1999) 'Is something rotten in the state of Denmark? Constructivism and European integration', *Journal of European Public Policy*, 6 (4): 669–81.

—— (2001) 'Constructivism and European integration: a critique, in T. Christiansen, K. E. Jørgensen and A. Wiener (eds) *The Social Construction of Europe*, London: Sage.

Muller, H. (2004) 'Arguing, bargaining and all that: communicative action, rationalist theory and the logic of appropriateness in international relations', *European Journal of International Relations*, 10 (3): 395–435.

Naurin, D. (2007) 'Safe enough to argue? Giving reasons in the Council of the EU', Arena Working Papers 11/07, Centre for European Studies, University of Oslo.

Naurin, D. and Wallace, H. (2008) *Unveiling the Council of the European Union: Games Governments Play in Brussels*, Basingstoke, UK: Palgrave Macmillan.

Nicolaïdis, K. and Howse, R. (2002) 'This is my EUtopia: narrative as power', *Journal of Common Market Studies*, 40: 767–92.

Nonneman, G. (2004) *Analysing Middle East Foreign Policies: The Relationship with Europe*, London: Frank Cass.

Nugent, N. (2003) *The Government and Politics of the European Union*, 5th ed., Basingstoke, UK: Palgrave Macmillan.

Nye, J. S. (1970) 'Comparing common markets: a revised neo-functionalist model', *International Organization*, 24: 796–835.

OECD (2001) *Multifunctionality: Towards an Analytical Framework*, Paris: Organisation for Economic Co-operation and Development.

Olsen, J. P. (2002) 'The many faces of Europeanization', *Journal of Common Market Studies*, 40: 921–52.

Ó'Tuathail, G. (1994) 'Problematizing geopolitics: survey, statesmanship and strategy', *Transactions of the Institute of British Geographers*, 19 (3): 259–72.

—— (2002) 'Theorizing practical geopolitical reasoning: the case of the United States' response to the war in Bosnia', *Political Geography*, 21: 601–28.

Ó'Tuathail, G. and Agnew, J. (1992) 'Geopolitics and discourse: practical geopolitical reasoning in American foreign policy', *Political Geography*, 11: 190–204.

Paasi, A. (2001) 'Europe as a social process and discourse: considerations of place, boundaries and identity', *European Urban and Regional Studies*, 8: 7–28.

—— (2005) 'Remarks on Europe's transforming metageography', *Geopolitics*, 10: 580–85.

Pace, M. (2004) 'The Euro-Mediterranean partnership and the common Mediterranean strategy? European Union policy from a discursive perspective', *Geopolitics*, 9: 292–309.

—— (2006) *The Politics of Regional Identity: Meddling with the Mediterranean*, London, UK: Routledge.

Pagden, A. (ed.) (2002) *The Idea of Europe: From Antiquity to the European Union*, Cambridge: Cambridge University Press.

Painter, J. (1995) *Politics, Geography and Political Geography: A Critical Perspective*, London: Arnold.

—— (2001) 'Space, territory and the European project: reflections on Agnew and Paasi', *European Urban and Regional Studies*, 8: 42–43.

Pardo, S. (2004) 'Europe of many circles: European Neighbourhood Policy', *Geopolitics*, 9 (3): 731–37.

Passerini, L. (2002) 'From the ironies of identity to the identities of irony', in A. Pagden (ed.) *The Idea of Europe: From Antiquity to the European Union*, Cambridge: Cambridge University Press.

Patten, C. (2001) 'Common strategy for the Mediterranean and reinvigorating the Barcelona Process', speech at the European Parliament, 31 January.

Peterson, J. and Bomberg, E. (1999) *Decision Making in the European Union*, Basingstoke, UK: Macmillan.

Piening, C. (1997) *Global Europe: The European Union in World Affairs*, Boulder, CO: Lynne Rienner.

Pieterse, J. (1999) 'Europe travelling light: Europeanization and globalization', *The European Legacy*, 4: 3–17.

PIU (1999) Rural Economies Report Performance and Innovation Unit (The Stationery Office).

Pollard, S. (1974) *European Economic Integration, 1815–1970*, London: Thames & Hudson.

Prodi, R. (2002) 'Europe and the Mediterranean: time for action', speech at Université Catholique de Louvain-la-Neuve, Nouvain-la-Neuve, 26 November, *EuroMed Report 52*.

—— (2003) 'Building a Euro-Mediterranean area', speech in Bologna, 17 May.

Puchala, D. (1972) 'Of blind men, elephants and international integration', *Journal of Common Market Studies*, 10 (3): 267–84.

Radaelli, C. M. (2000) 'Whither Europeanization? Concept stretching and substantive change', *European Integration Online Papers*, 4 (8). Online, available at: http://eiop.or.at/eiop/texte/2000-008a.htm.

—— (2003) 'The Europeanization of public policy', in K. Featherstone and C. Radaelli (eds) *The Politics of Europeanization*, Oxford: Oxford University Press.

—— 2004 'Europeanisation: solution or problem?', *European Integration Online Papers*, 8 (16). Online, available at: http://eiop.or.at/eiop/pdf/2004-016.pdf (accessed 9 April 2009).

Rhodes, R. A. W. (1997) *Understanding Governance*, Buckingham, UK: Open University Press.

Rieger, E. M. (2000) 'The Common Agricultural Policy: Politics against markets', in H. Wallace and W. Wallace (eds) *Policy-Making in the European Union*, Oxford: Oxford University Press.

Rieker, P. (2007) 'Europeanization of national security identity: the EU and the changing security identities of the Nordic states', *Journal of Common Market Studies*, 45 (1): 217.

Rodríguez-Pose, A. (2002) *The European Union: Economy, Society, and Polity*. Oxford: Oxford University Press.

Roederer-Rynning, C. (2007) 'Agricultural policy', in P. Graziano and M. P. Vink (eds) *Europeanization: New Research Agendas*, Basingstoke, UK: Palgrave Macmillan.

Rosamond, B. (2000) 'Globalisation and Europeanisation', *Yearbook of European Studies/Annuaire d'Études Européennes*, 14: 261–74.

Rose, G. (1996) 'As if the mirrors had bled: masculine dwelling, masculinist theory and feminist masquerade', in N. Duncan (ed.) *BodySpace: Destabilizing Geographies of Gender and Sexuality*, London: Routledge.

—— 1999 'Performing space', in D. Massey, J. Allen and P. Sarre (eds) *Human Geography Today*, Cambridge: Polity Press.

Rosenow, K. (2009) 'The Europeanisation of integration policies', *International Migration*, 47 (1): 133–59.

Ross, G. (2008) 'What do "Europeans" think? Analyses of the European Union's current crisis by European elites', *Journal of Common Market Studies*, 46 (2): 389–412.

Ruggie, J. G. (1993) 'Territoriality and beyond: problematizing modernity in international relations', *International Organization*, 47 (1): 139–74.

Rumelili, B. (2004) 'Constructing identity and relating to difference: understanding the EU's mode of differentiation', *Review of International Studies*, 30: 27–47.

Sack, R. (1986) *Human Territoriality: Its Theory and History*, Cambridge: Cambridge University Press.

Sadler, D. (1997) 'The role of supply chain management strategies in the "Europeanization" of the automobile production system', in R. Lee and J. Wills (eds) *Geographies of Economies*, London: Arnold.

—— (2000) 'Organising European labour: governance, production, trade unions and the question of scale', *Transactions of the Institute of British Geographers*, 25: 135–52.

Schalenburg, M. (2006) 'Europeanization and history: concepts, conflicts, cohesion', *German History*, 24: 106–10.

Scheipers, S. and Sicurelli, D. (2007) 'Normative power Europe: a credible utopia?', *Journal of Common Market Studies*, 45: 435–57.

Schimmelfennig, F. (2005) *The International Promotion of Political Norms in Eastern Europe: A Qualitative Comparative Analysis*, Central and Eastern Europe Working Paper 61, Center for European Studies, Harvard University.

Schimmelfennig, F. and Sedelmeier, U. (2007) 'Candidate countries and conditionality', in P. Graziano and M. Vink (eds) *Europeanization: New Research Agendas*, Basingstoke, UK: Palgrave Macmillan.

Schmidt, V. A. (2001) 'Europeanization and the mechanics of economic policy adjustment', *European Integration Online Papers*, 5 (6). Online, available at: http://eiop.or.at/eiop/texte/2001-006.htm.

Schmidt, V. A. and Radaelli, C. M. (2004) 'Policy change and discourse in Europe: conceptual and methodological issues', *West European Politics*, 27: 183–210.

Schneider, V. and Häge, F. M. (2008) 'Europeanization and the retreat of the state', *Journal of European Public Policy*, 15: 1–19.

Scott, J. W. (2002) 'A networked space of meaning? Spatial politics as geostrategies of European integration', *Space and Polity*, 6: 147–67.

—— (2005) 'The EU and wider Europe: toward an alternative geopolitics of regional cooperation?', *Geopolitics*, 10: 429–54.

Sedelmeier, U. (2004) 'Collective identity', in W. Carlsnaes, H. Sjursen and B. White (eds) *Contemporary European Foreign Policy*, London: Sage.

Sending, O. J. (2002) 'Constitution, choice and change: problems with the "logic of appropriateness" and its use in constructivist theory', *European Journal of International Relations*, 8 (4): 443–70.

Seton-Watson, H. (1985) 'What is Europe, where is Europe? From mystique to politique', Eleventh Martin Wight Lecture, *Encounter*, 65 (2): 9–17.

Shore, C. (2000) *Building Europe: The Cultural Politics of European Integration*, London: Routledge.

Shore, C. and Wright, S. (1997) *Anthropology of Policy: Critical Perspectives on Governance and Power*, London: Routledge.

Sifft, S., Bruggemann, M., Konigslow, K., Peters, B. and Wimmel, A. (2007) 'Segmented Europeanization: exploring the legitimacy of the European Union from a public discourse perspective', *Journal of Common Market Studies*, 45: 127–55.

Smith, A. (2002) 'Imagining geographies of the "new Europe": geo-economic power and the new European architecture of integration', *Political Geography*, 21: 647–70.

Smith, K. (2003) 'EU external relations', in M. Cini (ed.) *European Union Politics*, Oxford: Oxford University Press.

Smith, M. (1997) 'The Commission and external relations', in G. Edwards and D. Spence (eds) *The European Commission*, London: Catermill.

—— (2000) 'Conforming to Europe: the domestic impact of EU foreign policy cooperation', *Journal of European Public Policy*, 7 (4): 613–31.

—— (2004) 'Foreign economic policy', in W. Carlsnaes, H. Sjursen and B. White (eds) *Contemporary European Foreign Policy*, London: Sage.

Smith, N. (1987) 'Rascal concepts, minimalizing discourse, and the politics of geography', *Environment and Planning D: Society and Space*, 5: 377–83.

—— (1992) 'Geography, difference, and the politics of scale', in J. Doherty, E. Graham and M. Malek (eds) *Postmodernism and the Social Sciences*, London: Macmillan.

Soja, E. W. (1980) 'The socio-spatial dialectic', *Annals of the Association of American Geographers*, 70 (2): 207–25.

—— (1996) *Thirdspace: Journeys to Los Angeles and Other Real-and-Imagined Places*, Oxford: Blackwell.

—— (1999) 'Thirdspace: expanding the scope of the geographical imagination', in D. Massey, J. Allen and P. Sarre (eds) *Human Geography Today*, Cambridge: Polity Press.

Soysal, Y. N. (2002) 'Locating Europe', *European Societies*, 4: 265–84.

Spohn, W. and Triandafyllidou, A. (eds) (2003) *Europeanisation, National Identities and Migration: Changes in Boundary Constructions between Western and Eastern Europe*, London: Routledge.

Stone-Sweet, A, Sandholtz, W. and Fligstein, N. (eds) (2001) *The Institutionalization of Europe*, Oxford: Oxford University Press.

Stråth, B. (2002) 'A European identity: to the historical limits of a concept', *European Journal of Social Theory*, 5: 387–401.

Swyngedouw, E. (1997) 'Excluding the other: the production of scale and scaled politics', in R. Lee and J. Wills (eds) *Geographies of Economies*, London: Arnold.

—— (2000) 'Authoritarian governance, power and the politics of rescaling', *Environment and Planning D: Society and Space*, 18: 63–76.

—— (2005) 'Autocratic governance: the Janus-face of governance beyond the state', paper presented Royal Geographical Society Institute of British Geographers conference session on 'The Politics of Globalization', 31 August, London.

Taggart, P. (2006) 'Questions of Europe: the domestic politics of the 2005 French and Dutch referendums and their challenge for the study of European integration', *Journal of Common Market Studies*, 44: 7–25.

Taylor, S. (2009) 'New conservative parliamentary group formed', *European Voice*, 22 June.

Thomson, R. and Hosli, M. (2006) 'Who has power in the EU? The Commission, Council and Parliament in legislative decision making', *Journal of Common Market Studies*, 44 (2): 391–417.

Tilly, C. (1977) 'From mobilization to revolution', Working Paper Series CRSO Working Paper 156, Center for Research on Social Organization, University of Michigan.

—— (1992) *Coercion, Capital and European States, AD 990–1992*, Oxford: Wiley-Blackwell.

Töller, A. E. (2004) 'The Europeanization of public policies: understanding idiosyncratic mechanisms and contingent results', *European Integration Online Papers*, 8 (9). Online, available at: http://eiop.or.at/eiop/texte/2004-009a.htm.

Tonra, B. (2001) *The Europeanization of National Foreign Policy: Dutch, Danish and Irish Foreign Policy in the European Union*, Aldershot, UK: Ashgate.

Trondal, J. (2002) 'Beyond the EU membership–non-membership dichotomy?', *Journal of European Public Policy*, 9: 468–87.

—— (2005) 'Two worlds of Europeanisation: unpacking models of government innovation and transgovernmental imitation', *European Integration Online Papers*, 9 (1). Online, available at: http://eiop.or.at/eiop/texte/2005-001a.htm.

Tunbridge, J. and Ashworth, G. (1996) *Dissonant Heritage*, Chichester, UK: Wiley.

Vachudova, M. A. (2005) *Europe Undivided: Democracy, Leverage, and Integration after Communism*, Oxford: Oxford University Press.

Van Apeldoorn, B. (2002) 'The struggle over European order: Transnational class agency in the making of "embedded neo-liberalism"', in N. Brenner, B. Jessop, M. Jones and G. MacLeod (eds) *State/Space: A Reader*, Oxford: Blackwell.

Vetik, R., Nimmerfelft, G. and Taru, M. (2006) 'Reactive identity versus EU integration', *Journal of Common Market Studies*, 44: 1079–1102.

Vink, M. (2002) 'What is Europeanization? and other questions on a new research agenda', Second YEN Research Meeting on Europeanisation, 22–23 November, University of Bocconi, Milan. Online, available at: www.essex.ac.uk/ECPR/standinggroups/yen/paper_archive/2nd_yen_rm_papers/vink2002.pdf.

Vink, M. and Graziano, P. (2007) 'Challenges of a new research agenda', in P. Graziano and M. P. Vink (eds) *Europeanization: New Research Agendas*, Basingstoke, UK: Palgrave Macmillan.

Voyenne, B. (1964) *Histoire de l'idée européenne*, Paris: Petit Bibliothèque Payor.

Wallace, H. and Wallace, W. (1999) *Policy-making in the European Union*, Oxford: Oxford University Press.

Walters, W. (2004) 'The frontiers of the European Union: a geostrategic perspective', *Geopolitics*, 9 (3): 674–98.

Ward, N. and Lowe, P. (2004) 'Europeanizing rural development? Implementing the CAP's second pillar in England', *International Planning Studies*, 9: 121–37.

Ward, N., Donaldson, A. and Lowe, P. (2004) 'Policy framing and learning the lessons from the UK's foot and mouth disease crisis', *Environment and Planning C: Government and Policy*, 22: 291–306.

Weale, A. (2007) Review of *Rethinking Europe: Social Theory and the Implications of Europeanization* by G. Delanty and C. Rumford, *Journal of Social Policy*, 36: 157–58.

Western, J. (2007) 'Neighbors or strangers? Bi-national and transnational identities in Strasbourg', *Annals of the Association of American Geographers*, 97: 158–81.

Wolff, L. (1994) *Inventing Eastern Europe: The Map of Civilization on the Mind of the Enlightenment*, Stanford, CA: Stanford University Press.

Youngs, R.(2004) 'Normative dynamics and strategic interests in the EU's external identity', *Journal of Common Market Studies*, 42 (2): 415–35.

Zielonka, J. (ed.) (2002) *Europe Unbound: Enlarging and Reshaping the Boundaries of the European Union*, London: Routledge.

Index

Page numbers in *italics* denotes a table